BASEBALL FIELD GUIDE

BECAUSE EVERY BOOK IS A TEST OF NEW IDEAS

BASEBALL FIELD GUIDE

An In-Depth Illustrated Guide to the Complete Rules of Baseball

Third Edition

Dan Formosa & Paul Hamburger

THE EXPERIMENT
NEW YORK

BASEBALL FIELD GUIDE: *An In-Depth Illustrated Guide to the Complete Rules of Baseball*—Third Edition

The Experiment, LLC
220 East 23rd Street, Suite 301
New York, NY 10010-4674

www.theexperimentpublishing.com

Library of Congress Cataloging-in-Publication Data

Names: Formosa, Dan, author. | Hamburger, Paul, author.
Title: Baseball field guide : an in-depth illustrated guide to the complete rules of baseball / Dan Formosa & Paul Hamburger.
Description: Third edition. | New York, NY : Experiment, LLC, [2016] | Includes index. | Description based on print version record and CIP data provided by publisher; resource not viewed.
Identifiers: LCCN 2015047712 (print) | LCCN 2015042027 (ebook) | ISBN 9781615193295 (ebook) | ISBN 9781615193288 (pbk.) | ISBN 9781615193295 (Ebook)
Subjects: LCSH: Baseball--Rules.
Classification: LCC GV877 (print) | LCC GV877 .F596 2016 (ebook) | DDC 796.35702/022--dc23
LC record available at http://lccn.loc.gov/2015047712

Interior and cover design, and typesetting, by Dan Formosa and Paul Hamburger

Manufactured in China
Distributed by Workman Publishing Company, Inc.
Distributed simultaneously in Canada by Thomas Allen & Son Ltd.

First printing March 2016

10 9 8 7 6 5 4 3 2 1

Pete Coscarart Striking Out at Ebbets Field

With a wild swing, Pete Coscarart of the Brooklyn Dodgers strikes out in the fifth inning as Cincinnati pitcher Johnny Vander Meer hurled his second consecutive no-hit, no-run game within a week to trounce the Dodgers 6-0. The game played beneath the floods was the first big-league night game in New York, June 15, 1938.

Baseball Field Guide: Table of Contents

Introduction: How to Use This Book

Overview: We designed the *Baseball Field Guide* to be a quick and easy-to-use reference guide to the complete rules of Major League Baseball. Our goal is to organize and explain the vague, misleading, confusing, inconsistent, and obscure rules of America's favorite pastime.

While the basic rules of baseball are second nature to anyone born in the USA (or any other baseball-friendly country), the official rules can be surprisingly complex. Since the inception of professional baseball in the late 1800s the official rule book has evolved somewhat haphazardly — revised, appended, patched together, reorganized, and renumbered by committees throughout the decades. The rules are worded to cover every angle and circumstance — but they are not easy to read.

In the *Baseball Field Guide* we set out to explain the rules in plain English, adding lots of examples and illustrations where we felt they would help. The result is an easy-to-use reference guide that will help everyone, beginner to expert, understand every play in the game.

This book is intended to be used as a reference guide.

The *Baseball Field Guide* is built for speed, each chapter covering a major topic.

As a reference book we didn't think you would read it from cover to cover — although you certainly may. Instead we designed it to allow you to find quick and clear answers to events as they happen on the field. It's a handy book to have around while watching a game — to answer a question, settle an argument, or perhaps win a bet about the true nature of the Infield Fly Rule.

Chapters begin with a list of contents and brief descriptions — you may be able to immediately find answers to some of your questions there.

Because many of the rules apply to several topics, you'll notice that we'll often explain the same rule in more than one chapter. We opted to do this in order to give you answers quickly rather than send you to many different parts of the book to complete a thought.

Where rules are repeated, we discuss them from a point of view relevant to that chapter.

Note that the rules of baseball are gender-neutral, so any time we refer to "he," "him," or "his" — which we do a lot — please consider it to also mean "she," "her," or "hers."

Also note that you may read a rule and say, "Hey, wait a minute..." Not every rule in baseball is strictly enforced. Don't blame us, we're just reporting on the rules as stated by the authorities at Major League Baseball.

Ultimately, we hope this book helps you enjoy the beautiful game of baseball.

1 Basic Rules of Baseball

This chapter provides preliminary insight into the rules of the game. The first two pages show the basic rules at a glance. Subsequent pages go a bit further — but not much, since this chapter is meant to be a quick guide.

Chapters later in this book discuss the rules of baseball in detail. This chapter is intended to get new fans started.

Basic Rules of Baseball: contents

Baseball Basics

Overview: This section will be useful for those who are new to the game. It provides a quick description of the field, the players, and the equipment, and how the game is played. A more in-depth description of the rules can be found in the chapters to follow.

Baseball, a quick description

Baseball is played by two teams of nine players each. The objective of the game is to score more runs than the opposing team. A baseball field is arranged with four bases. In counterclockwise order, they are first base, second base, third base, and home plate. A run is scored when a runner touches all bases, reaching home plate.

A baseball game lasts nine innings (additional innings will be played if the score is tied). In each inning both teams will have a chance to bat.

To start the inning, nine fielders will take their positions. The pitcher will pitch the ball to a batter from the opposing team, who will try to hit it. The batter will get a strike if he swings and misses, or fails to swing at a perfectly good pitch. If he gets three strikes, he is out. He will also be out if he hits the ball but his hit is caught by a fielder before it touches the ground. If his hit touches the ground first, however, the batter begins his run around the bases. If other runners are on base they may run as well.

The fielders will attempt to put out the batter or runners as they advance. A runner touching a base, however, is safe on that base and cannot be put out. A team is allowed three outs before the next team will come to bat.

The winning team will be the team with the most runs scored at the end of the game.

The field and players:

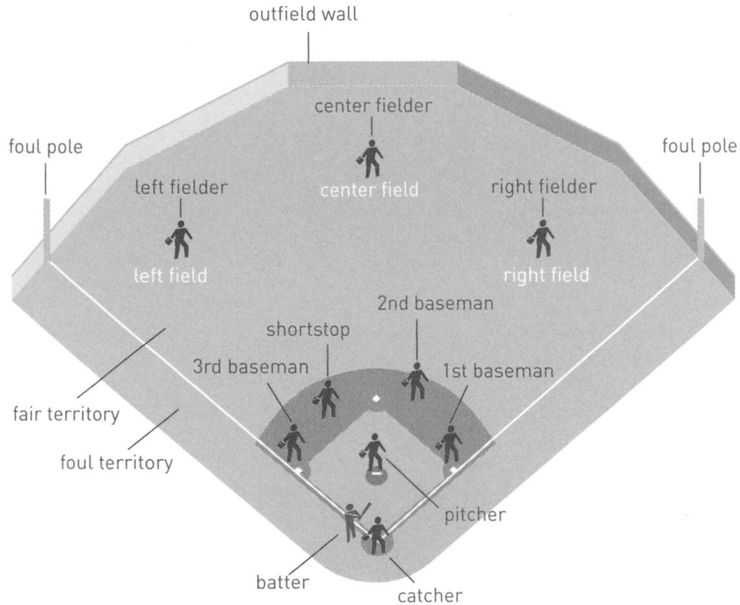

The infield

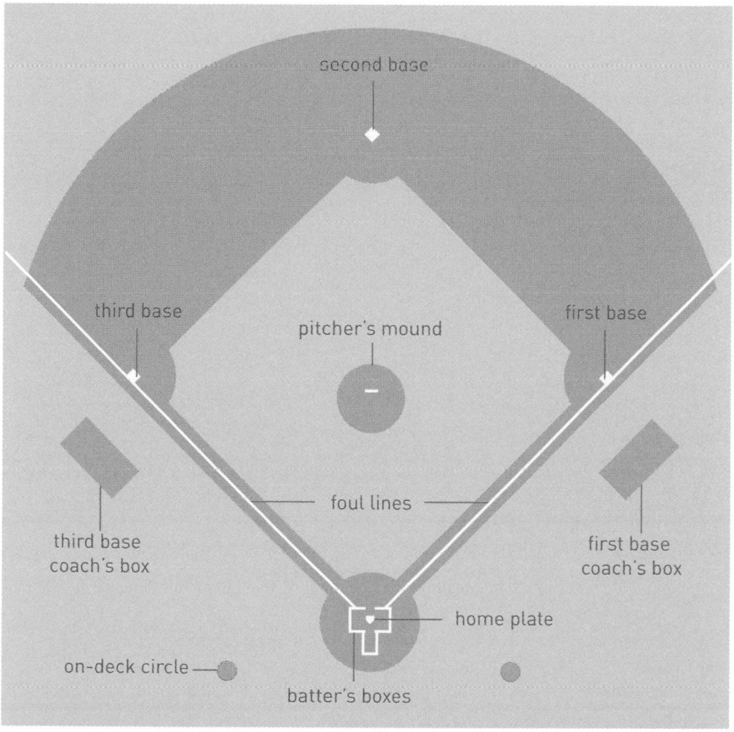

second base

third base

pitcher's mound

first base

foul lines

third base coach's box

first base coach's box

home plate

on-deck circle

batter's boxes

Baseball: Basic Rules

Overview: The goal of the team at bat is to reach the next base — hence the name "baseball." If a runner safely reaches first, second, third, and home plate he will score a run for his team.

How to score: The first thing a batter wants to do is to get on a base safely. There are many ways to get on base, but the most typical way is to hit the ball so that none of the fielders can catch it. If the batter does that, he can try to run to a base before a fielder tags him with the ball. If he can continue to advance to all the bases until he makes it back to home plate (where he started), he will score a run for his team.

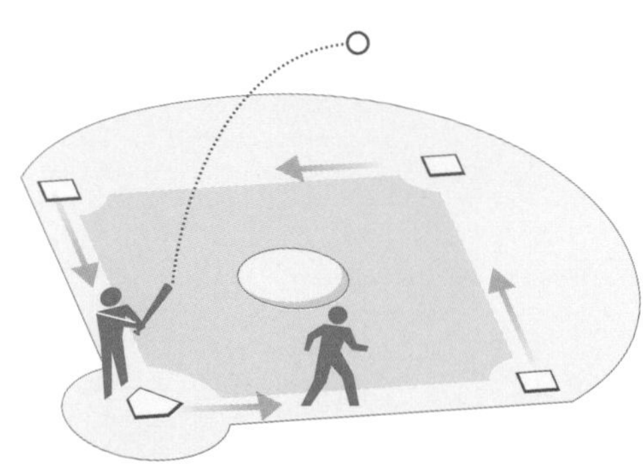

Pitching

The pitcher's job is to pitch the ball to the batter, in an attempt to put him out. The pitcher may throw the ball into the strike zone, or may try to throw the ball just outside of the strike zone in hopes the batter will swing but miss. Each pitch thrown by the pitcher will result in either:

- a strike
- a ball
- a hit
- an awarded base

Three strikes: the batter is out.

Four balls: the batter is "walked."

If the batter swings and misses it will count as a strike. A ball hit into foul territory will also be considered a strike — unless it is caught before it touches the ground for an out, or it occurs on the third strike. On the third strike, a hit into foul territory that is not caught for an out is ignored.

If the pitcher throws four balls (four pitches outside of the strike zone) at which a batter does not swing, the batter will be walked, meaning he will advance to first base.

If the batter hits the ball, what happens next depends on where the ball goes and what happens to the ball when it gets there.

The strike zone

The strike zone is an area in space over home plate. If a pitch passes through the strike zone, it's a strike. If it misses the strike zone, and the batter does not swing at it, it's a ball.

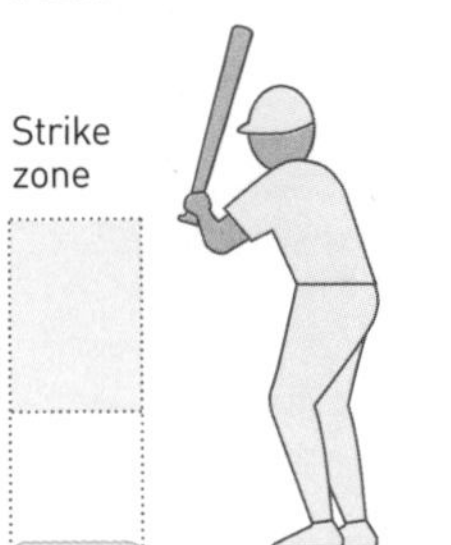

Note: If a pitch touches the ground, bounces, then passes through the strike zone, it's a ball — unless the batter hits the ball, in which case the bounce will be ignored. If a bouncing pitch hits the batter he will be awarded first base.

Basics

Batting

Batters come to bat according to the "batting order" — a sequence of players established by the team's manager at the beginning of the game. The batting order (also called the "lineup") is a significant part of the team's strategy. Stronger and weaker batters are arranged with purpose.

At bat, a batter will try to hit the pitch into fair territory. He may choose to swing at a pitch or not swing. If the ball is hit, the batter becomes a runner and will try to safely run to first base or beyond. Runners in front of him, if any, may also run — or will be forced to run because the batter needs that base.

Example: If the batter gets a hit that sends him to first base, a runner on first base is forced to run to second.

Sacrifice

While typically a batter's objective will be to safely reach a base, at times the batter's goal may be to advance a teammate already on base — even if it means putting himself out on the play.

If the ball is hit, several things may happen:

- **Safe on base:** the batter may safely reach first base or beyond.
- **Awarded bases:** the batter and possibly the runners, for a number of reasons, may be awarded one or more bases.
- **Out:** the batter or another runner may be put out by the fielders.
- **Foul:** the ball may go into foul territory.

Safe on base

By hitting the ball into fair territory, uncaught, the batter becomes a runner. If he reaches first base, or any base beyond, he will be safe as long as he is touching that base.

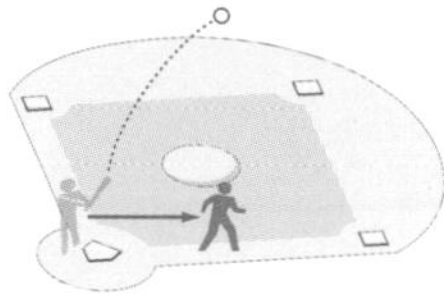

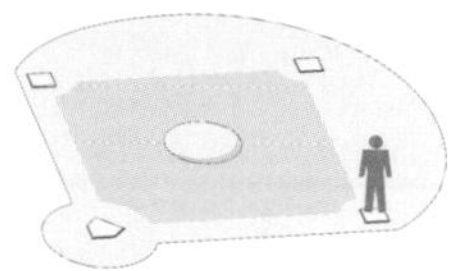

Awarded bases

A batter may be awarded one, two, or three bases, for a number of reasons. For example, he may be "walked" (see the next page), or he may be hit by a pitch, allowing him to advance to first base. Or he may hit a ball that bounces out of the playing field, receiving an award of two bases. Alternatively a fielder may commit a violation of the rules by obstructing the batter as he tries to advance, in which case the umpire will determine the number of bases awarded. Awarded bases are discussed in the Batting chapter.

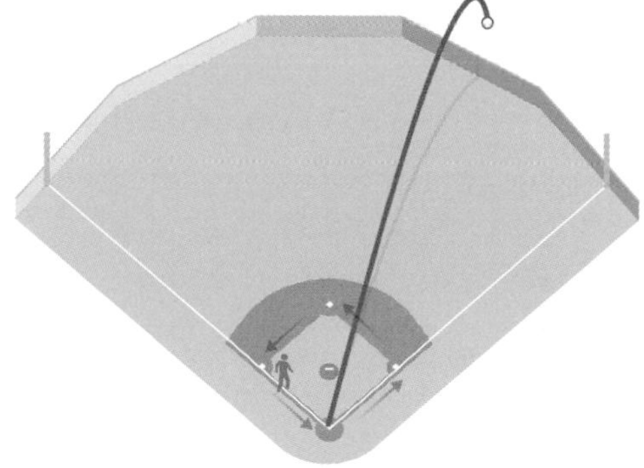

A home run. If the batter hits the ball over the wall in fair territory, he may freely run all the way home to score. Any other runners on base will score as well.

(continued...)

Basics

Batting

continued

How to be put out

After the batter hits the ball, there are several ways he or his teammates can be put out:

1. If a fielder catches the ball on a "fly" (meaning before it touches the ground), in fair or foul territory — or even in the stands — the batter will be out.

2. The batter or another runner will be out if a fielder who catches the ball in fair territory after it touches the ground, while in possession of the ball does any of the following:

- tags the batter with the ball before the batter reaches his base.
- tags first base (by stepping on it while holding the ball).
- tags out another runner with the ball, while that runner is running between bases.
- tags a base to which another runner is forced to run.

Or that fielder can throw the ball to another fielder, who will make an out as described above.

Double plays and triple plays

A double play or a triple play takes place when two or three runners are put out on a play.

Walks

After three strikes the batter will be out. After four balls the batter is considered "walked" — he will be awarded a base. This means the batter will be allowed to freely advance to first base. If there is already a runner at first base, that runner will freely advance to second, and so on. If there are runners on first, second, and third when the batter was walked, the runner from third will freely advance to home plate to score.

Fair or foul

With 0 or 1 strike in the count, if the batter hits a ball that lands in foul territory it will count as a strike. If there are already two strikes in the count, a hit that lands in foul territory will be ignored.

A hit ball that is caught in foul territory before it touches the ground, however, will be an out.

Examples: **Fair balls**

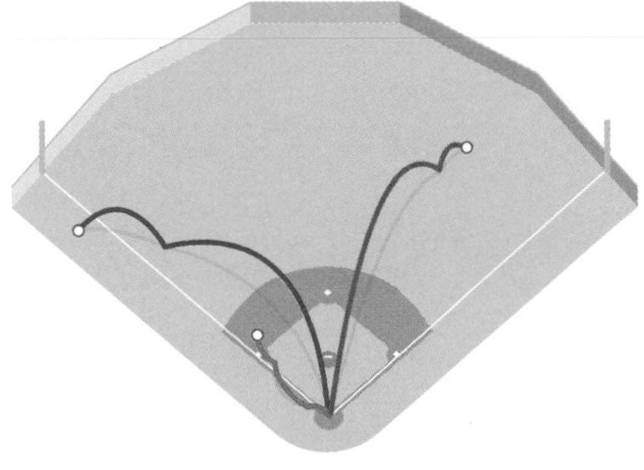

Examples: **Foul balls**

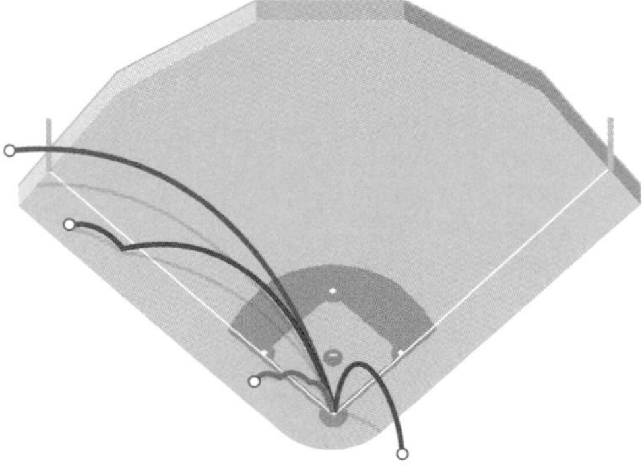

Basics

Running

A runner's goal is to keep advancing bases without being put out, until he reaches home to score. While the ball is in play, a runner can be put out whenever he is not touching his base. He can be put out in many other ways as well. He can be called out because he missed touching a base as he was running. Or he may have misbehaved by interfering with a fielder making a play. The many ways a runner can be put out during his journey around the bases are discussed in detail in the Running chapter.

Stealing a base

Instead of waiting for a batter to get a hit, a runner can "steal" a base by running to it while the pitcher is making his pitch. Stealing a base is risky. If the runner isn't fast enough he can be put out. A runner may also be "picked off" the base to be put out. A runner will commonly take a lead off of his base, standing several feet away from the base in the direction of the next base. If the pitcher is alert he can throw to that base before the runner has a chance to return. He cannot do this, however, after he has started his pitching motion toward home.

The pitcher or the catcher typically makes the throw to a base to catch a runner who is stealing. They therefore need to constantly monitor the runners.

Example: Stealing a base

Taking a lead: The runner takes a lead off his base while the pitcher is pre-occupied with the batter.

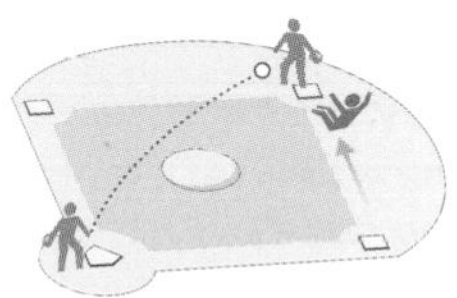

Stealing a base: The runner tries to reach the base he is stealing before the catcher's throw reaches the fielder and the fielder can tag him out.

Tagging up

If a ball hit fair or foul is caught on a fly for an out, a runner may still try to reach the next base — as long as he touches his original base after the ball is caught for the out (or more accurately, after that ball is first touched by the fielder). If a runner took a lead off of his base to get a head start on his run, he must retreat to touch his base before advancing.

Example: Tagging up

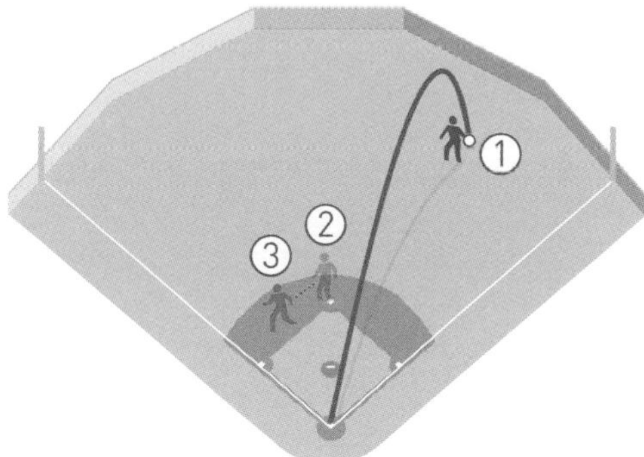

1. The ball is hit and the right fielder catches it on a fly, putting the batter out.

2. The runner waits until the fielder first contacts the ball before leaving his base.

3. He can now attempt to reach the next base, hopefully before a fielder can tag him with the ball to put him out.

(continued...)

Basics

Running

continued

Scoring a run

One run scores every time a runner safely reaches home plate — the base from which he started when batting. On becoming a runner, either by getting a hit or by being awarded a base, the batter needs to safely reach first, second, third, then home.

Example: Scoring a run

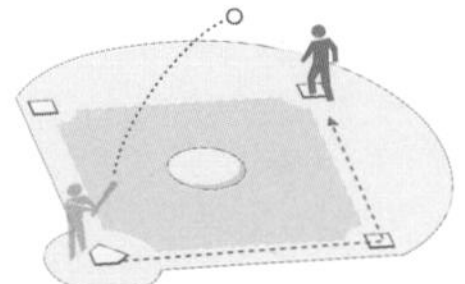

A batter gets a hit and runs safely to second base.

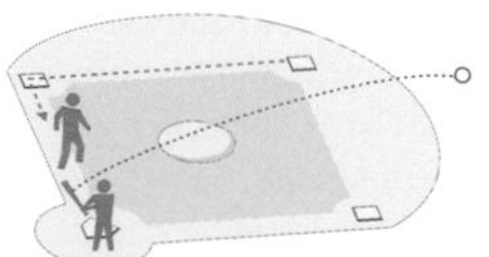

The following batter also gets a hit and the first batter is able to run to home plate to score a run.

Runs may or may not score on a third out

A run usually will not score if the runner reaches home on a play that results in the third out, ending his team's time at bat for that inning. A runner will not score when, on the third out:

- a batter hits the ball but is put out before he reaches first base.
- any runner is forced out during the play (forced to run to make room on the base for the runner behind him).
- a runner behind the scoring runner missed touching a base he was forced toward on the same play.

In any other situation where a runner behind a scoring runner is put out for the third out, the run is allowed as long as home plate was touched before the third out was made.

Note: If a runner is scoring the winning run in a game (because it is the last half of the last inning of the game and his run will put his team ahead), the batter in that play must also touch first base. The batter cannot give up running because he thinks his team has already won.

Hitting a single, double, triple, or home run

Single: the batter safely reached first base.

Double: the batter safely reached second base.

Triple: the batter safely reached third base.

Home run: the batter hit the ball in fair territory over the wall, or (a rare occurrence) hit a ball in the infield but managed to run all the way home on the hit.

Basics

Fielding

Fielders may put out the batter by catching a hit ball before it touches the ground. A fielder holding the ball may put out a runner, including a batter running to first, by tagging him with the ball, or by tagging the base to which he is "forced" to advance.

When a batter gets a hit he is forced to run to first base. If there is a runner already on first base, that runner is forced to run to second. Other runners are similarly forced to run if they need to vacate their base for a forced runner directly behind them.

Example: Catching a hit

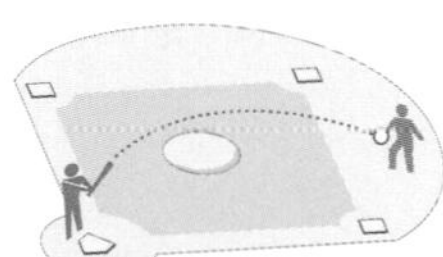

The batter hits a fly ball. A fielder catches it before it touches the ground. The batter is out.

Example: Tagging the player

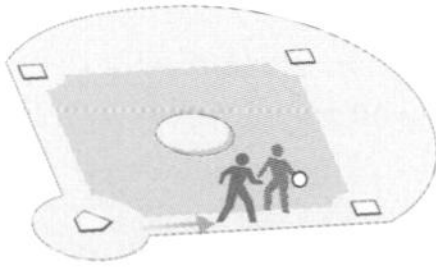

The batter hits a ground ball and must run to first base. A fielder can put him out by tagging him with the ball before he reaches the base.

Example: Tagging the base

Instead of tagging the batter, a fielder with the ball can tag first base by stepping on the base before the batter reaches it.

Example: Force play

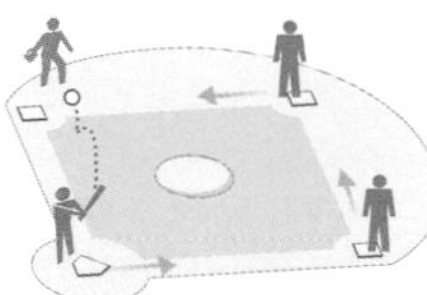

With runners on first and second bases, the batter hits a ground ball toward third base. The batter and runners are forced to run.

The third baseman, holding the ball, touches (tags) third base before the runner reaches it, putting the runner out.

Explanation: Since the runner is forced to run, the fielder only needs to tag the base to put the runner out.

Example: Double play

With a runner on first base, the batter hits the ball, forcing that runner to run to second base.

After forcing out the runner at second base by tagging the base, the second baseman throws the ball to the first baseman.

The first baseman catches the ball and tags first base before the batter reaches it, putting the batter out for a double play — two outs.

Basics

The Length of the Game

Games are nine innings long

A game typically lasts for nine innings. The winning team will be the team with the most runs at the end of the ninth inning. More specifically, the game will conclude in the ninth inning when:

- either the home team or the visiting team is ahead in the score at the conclusion of the ninth inning, or...
- the home team is ahead in the score, either at the start of their turn at bat in the ninth inning or anytime during that half-inning. In the latter case, the game will end as soon as the winning run scores.

If the score is tied or if the visiting team is ahead in the middle of the ninth inning

If, when the home team comes to bat in the ninth inning (they always bat in the second half of an inning), and the score is tied or the visiting team is ahead, the inning will end as soon as the home team takes the lead. The game will be over when the winning run reaches home plate. Even if other runners can score on that last play, the home team will only win by one run — the run that puts them ahead ends the game. However, if the game ends with a winning home run, the batter and any runners on base at the time will score, and the home team may win by more than one run.

Scoreboard showing the home team winning in the ninth inning

	1	2	3	4	5	6	7	8	9
VISITING TEAM	0	1	0	1	0	0	0	0	0
HOME TEAM	0	0	1	2	0	0	1	0	-

Because the home team is ahead by a score of 4 to 2 when the visiting team completes their turn at bat in the ninth inning, there is no need for the home team to come to bat. The game is over and they win.

Basics

Extra Innings

Winning the game if the score is tied after nine innings

Baseball games cannot end in a tie. A game that is tied at the end of the ninth inning will continue into extra innings. The game continues until:

- the visiting team is ahead in the score at the end of the inning (after the home team concludes their time at bat), or...
- the home team pulls ahead in the score.

Scoring in an extra inning is treated like the ninth inning — if the home team scores a run to take the lead, the game will end as soon as the runner reaches home plate, winning by one run. If the game ends with a home run, the batter and all runners will score.

Therefore, if the visiting team is ahead when they complete their half of the ninth inning, or their half of an extra inning, the home team will have a chance to catch up.

An Example of a Half-Inning

Below is an example of one-half of an inning, showing a team's time at bat, concluding when they make their third out.

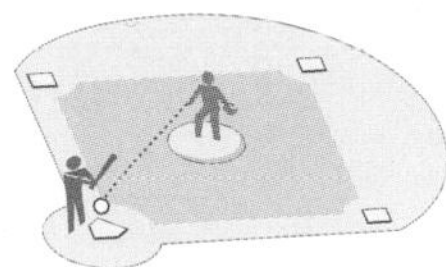

1. The first batter comes to bat and is struck out (receives three strikes). **One out.**

2. The next batter is walked and advances to first base.

3. The third batter flies out. The runner remains on first base. **Two outs.**

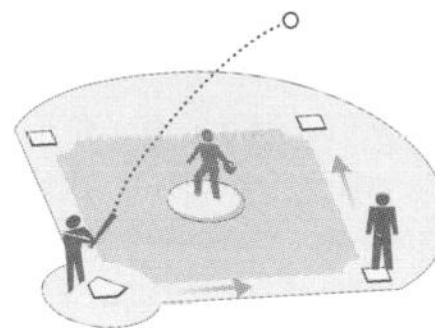

4. The fourth batter gets a hit and goes to first base, forcing the runner to second base.

5. The fifth batter hits a line drive deep into the outfield. The ball touches the ground.

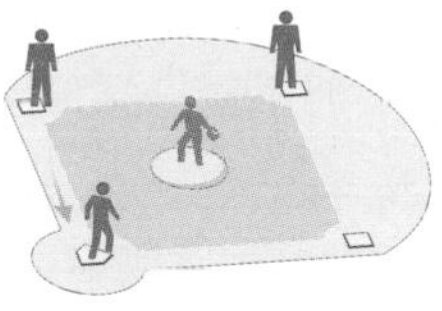

6. The runner from second base scores. The runner from first base goes to third, and the batter goes to second. **One run scores.**

7. The sixth batter grounds the ball toward the shortstop.

8. The shortstop throws the ball to the first baseman, who steps on the base for a force out. **Three outs, and the inning is over.**

Regulation games

A game will only count as an official "regulation game" if at least half of the game has been played. Basically this occurs when the losing team has completed five or more innings. See "Regulation Games" on page 200 for more details.

2 | Teams and Leagues

Major League Baseball oversees two leagues — the American League and the National League. This chapter discusses how teams play their many games throughout the regular season, and into the Division Championships, League Championships, and the World Series.

The leagues abide by an agreement with Major League Baseball called the Major League Constitution. Selected items from that agreement are included in this chapter.

Teams and Leagues: contents

Teams and Leagues: Basics

Overview: Major League Baseball is the organization that controls the two professional baseball leagues in North America — the American League and the National League. The two leagues encompass thirty teams — fourteen in the American League and sixteen in the National League. Both leagues divide their teams into three divisions: East, Central, and West.

Established in 1876, the National League predates the American League by twenty-four years. At its founding it included eight teams. The American League also consisted of eight teams when it was established in 1900. Major League Baseball brought the two leagues together in 1920.

The American League consists of fourteen teams

East	Central	West
Baltimore Orioles	Chicago White Sox	Anaheim Angels
Boston Red Sox	Cleveland Indians	Oakland Athletics
New York Yankees	Detroit Tigers	Seattle Mariners
Tampa Bay Rays	Kansas City Royals	Texas Rangers
Toronto Blue Jays	Minnesota Twins	

The National League consists of sixteen teams

East	Central	West
Atlanta Braves	Chicago Cubs	Arizona Diamondbacks
Florida Marlins	Cincinnati Reds	Colorado Rockies
New York Mets	Houston Astros	Los Angeles Dodgers
Philadelphia Phillies	Milwaukee Brewers	San Diego Padres
Washington Nationals	Pittsburgh Pirates	San Francisco Giants
	St. Louis Cardinals	

Basics

The Major League Constitution

Major League Baseball's agreement with the two leagues is called the Major League Constitution. This agreement covers topics ranging from the number of games played, to minimum salaries for players, to treatment programs and penalties for the use of steroids and other drugs.

Many of the items discussed in this chapter come from the Major League Constitution, not the Official Baseball Rules.

The team's roster

Major League Baseball requires that each team maintain an active roster that includes a minimum of twenty-four and a maximum of twenty-five players from opening day through August 31. If that number drops below twenty-four, due to unforeseen events, the team is required to bring that number back up to twenty-four within forty-eight hours.

The Regular Season

Overview: Baseball starts the year with spring training and preseason games. The regular season runs from late March or early April to October. Postseason championship games take place in October: the Division Series, the League Championships (the "Pennant"), and the World Series. The regular season is discussed here.

162 games

The "regular season" (also called the championship season) is Major League Baseball's term for the games that lead to the Division Series Championships in October. During the regular season each team plays 162 games. The season lasts from 178 to 183 days — up to half of a year. Opening day typically takes place in early April. The final game of the regular season takes place in early October, when the postseason playoff games begin.

As an effort to spur interest in baseball worldwide, since 1996 some regular season games have been scheduled to take place outside the United States and Canada. Venues have included Puerto Rico, Mexico, and Japan. When an opening-day game is scheduled as an "international opener," in Japan for instance, the opening game may be scheduled earlier in the season — possibly in late March. When this is the case, the 183-day limit may be extended.

2,430 games

An incredible number of games take place in the regular season. Each of the thirty Major League teams plays 162 games, not including preseason or postseason games, or the All-Star Game.

162 games played by 30 teams = 2,430 games in the regular season

Games between American League and National League teams

Historically, American and National League teams would not face each other until the World Series championship at the end of the season, when the pennant-winning teams from each of the leagues vie for the World Series title. That changed in 1997, when games in the regular season were scheduled between teams from the two leagues. Of 162 games scheduled for each team in the regular season, up to 18 may be inter-league games. When an inter-league game takes place, the rules of the home team's league will be followed.

Spring training and preseason games

Baseball activities begin in February and March with the start of spring training. Preseason exhibition games take place throughout March and lead right up to opening day.

The All-Star Game

Overview: The All-Star Game is an exhibition game played in the middle of the regular season. The American League plays the National League, with players chosen from every team.

The American League vs. The National League

At approximately midseason, sometime in mid-July, Major League Baseball stages the All-Star Game. This is an exhibition game between American League and National League teams composed of players selected by fans. Starting players are selected by vote. At least one player from each team will be included in the game.

The "fan vote" process, of course, raises the question as to whether the selected players are the best in baseball, or simply the most popular.

The winning league gets home-field advantage at the World Series

Beginning in 2003, to give the All-Star Game more purpose, Major League Baseball declared that the winning league will be given home-field advantage in the World Series. That is, of the two teams participating in the World Series, the team whose league won the All-Star Game will have four of the seven World Series games scheduled to take place at their ballpark.

Postseason Championships

Overview: Two postseason playoffs take place prior to the World Series: the Division Series and the League Championship Series (the "Pennant").

Postseason | Division Series

Three winning teams, and a "wild card"

Each Division Series is a best-of-five-game event. As implied by its name, it puts teams with the best win-loss records from each division in competition. This means that, within each league, one team each from the East, Central, and West divisions will compete. A fourth team is also selected — the *wild card* team. To select the wild card team:

1. The teams with the second-best win-loss percentage are identified in each division.

2. Of these three teams, the one with the best win-loss percentage is chosen.

Note: The win-loss percentage is simply the number of games won divided by the total number of games played (the total number of games played is 162 at the end of the regular season).

Four teams will enter the Division Series

Within each league, four teams pair off to compete in two separate Division Series. The four teams divide into pairs according to the following rules:

- the team with the highest win-loss percentage will play the team with the lowest win-loss percentage.
- if this places two teams from the same division against each other, the pairs will be rearranged — the team with the highest win-loss record will play the team with the second-to-lowest win-loss record.

Two teams will advance in each league

The two winning teams in each league will advance to play each other for their League Championship.

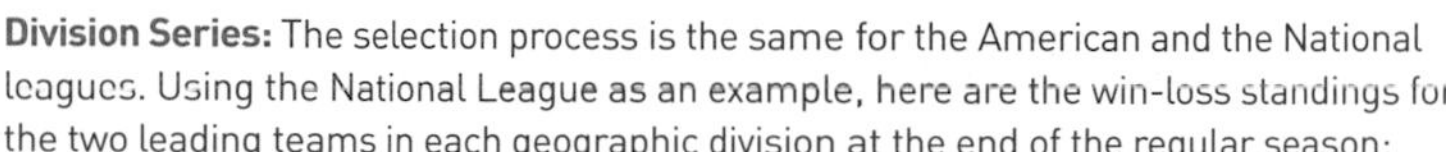

Division Series: The selection process is the same for the American and the National leagues. Using the National League as an example, here are the win-loss standings for the two leading teams in each geographic division at the end of the regular season:

East	Wins	Losses	Win-Loss Percentage
1. Atlanta Braves	96	66	.593
2. Philadelphia Phillies	86	76	.531
Central			
1. St. Louis Cardinals	105	57	.648
2. Houston Astros	92	70	.568
West			
1. Los Angeles Dodgers	93	69	.574
2. San Francisco Giants	91	71	.562

The Atlanta Braves, St. Louis Cardinals, and Los Angeles Dodgers ended the regular season with the best records in their division, so they will participate in the Division Series. Of the three second-place teams, the Houston Astros have the best record, making them the wild card. The Astros will become the fourth team to play.

Of these four teams, the St. Louis Cardinals have the highest win-loss percentage (.648), and the Houston Astros have the lowest (.568). However, because they are in the same division, they will not play each other. The Cardinals will play the Dodgers, who have the second-to-lowest record. The Braves will play the Astros.

Home-field advantage

Since the Division Series is a best-of-five game set, the series ends as soon as one team wins three games. Three of the five games will be scheduled to take place at the home of the team with the highest win-loss percentage, giving that team the home-field advantage. Games one, two, and five will be played at their stadium. If the series goes to five games, they will have the advantage of playing three of the games in their own ballpark.

Postseason

League Championship Series (Pennant)

Each league next holds a League Championship Series (the "Pennant"), to be played by the two winning teams from the Division Series. This is a best-of-seven game series. In scheduling the games, the home-field advantage will be given to the team that had the highest win-loss percentage in the regular season. That team will be scheduled to host games one, two, six, and seven.

In each League Championship Series, the first team to win four games will win the pennant.

Postseason

The World Series

The World Series places the winners of the American League Championship Series and the National League Championship Series in competition.

The World Series is a best-of-seven game series. The home-field advantage for the World Series goes to the team whose league won the All-Star Game. That team will host games one, two, six, and seven.

In addition to the notoriety of becoming World Series champions, the winning team receives a World Series trophy, and its players receive World Series rings.

Postseason

Steps to the World Series: Example

The Regular Season

Best of 162 games

In the regular season, each team plays 162 games, vying for a place in their league's Division Series.

The Division Series

Best of five games

Within each league, the teams with the highest win-loss percentage in each division will advance. So will a fourth "wild card" team, the team with the next-best record.

The four teams will pair off, creating two different Division Series within each league. A team needs to win three out of five games.

The League Championship

Best of seven games

Also known as "the Pennant," the two winning teams from the Division Series will play each other. A team needs to win four out of seven games.

The World Series

Best of seven games

The team that wins the National League pennant will play the American League's pennant winner in the World Series. Four out of seven World Series games must be won to become the World Series champions.

Example: This diagram shows steps to the World Series, using the National League as an example. The American League's process is identical.

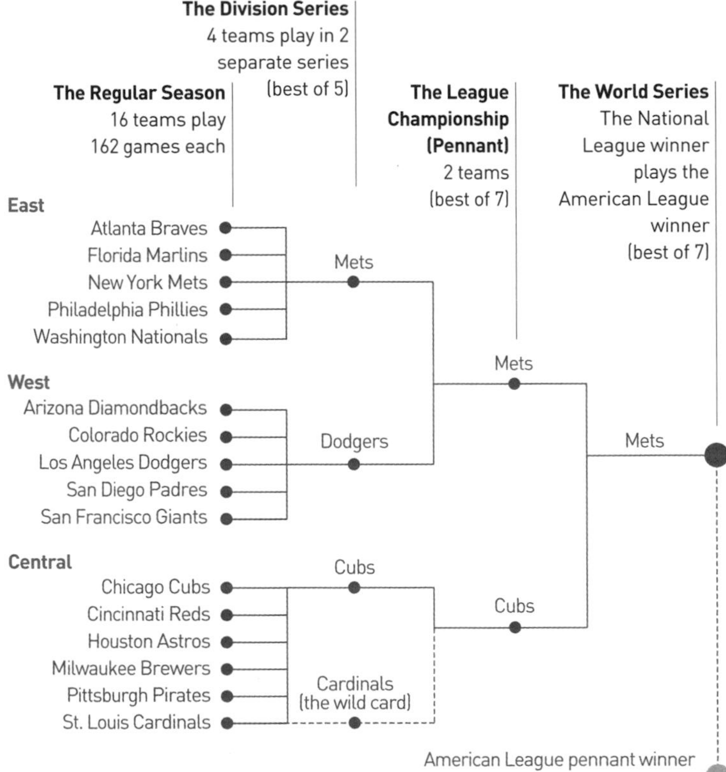

Minor League vs. Major League Rules

Overview: MLB's Official Baseball Rules identify several differences between rules used in the Minor Leagues and the Major Leagues.

1. **Helmets must have double earflaps:** Minor League players are required to use helmets protecting both ears. Major League players may use single earflap helmets, protecting only the ear that faces the pitcher.

2. **Doubleheader games may be seven innings:** In the Minor Leagues each game of a doubleheader may be limited to seven innings. Rules that typically apply to the ninth inning will apply to the seventh inning. For example, because the seventh inning is now the last scheduled inning of the game, the game will end at the conclusion of the first half of the seventh inning when the home team (who always bats after the visiting team) is in the lead, or as soon as the home team pulls ahead in that inning.

3. **Rules regarding suspended and terminated games:** If a Minor League game is suspended due to weather or other factors, and played on another day prior to another game, the regularly scheduled game that day will be seven innings. (See page 201 for more information.)

4. **Penalties for ball tampering:** In the Minor Leagues the pitcher's penalty for pitching with a tampered ball, or having a foreign substance in his possession, is ejection and a specified ten-game suspension. In the Major Leagues the penalty is also ejection, but the length of suspension is up to the commissioner.

5. **Leaving the batter's box:** In the Minor Leagues a batter must keep one foot in the box during his entire time at bat. He may only leave the box when:

- he swings at a pitch
- a pitch forces him out
- the other team calls "time"
- a play is made on a runner
- he fakes a bunt
- a wild pitch or passed ball takes place
- the pitcher, in possession of the ball, leaves the mound
- the catcher exits the catcher's box to give signals

6. **Requirements for the individual pitching championship:** At the end of the season each league names an individual pitching champion, the pitcher with the best earned run average (ERA).

Major League rules require the selected pitcher to have pitched the number of innings equal to or greater than the total number of games played in the season (162 innings or more). Minor League rules require their pitchers to have pitched innings equal to only 80 percent of the number of games (.80 x 144 games in a Minor League season = 115 innings or more).

7. **Requirements for individual batting, slugging, and on-base percentage championships:** Players must appear in a minimum specified number of plate appearances to qualify for these individual championships. In the Major Leagues that number is 3.1 times the number of games in the regular season. In the Minor Leagues it's 2.7 times the number of games in the regular season.

Note: The Minor Leagues are also known as the National Association, the term used in the Official Baseball Rules. To avoid any confusion between the terms National Association and National League, we are using the term Minor Leagues in our discussions of the rules.

3 | Before the Game Starts

Although the game officially starts when the umpire calls "play," the rules require a number of activities to take place beforehand. These range from the home team's manager determining if the game will take place due to weather, to the exchange of batting orders that will lock in the sequence by which players will come to bat.

Before the Game Starts: contents

Before the Game Starts

Overview: Before the game, umpires need to make sure the field and the equipment being used meet the specifications laid out in the rules.

Umpire's tasks before the game starts

Before the game begins the umpire is responsible for checking the equipment used in the game. The official rules of baseball require that gloves be within specific size limits, that bats and balls conform to official standards, and that uniforms meet certain requirements. The umpire is responsible for ensuring that:

- bats, balls, uniforms, and gloves meet specifications.
- the white lines marking the field are correct and intact. Lines must be in place to indicate:
  - baselines
  - foul lines
  - the batter's box
  - the catcher's box
  - the coaches' boxes
- the pitcher's mound and pitcher's plate are correct.
- he receives the game's supply of baseballs, provided by the home team. The baseballs need to meet the specifications of Major League Baseball.
- there are at least a dozen more baseballs available for use in the game if required.
- he has at least two baseballs in his possession to be put into the game when:
  - a batter hits the ball into the stands or somewhere else out of play.
  - the ball is worn out or otherwise unacceptable for use — for instance, because it has become discolored, scratched, or frayed.
  - the pitcher asks for a new ball to be put into play.

Weather and field conditions

Before the start of the game the home team manager is in charge of the field. This means he decides if weather or poor field conditions will be cause for the game to be delayed or rescheduled for another day.

When a manager or umpire-in-chief is in charge of the field it means he is also in charge of the ground crew and field assistants. If field conditions need to be improved, the manager (before the game) or the umpire-in-chief (during the game) is responsible for the maintenance activities.

Just before the game, and throughout the remainder of the game, the umpire-in-chief takes authority. He assumes this responsibility as soon as he receives the batting orders, several minutes before the game's start.

Doubleheaders

The umpire-in-chief remains in charge between games in a doubleheader. He becomes the sole judge concerning whether or not the second game of a doubleheader should be delayed or rescheduled.

Toward the end of the season

If a home team manager decides to postpone a game, or decides not to, the visiting team may appeal this decision to the League President, asking him to override the home team manager's authority to decide whether or not to start the game — on the basis that the home team manager's decision could be biased. Alternately, each league may relieve all its managers of this authority in the closing weeks of the season, automatically transferring this authority to the League President for each game.

Thirty Minutes Before

Each team must identify its manager.

Each team is required to identify a manager at least thirty minutes prior to the start of the game. Although not common practice, the manager may also be a player on the team. The manager has many responsibilities identified in the rules. However, he may delegate some of his responsibilities to players or members of his coaching staff. If he does, he will notify the umpire-in-chief sometime before the start of the game that, in specific situations, a player or coach will be acting on his behalf.

Team members cannot mingle.

Players in uniform are not allowed in the stands before the game. The rules prohibit managers, coaches, or players from interacting with spectators or members of the opposing team before, during, or after the game.

Preparing the Baseballs

Overview: Behind the scenes, the umpire must inspect each of the many baseballs supplied for the game. He also plays with mud.

The home team supplies the umpire with a large supply of baseballs for each game. This can total sixty baseballs or more. The balls must be delivered in sealed boxes, with the seals intact. Each package displays the signature of the League President. On receiving the baseballs an umpire inspects and prepares each one. This entails removing the gloss from the new ball by rubbing it with a special type of mud.

Lena Blackburne Rubbing Mud

The rules require the umpire, on opening each sealed package containing a baseball, to inspect the baseball and to "remove its gloss." This, by tradition, is accomplished by rubbing each ball with mud.

Since the 1930s, umpires have been using a very specific type of mud. In the 1910s and 1920s, Russell Aubrey "Lena" Blackburne played infield for the Chicago White Sox. He later was hired as the third base coach for the Philadelphia Athletics. In previous years umpires used a variety of substances to remove the shine from baseballs. In 1938, Lena came across something that was perfect. Somewhere in New Jersey, at an undisclosed location along the Delaware River, he found a fine, chocolate-pudding-like mud. The mud could be rubbed on a baseball, removing the gloss without discoloring it or otherwise affecting the ball. It worked perfectly. Within a few years every American League team was using it, and by the late 1950s, every team in the National League as well.

Lena Blackburne Rubbing Mud is still being collected from the banks of the Delaware River and is used by every Major League umpire today.

Note: While the rules call for the umpire to prepare the baseballs, today this task is typically carried out by the clubhouse attendant.

Forfeits

Overview: Teams can win or lose even before the game starts. A team can forfeit a game — a situation in which the umpire-in-chief, as penalty for a team's flagrant violation of the rules, can award the game to the opposing team. Forfeited games are automatically assigned a score of 9 to 0.

A game can be over before it even starts.

The following causes will lead to forfeiture of the game, possibly before a first pitch is even thrown.

A forfeit of a game must be called by the umpire-in-chief. He is the sole decision maker on forfeits.

1. Unfit field conditions. If the umpire-in-chief determines the field is not in proper playing condition, he can call a forfeit in favor of the visiting team.

2. The home team's failure to provide police protection for the field. If one or more fans come onto the field, interfering with players or the play, the visiting team may refuse to play until the fan or fans have been ejected. The home team will be allowed at least fifteen minutes, possibly more, for police or security personnel to clear the field. If not cleared, at any point after the fifteen-minute period the umpire-in-chief may declare a forfeit in favor of the visiting team.

3. A team does not enter the field, or they refuse to start the game within five minutes of the call of "play" by the umpire. If the delay is due to a reason that cannot be avoided, the umpire-in-chief may forgive the delay.

4. A team fails to show up on the field for game two of a doubleheader following the twenty-minute interval normally scheduled between the games (unless the interval that day has been extended).

5. A team tries deliberately to delay the game or to shorten the game's duration.

6. A team refuses or is unable to place nine players on the field.

Five Minutes Before

The umpire-in-chief will enter the field five minutes prior to the start of the game and proceed to home plate, where:

- the home team's manager hands two identical copies of the home team's batting order to the umpire.
- the visiting team's manager hands two identical copies of the visiting team's batting order to the umpire.

  Note: A manager may designate a team member to deliver the batting order.
- the umpire checks both lists to make sure they are identical, and looks for obvious mistakes.
- on delivering the lists to the umpire the batting orders are established for the entire game. Substitutions can only be made as provided by the rules.

  Teams are not bound by obvious unintentional errors or omissions. For instance, if the list contains only eight names instead of nine, or if it shows two players with identical names without identifying which player was intended, the error should simply be corrected. The team's manager or captain should be notified of the error and the team will be allowed to correct it prior to the start of the game.

  Note: MLB rules ask "as a courtesy" that the field positions of each player, as well as the names of possible substitute players, be identified.
- confirming that the lists are identical and with no mistakes detected, the umpire retains one copy of each list and hands the opposing team's list to each manager.
- The umpires assume their authority over the game and the field. This means the umpire-in-chief now has the authority to suspend or postpone a game due to poor weather or unfit conditions of the field, and to determine when and if a game will be resumed.

Note: If a designated hitter will come to bat in place of the pitcher, that designated hitter must be identified in the batting order handed to the umpire-in-chief. Although either league is free to adopt the rule allowing designated hitters, only the American League is using it.

Ground rules

Each ballpark has its own set of ground rules covering issues specific to that field. Ground rules are specific to the current game and stadium, and address situations not covered in the official rule book. Rules range from balls getting trapped under rolls of tarp, to the use of retractable roofs. The manager of the home team may wish to impose other special ground rules prior to the start of the game. If the visiting team's manager agrees, the ground rules will go into effect. If not, the umpire may impose his own ground rules to cover special circumstances associated with the game that day.

The visiting team wears darker uniforms and always bats first.

If you are sitting in a stadium there should be no confusion over which team is the visiting team — just read the logos on the uniforms. If glancing at a game on television, however, it's easy to quickly identify the home team and visiting team.

Each team owns two sets of uniforms — one set is white and the other darker — a light gray or beige. The home team wears white. The visiting team's uniforms will be darker. In every game, the visiting team comes to bat first.

Starting the Game

The starting pitcher

The batting order names a starting pitcher who will be required to pitch to at least one batter. The starting pitcher, unless he becomes sick or injured, making him unable to pitch, must pitch at least until the first batter completes his turn at bat — by reaching a base or by being put out.

At the start of the game:

- **The nine members of the home team take their positions on the field.** This means eight players, including the pitcher, will be in fair territory. The catcher will take his position in the catcher's box, behind home plate — therefore the only fielder not stationed in fair territory.
- **The pitcher will complete his warm-up pitches.** The pitcher is allowed up to eight warm-up pitches, not to exceed one minute. However, if there are delays in the game for other reasons, including a commercial break if the game is being televised, the umpires may be lenient on this rule.
- **The first batter in the visiting team's batting order takes his position in the batter's box.** He must be in position when the pitcher starts his pitch (see the Batting chapter for information on the batter's box, page 86).
- **The first and third base coaches will be in their positions.** The base coaches are the two members of the offensive team who, in addition to the starting batter, will take their positions at the start of the game. The coaches' boxes are located fifteen feet to the sides of first base and third base (see the Manager and Coaches chapter, page 166).
- **The umpire will call "play."** On this call the ball becomes live (or "in play") and the game has officially started.
- **The pitcher will deliver his first pitch,** which must be thrown within twelve seconds of the call of "play."

Of the nine fielders, only the pitcher and the catcher have defined locations. The other seven fielders may position themselves anywhere in fair territory. Their "typical" positions are not required by the rules — but make perfect sense if the team is going to adequately cover the field.

Restarting a suspended or a protested game

If the game being played is actually the remainder of a game from a previous day that was suspended because of rain or other reasons, the game will resume from the point at which the game was suspended. The next batter, the fielders, and the batting order will be the same — although player substitutions may be made as provided in the rules.

Teams can protest a game to the League President if they believe the umpire made a crucial decision in error, one that may have affected the outcome of the game. The umpire's call may not have been in accordance with the official rules of baseball. If the League President upholds the protest, the game will be rescheduled. The game will be replayed, starting from the play in which the protested call was made.

For more on protested games see pages 151 and 172.

4 | Equipment

Baseball equipment is strictly regulated. Every bat must be a solid piece of wood (no cork allowed) and the size and weight tolerances of each Major League baseball are specified.

This chapter will discuss equipment dimensions and specifications.

Equipment: contents

The Ball

Overview: Although the official rules cover the basic specifications for the baseball, they go into remarkably little detail. However, all baseballs used in Major League Baseball are made by one manufacturer, by hand, with exacting specifications and consistency.

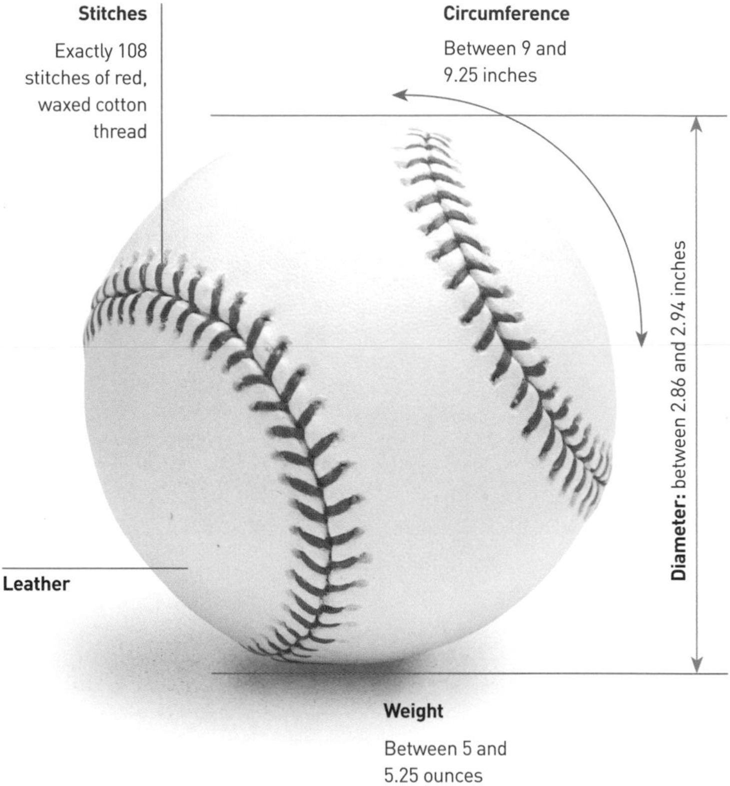

Stitches
Exactly 108 stitches of red, waxed cotton thread
Circumference
Between 9 and 9.25 inches
Diameter: between 2.86 and 2.94 inches
Leather
Weight
Between 5 and 5.25 ounces

Layers and construction

The core
Red rubber outer layer
Black rubber inner layer
Rubber and cork core
Outer layers
White horsehide or cowhide
Cotton winding
4-ply gray wool
3-ply white wool
4-ply gray wool

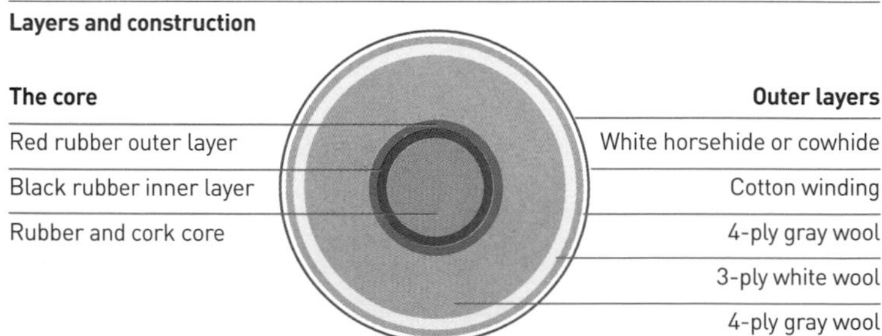

The Bat

Overview: The official rules concerning bats begin, "The bat must be a smooth round stick...."

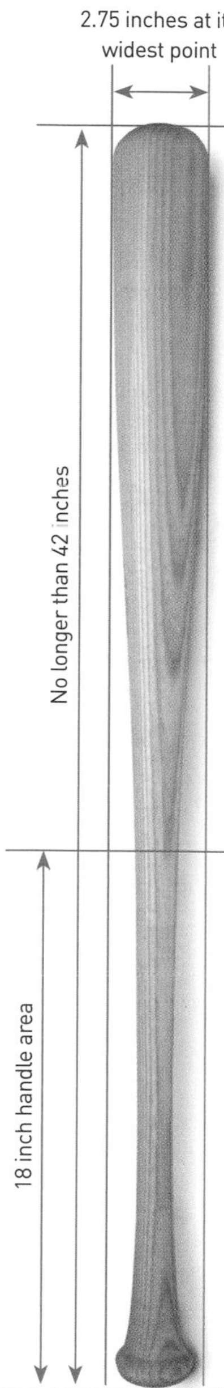

One solid piece of wood

While college baseball allows metal bats, Major League rules only allow one-piece wood bats.

The rules state that no laminated or experimental bat can be used unless it has been cleared by the Rules Committee.

The handle

The handle area can be treated with any substance or material to improve the grip. Typically, pine tar is used for this purpose, applied to the bat with a rag.

Whatever material is used, it may not extend more than eighteen inches from the bottom end, or the bat will be banned from the game unitil the substance is removed.

If a bat that has already been used in a game is discovered to have broken the eighteen-inch rule, it will not be grounds for ejecting or even calling the batter out, and any play will stand.

Note: Since home plate is seventeen inches wide, umpires will often check pine tar on a bat handle by measuring it against the plate.

Cupped bats

It's permitted to make an indentation at the head of the bat. This is called a cupped bat or a teacup bat. It must be a curved indentation no deeper than one inch and between one and two inches in diameter. It should never contain a foreign substance.

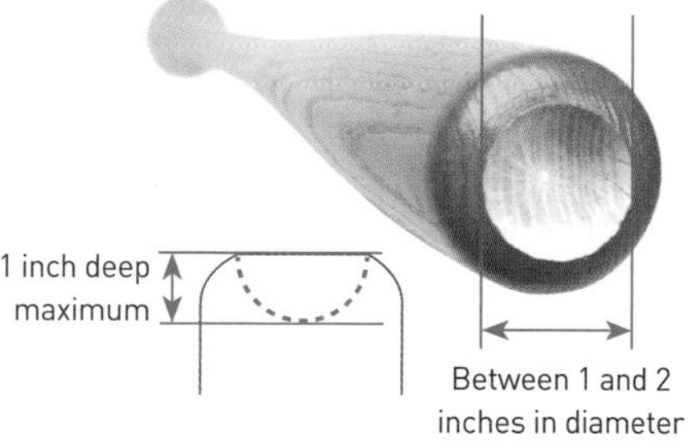

The color of bats

Bats are typically a natural color: brown, black, reddish, or white. Colored bats can be used with approval of the rules committee. On Mother's Day pink bats have been used to raise awareness of breast cancer.

Gloves and Mitts: Basic Anatomy

Overview: The following shows basic terms and requirements that are applied to all gloves and mitts. In the next pages we will discuss the measurements for each specific glove or mitt.

The Crotch

This is the term for the area between the thumb and index finger. It is where the web sits.

Measurements

The measurements listed in the rules are taken by placing a tape measure directly against the surface, measuring every contour of the glove or mitt.

Mitts vs. gloves

Mitts are generally larger than gloves and have a single area for all the fingers (like a mitten). Mitts can only be used by the catcher and (at his option) the first baseman.

A glove has individual finger sections and can be used by all other fielders, however, there are a few more constraints applied to the pitcher's glove.

If the glove fits....

The size of the glove depends both on a player's preference as well as the rules. Most shortstops and second baseman like a smaller glove so they can catch and throw quickly. Outfielders typically like bigger gloves to make the catch a bit easier. Pitchers like a bigger glove with closed webbing to hide the ball from the view of the batter.

The Web

The web must be secured and constrained completely on all sides including the top. If the lacing stretches or becomes loose, it must be repaired to meet the proper requirements.

Palm

Weight

While there are strict size and material limitations, there are no weight requirements for gloves or mitts.

Base or heel

Webbing variation

The webbing can be constructed in a number of different ways. In all cases, the web must control and limit the space between the thumb and fingers. A web that is constructed to expand or give like a net is not allowed. The idea is to make the glove flexible without allowing it to expand to "net" or "trap" the ball.

Rules are rules?

In the spirit of "rules are meant to be broken..." the following pages show glove dimensions as specified by the rules of Major League Baseball. Whether or not these rules are enforced is another matter.

Catcher's Mitt

Overview: The catcher's mitt is allowed to be bigger than any other type of glove. The design of this glove has evolved over the years to handle everything from 100-miles-per-hour fastballs to awkward and unpredictable knuckleballs.

Reinforced web

A catcher's mitt is typically reinforced in the webbing and padded through the palm.

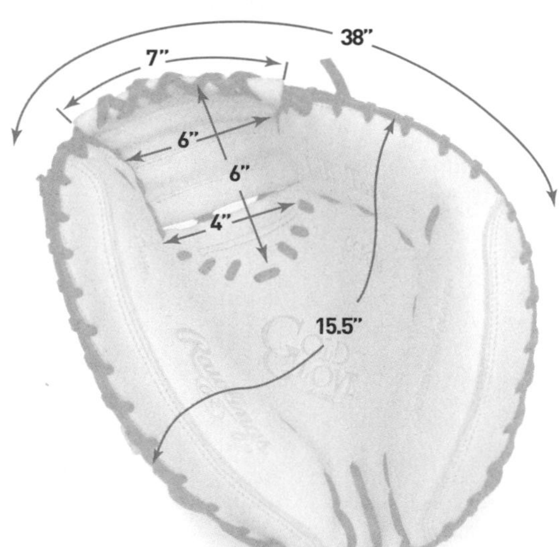

Maximum dimensions

The mitt must not exceed the following dimensions:

Overall height	15.5"
Circumference	38"
Top edge of web	7"
Web height	6"
Top web width	6"
Bottom web width	4"

First Baseman's Mitt

Overview: In a typical game, the first baseman will catch more balls than anyone aside from the catcher and pitcher. He has a choice of using a mitt or a glove. Specifications for the size of the web are different from the specs for other fielders.

Leather tubes

This typical style of webbing is constructed out of a lattice of leather tubes threaded together with leather lacing.

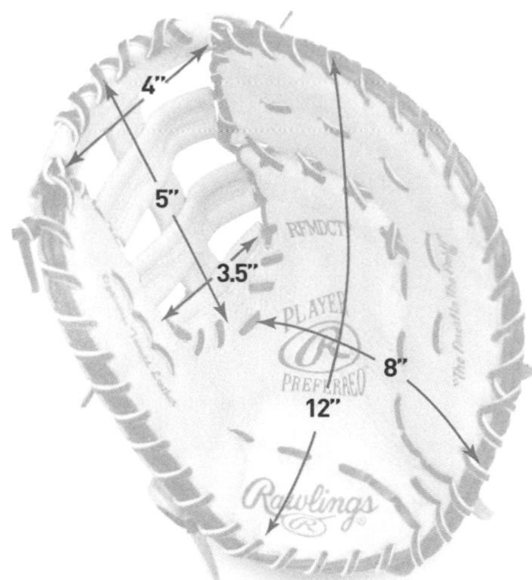

Maximum dimensions

The mitt must not exceed the following dimensions:

Overall height	12"
Palm width	8"
Web height	5"
Top web width	4"
Bottom web width	3.5"

Fielder's Glove

Overview: Every player except the catcher and first baseman will wear a glove that falls within these specifications. While maximum dimensions are shown, infielders other than the first baseman typically prefer smaller, "faster" gloves.

Glove color

The official rules reference the Pantone® color system as a guide. All gloves, no matter what field position, need to be equivalent or darker than the Pantone 14 series of colors — which essentially means "medium" in color.

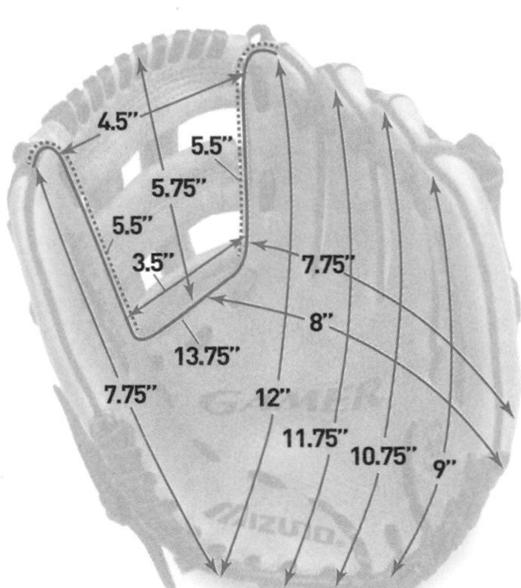

Maximum dimensions

The glove must not exceed the following dimensions:

Overall height	**12"**
Palm width	**7.75"**
Web height	**5.75"**
Top web width	**4.5"**
Bottom web width	**3.5"**

Pitcher's Glove

Overview: The pitcher's glove must conform to the same specifications as a fielder's. Additionally, it must minimize distractions to the batter, and cannot be white or gray — colors that could hide the ball.

Protecting the batter

The pitcher's glove can be multi-colored, but cannot distract the batter or make it too easy to hide the ball. Except for the stitching, lacing, and webbing, the pitcher's glove may not be white or gray. The pitcher is not allowed to attach a foreign material to his glove that's a different color than his glove.

If the umpire-in-chief feels the glove is illegal (by his own initiative or based on a tip from the opposing manager), the glove will be removed from the game.

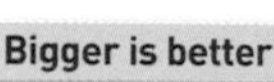

Bigger is better

Pitchers prefer big gloves with closed webbing (as shown) to help them hide the ball from the batter.

Maximum dimensions

The pitcher's glove dimensions are the same as those for a fielder's glove:

Overall height	12"
Palm width	7.75"
Web height	5.75"
Top web width	4.5"
Bottom web width	3.5"

The Uniforms

Overview: All team members must wear matching uniforms, identical in the style, colors, trim, and graphics.

Home and visiting team colors

Every team must have two sets of uniforms. A white uniform is worn for home games, and a uniform of a distinctly darker color must be worn for away games.

Player identification

The number of each player must be on his back in digits that are at least six inches tall.

The rules state that each league can create guidelines for displaying a player's name on their uniform. Typically, players have their last name printed on their back. The rules note that a name other than the player's last name (like a nickname) may be used by permission of the League President.

Commercialization

Company logos, patches, and labels for the purpose of commercial promotion are not allowed on the uniforms.

Labels and logos on the equipment must be reasonably small and not overly prominent.

Distractions

Players must never attach items to their uniform that differ in color or that may prove distracting. Shiny buttons or details are illegal for the same reason.

No one can wear a graphic or a detail of clothing that depicts or resembles a baseball "to prevent players from ever seeing more than one baseball at a time on the field."

Example: A uniform of the 1955 New York Giants worn by Willie Mays.

Caps

Every player has one, fans all over the world wear them, but the rules don't mention them.

Sleeves

Sleeve lengths can vary according to a player's preference as long as both sleeves are the same length and they are not frayed, ragged, or slit.

Undershirts

Undershirts can be exposed and can have logos, letters, or numbers on the sleeves, but they must be a solid color and the same color for everyone on the team.

Note: The pitcher's undershirt must not have any markings because they could distract the batters.

Evolution of the uniform

Like so many aspects of the game, the rules have changed very little over the years in regard to the uniform. This uniform of the world champion Red Sox team of 1903 would be acceptable today (according to the rules).

Helmets

Overview: The modern helmet is a hard plastic shell with foam padding inside.

Helmets are mandatory for batters, catchers, base coaches, and bat and ball girls and boys while performing their duties. Players are required to wear one when batting and while running the bases. If after a reasonable warning someone refuses to wear the appropriate head gear, the umpire will eject the culprit from the game. Further disciplinary action may be warranted.

Earflaps

Helmets come with either one or two earflaps.

Major Leagues: Players can choose to wear a helmet with either single or double earflaps.

Minor Leagues: All players must wear a helmet with double earflaps.

Catcher's helmet and mask

The catcher must wear a helmet when receiving pitches.

He must also wear a mask to protect his face. Some catcher's helmets come with an integrated hockey-style mask. Other more traditional masks are designed as a separate piece.

Shoes

Overview: For obvious safety reasons, baseball shoes cannot have pointed spikes (like golf shoes).

Plastic or metal treads

Baseball cleats are approximately one-half inch tall. They come in a variety of configurations and materials, but they must never come to a point at the bottom.

Ty Cobb

Ty Cobb, who was not known for his good sportsmanship, was said to sharpen his cleats so infielders would think twice before attempting to hold their ground as he slid into a base.

5 | Field Specifications

Baseball is a game of inches. A change in any of the critical dimensions in the infield, even by a small amount, could change the game dramatically.

While the infield dimensions are specified, outfields and foul areas vary widely. This chapter will show the specifications for the infield, including the bases and the pitcher's mound. It will also show the vast differences in sizes and shapes of outfields and foul areas at existing Major League ballparks.

Field Specifications: contents

The Field

Overview: The infield portion of all baseball fields must be identical, but the outfield can vary a great deal from one stadium to the next.

The Field |

The Infield

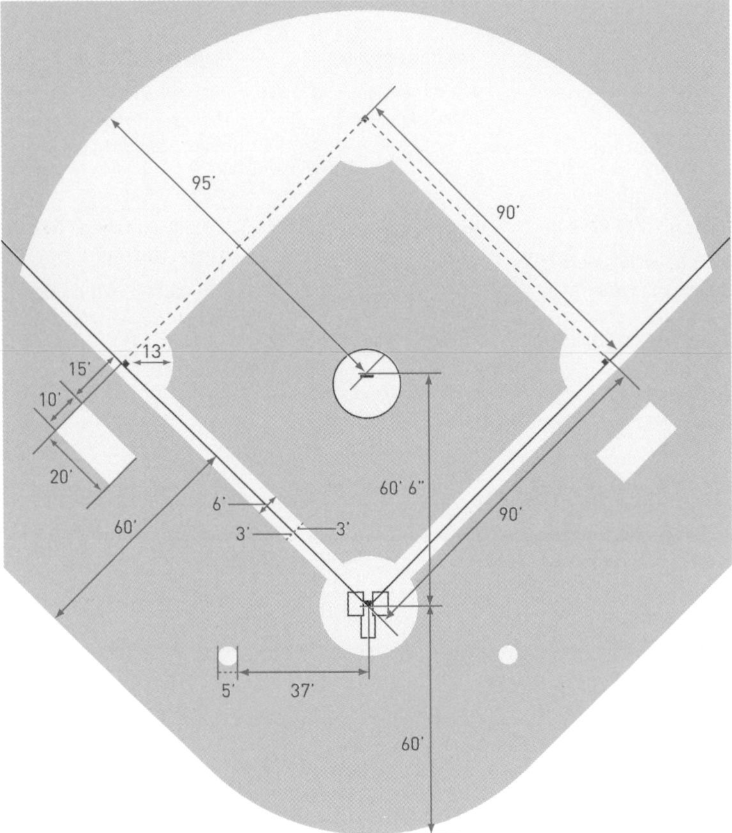

Optional dimensions and specifications

Not all of the standard dimensions are mandatory. The following points are preferable but not enforced as a rule:

- Ballparks should face east-northeast (meaning the batter looking toward the pitcher).
- The distance from home base to the backstop (the wall behind home plate) should be a minimum of sixty feet. The same goes for the distance between the infield foul lines and the surrounding fences or walls.
- It is up to the home ball club to decide which areas are covered by grass or dirt. The diagram shows a standard layout.

The Field

The Outfield

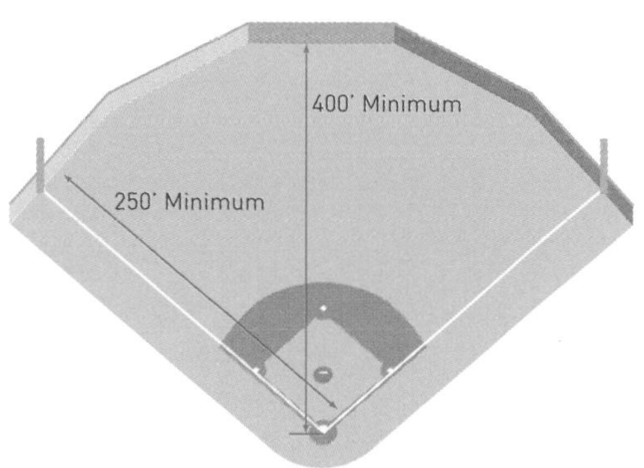

Outfield requirements

There must be a minimum of 325 feet from home plate to the nearest fence, stand, or wall along the right and left field foul lines. There should be a minimum of 400 feet to the center field wall.

Fields prior to 1958

Older ballparks were more varied in dimensions, and the restrictions were looser. The current regulations only apply to fields constructed after June 1, 1958. If an existing field pre-dates that period, then the closest distance between home plate and any wall or fence in fair territory must be 250 feet.

It is "desirable" for right and left field to be at least 320 feet, and center field to be at least 400 feet.

Remodeling. Any changes made to an existing ballpark should not cause the field to shrink below the minimum distances.

An endless outfield

While there are rules regarding the minimum sizes for the field, nothing prevents the outfield from extending outward from home plate indefinitely.

The Batter's Box

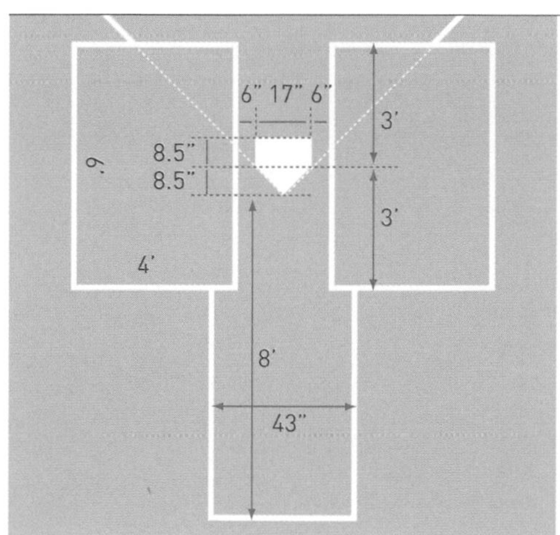

Each batter's box (one on each side of home plate) is six feet deep and four feet wide.

The catcher's box extends eight feet behind the back of home plate. It's enough room for the catcher and umpire to be out of the way of the batter's swing.

The Pitcher's Mound

Overview: The pitcher's mound is ten inches tall, eighteen feet in diameter. The "rubber" (also called the pitcher's plate) is six inches by twenty-four inches and is sixty feet six inches from the back (the point) of home plate.

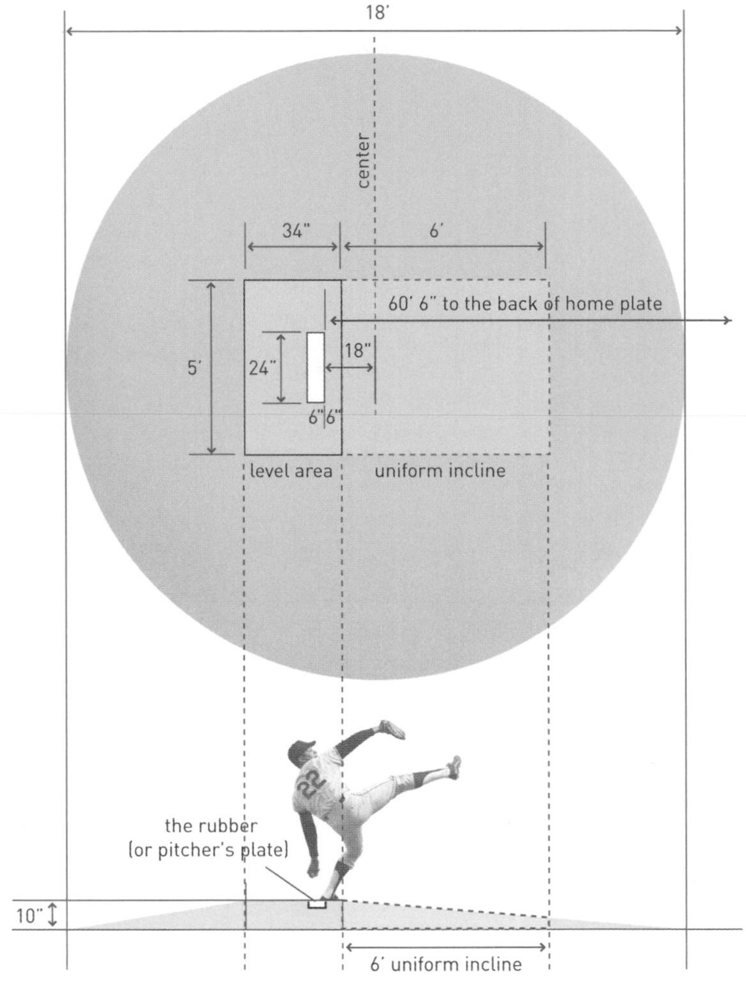

The pitcher's mound is ten inches tall. The rubber is set into a flattened area on top of the mound.

In front of the flattened area (toward home plate) is a uniform incline that extends for six feet and drops one vertical inch for every horizontal foot.

The degree of slope on all other areas of the mound is not critical and can slope gradually to field level.

The Bases

Overview: First, second, and third bases are identical squares, while home plate is an irregular five-sided shape. Each base is placed ninety feet apart. Together they describe the infield diamond.

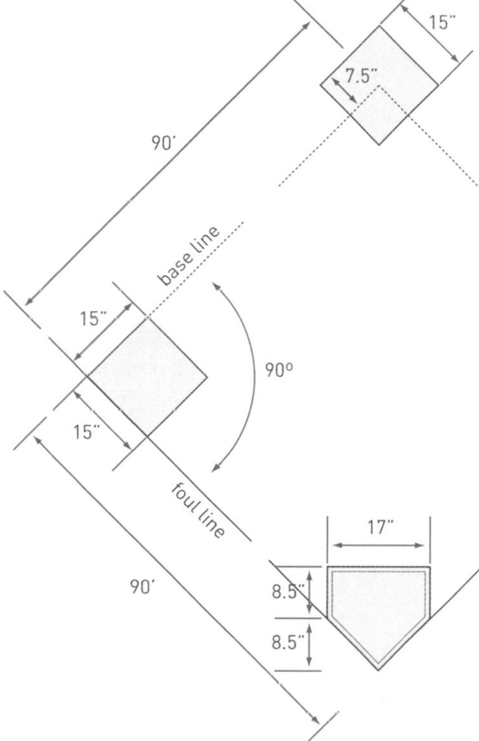

Base placement

First and third bases are placed with their outer edges against the foul lines and baseline.

Second base is placed so that its center is on the point at which the baselines intersect.

Home plate

Home plate is fixed securely so that the bottom is flush with the ground. The edges are beveled down.

The bases are secured in place by slipping a square pipe under the base (called the "anchor") into a fitting in the ground.

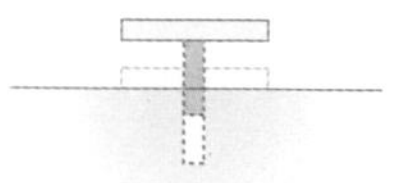

Steal a base. Really.

First, second, and third bases are not fixed in place and can be easily pulled free and carried away. This was demonstrated in 2001 by Pirates manager Lloyd McClendon when he disagreed with an umpire's call. In protest, McClendon picked up first base and carried it away into the dugout after being ejected.

Major League Fields

Overview: All baseball fields must have identical infield dimensions, but the outfield and foul territory can differ greatly. In this section, you can compare the basic shapes and sizes of the current Major League stadiums.

The required dimensions

Every field must have the same specifications in the infield. Fields built after 1958 must have a minimum distance of 325 feet from home plate to the outfield wall along the left and right foul lines and a minimum of 400 feet to the center field wall. There must be no obstructions in fair territory (fences, stands, or walls) closer than 250 feet from home plate. It is recommended, but not mandatory, that the foul area all the way around the infield be a minimum of 60 feet from the baselines. Aside from these specifications, every field can be designed differently.

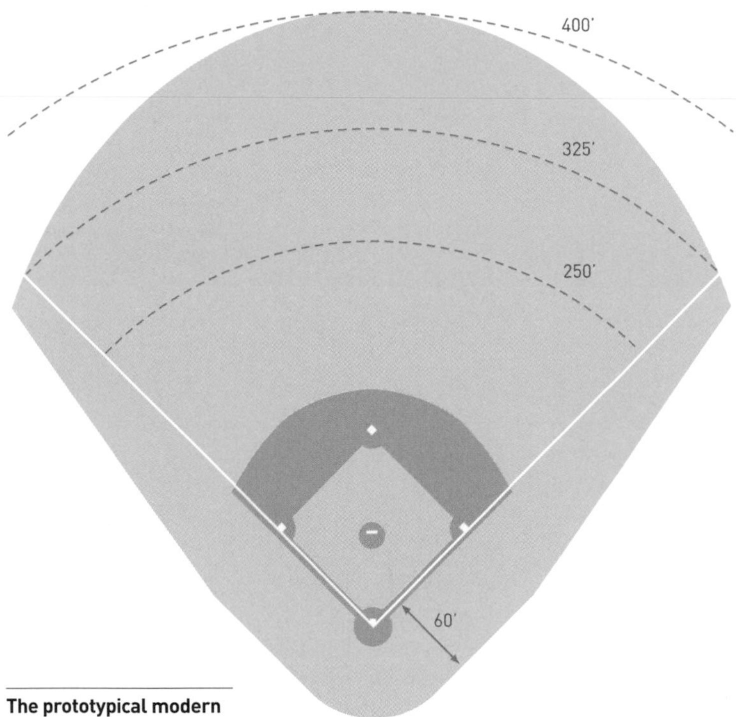

The prototypical modern baseball field

This diagram shows a symmetrical field that meets all the Major League requirements and recommendations.

Note: Every field illustrated in this section is shown at the same scale. The dotted blue lines in each diagram show arcs drawn 250, 325, and 400 feet from home plate for reference.

MLB Fields | Field Comparisons

American League East

Baltimore Orioles

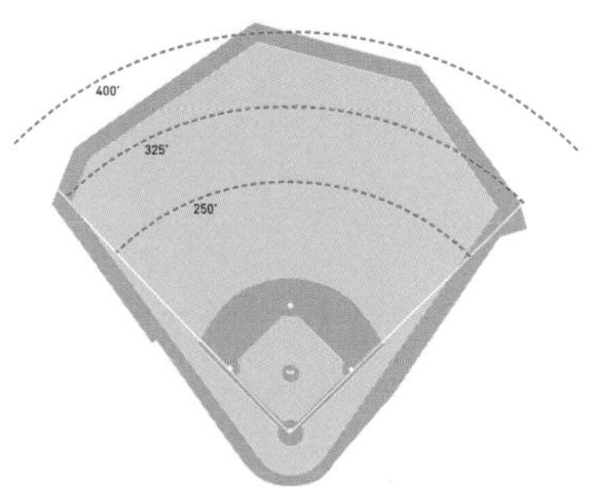

Tampa Bay Rays

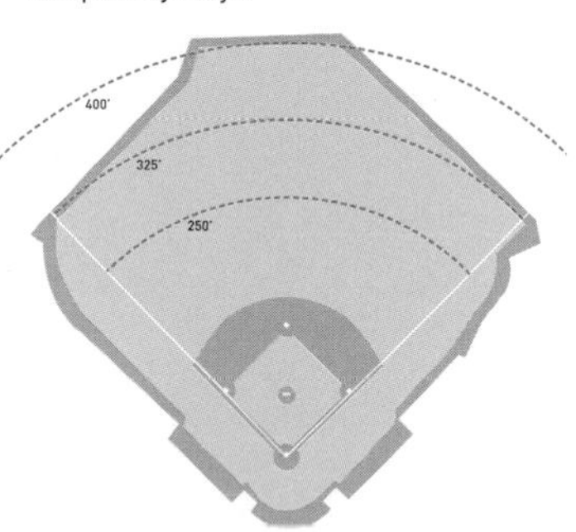

Boston Red Sox

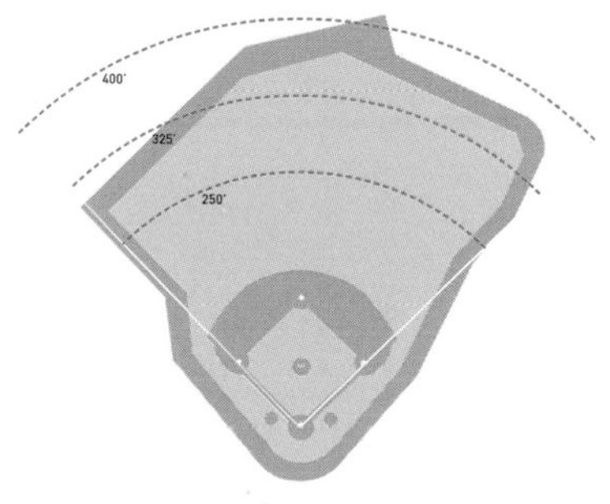

Toronto Blue Jays

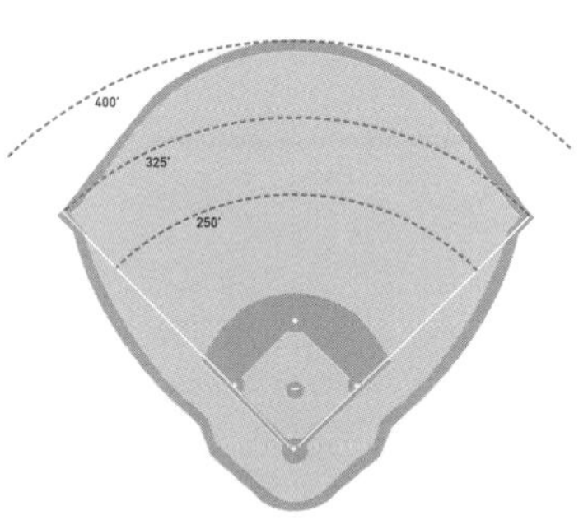

New York Yankees

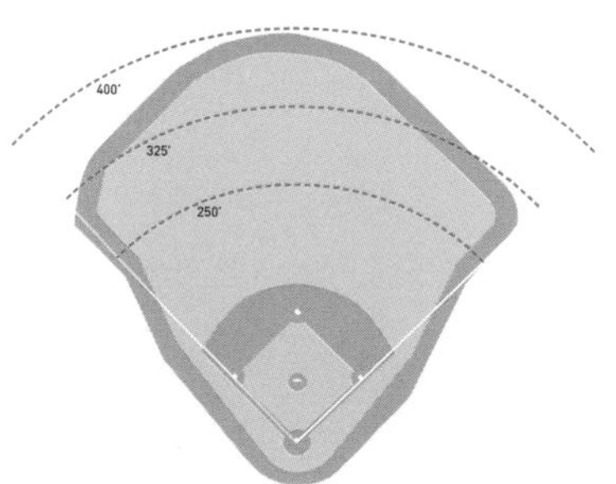

American League Central

Chicago White Sox

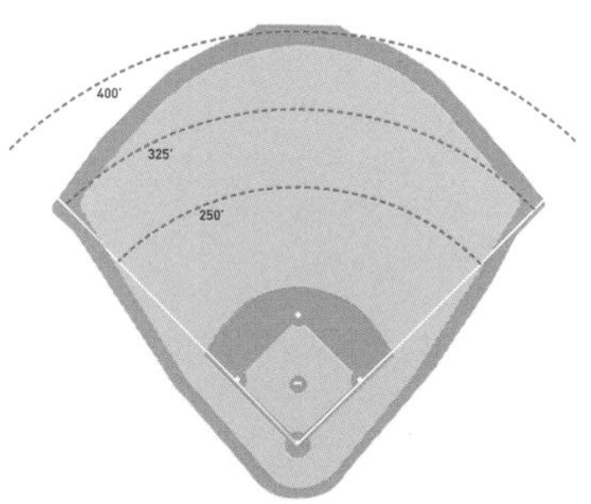

MLB Fields | # Field Comparisons

American League Central

Cleveland Indians

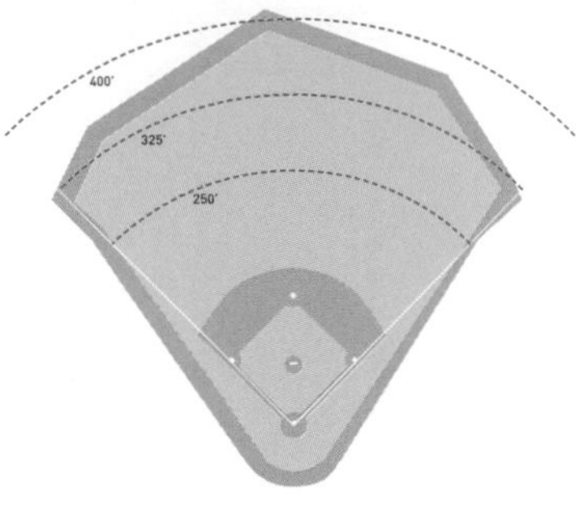

Minnesota Twins

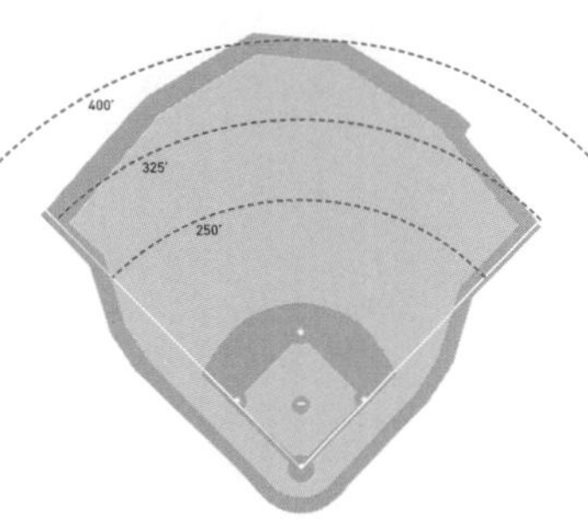

Detroit Tigers

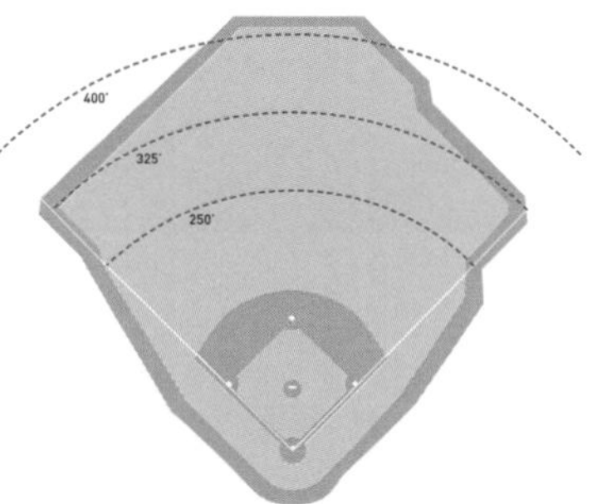

Kansas City Royals

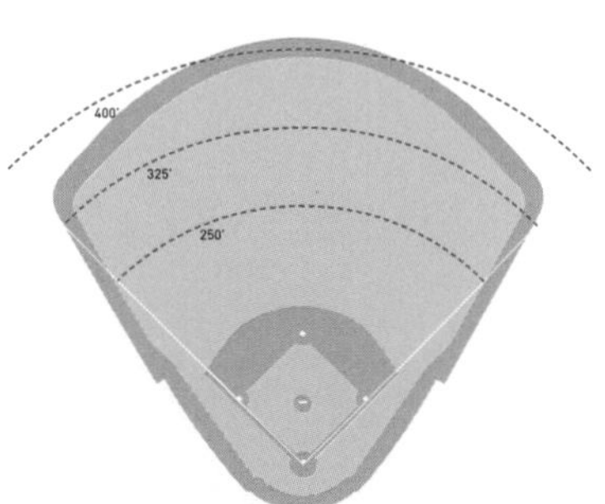

American League West

Anaheim Angels

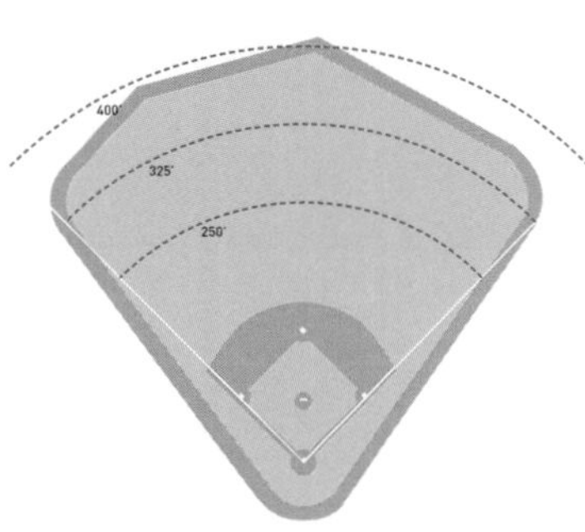

Oakland Athletics

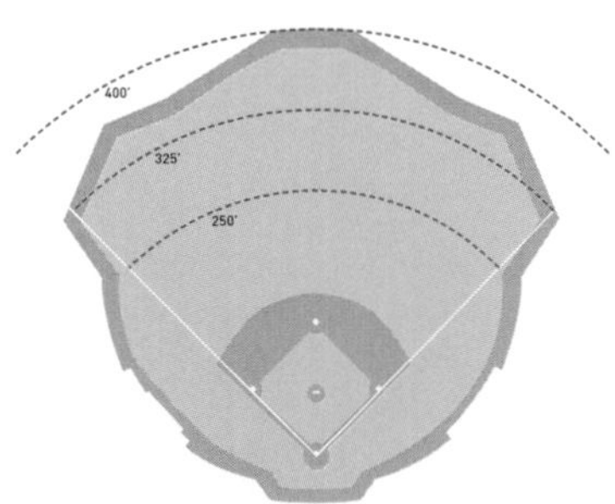

MLB Fields | Field Comparisons

American League West

Seattle Mariners

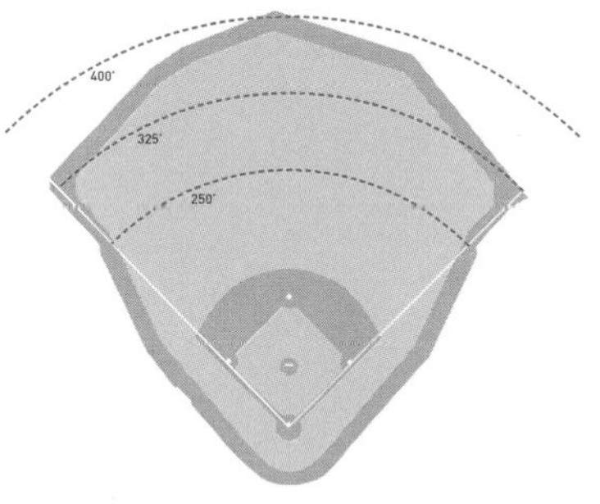

Texas Rangers

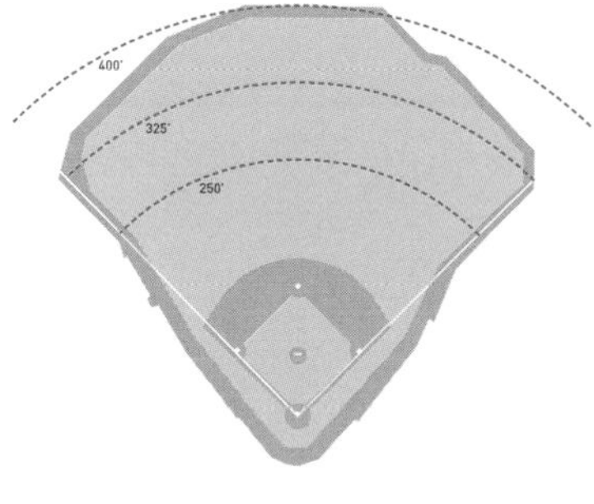

National League East

Florida Marlins

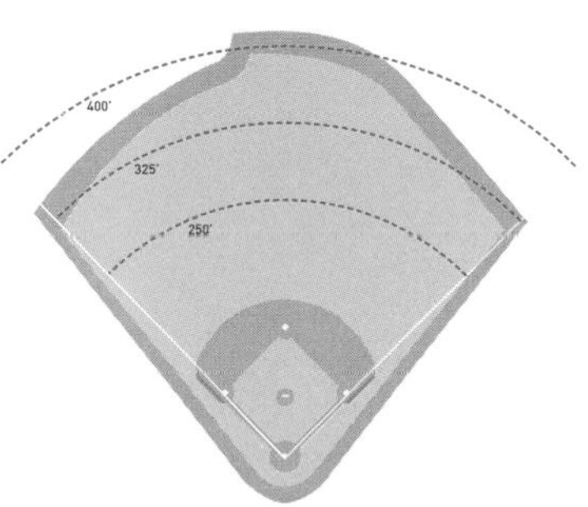

New York Mets

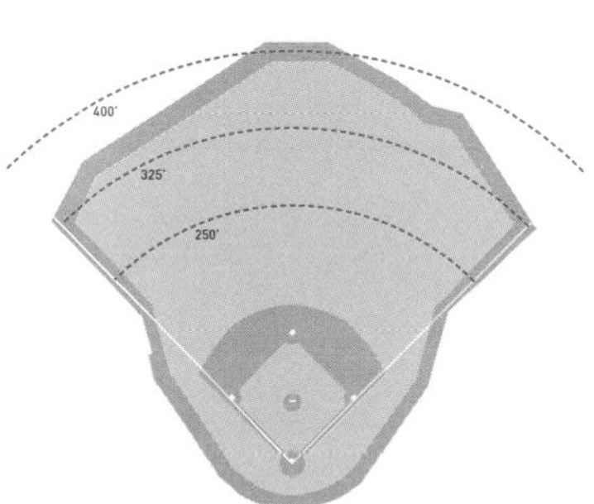

National League East

Atlanta Braves

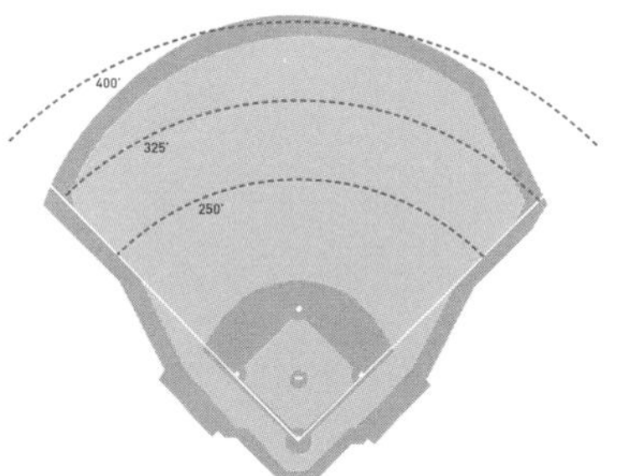

Philadelphia Phillies

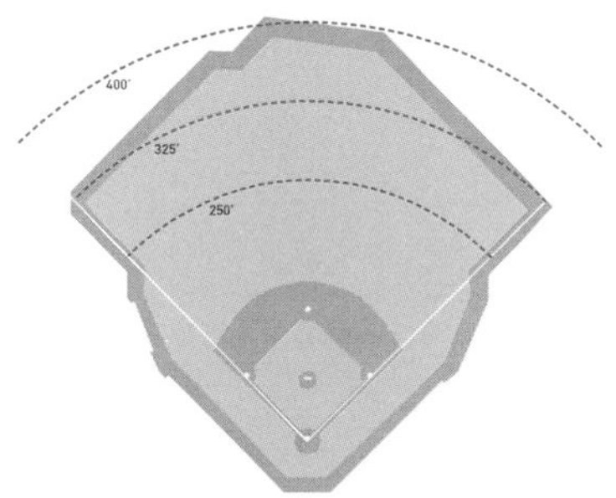

MLB Fields

Field Comparisons

National League East

Washington Nationals

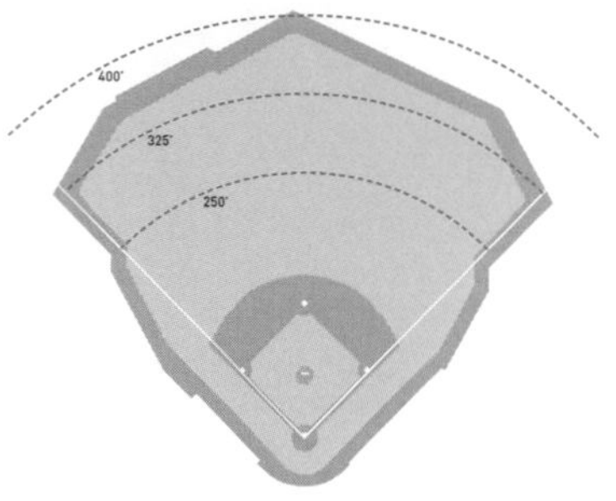

National League Central

Houston Astros

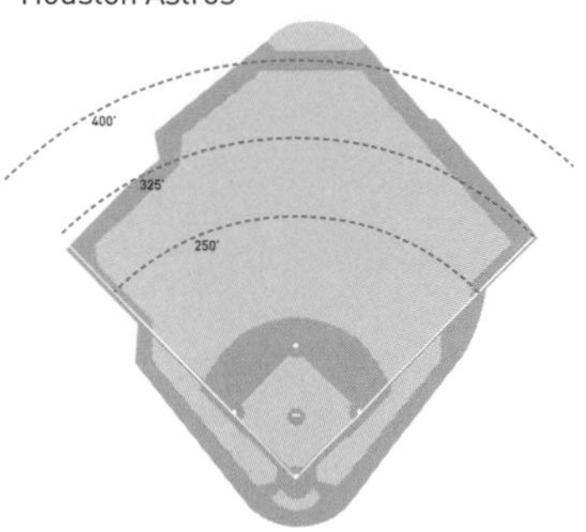

Chicago Cubs

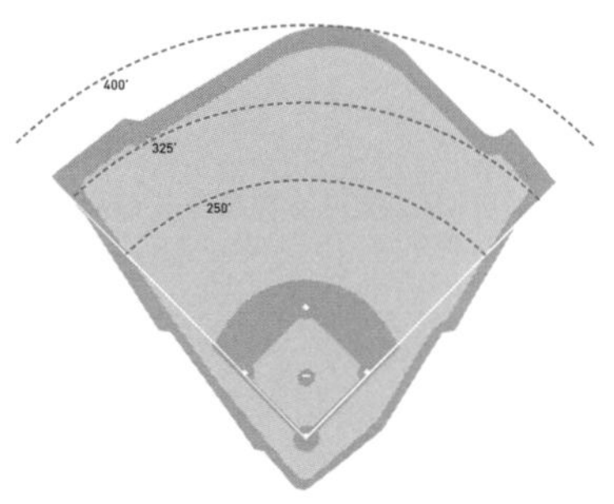

Milwaukee Brewers

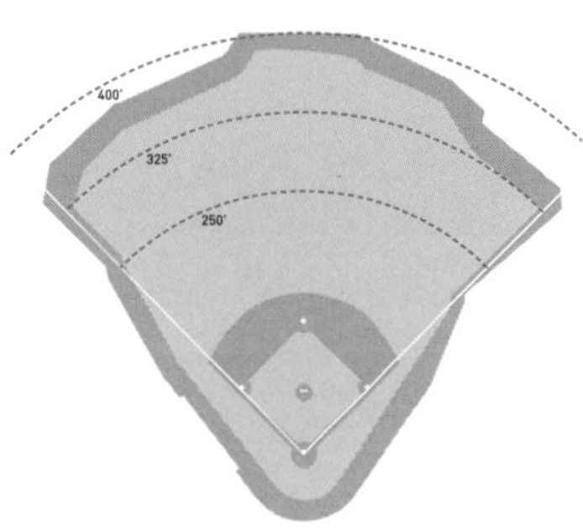

Cincinnati Reds

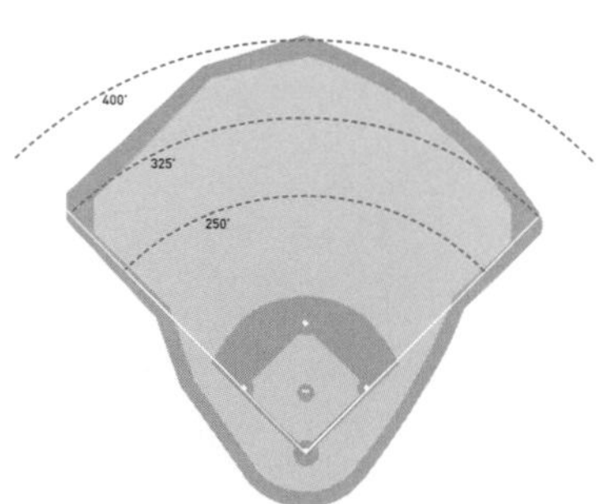

Pittsburgh Pirates

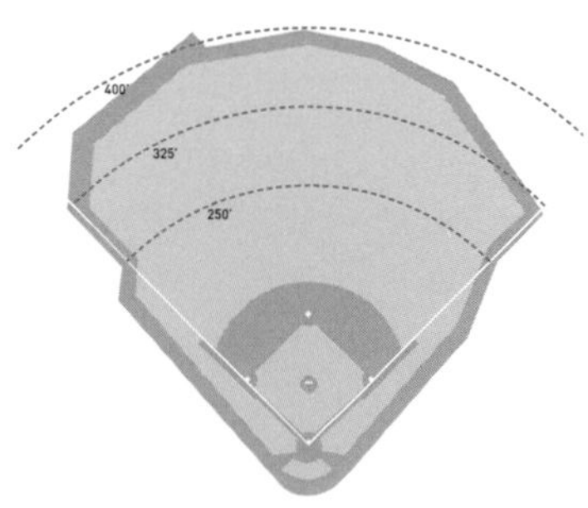

MLB Fields | # Field Comparisons

National League Central

St. Louis Cardinals

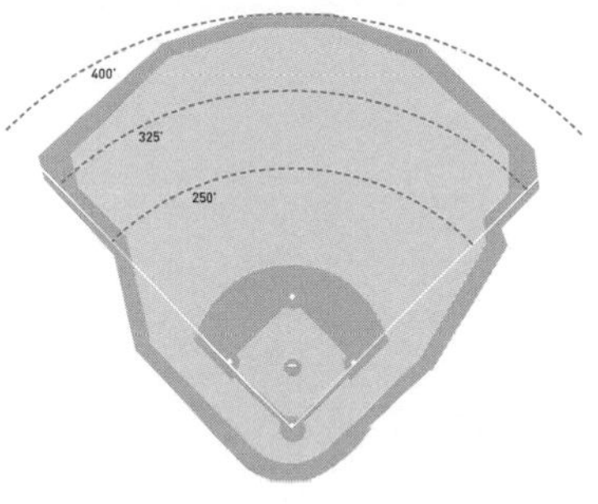

National League West

Los Angeles Dodgers

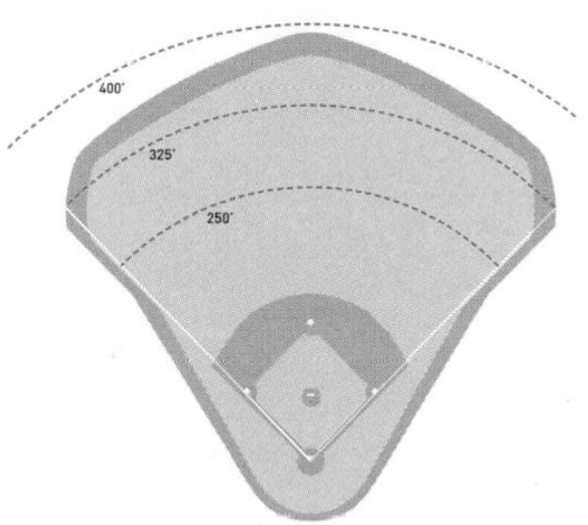

National League West

Arizona Diamondbacks

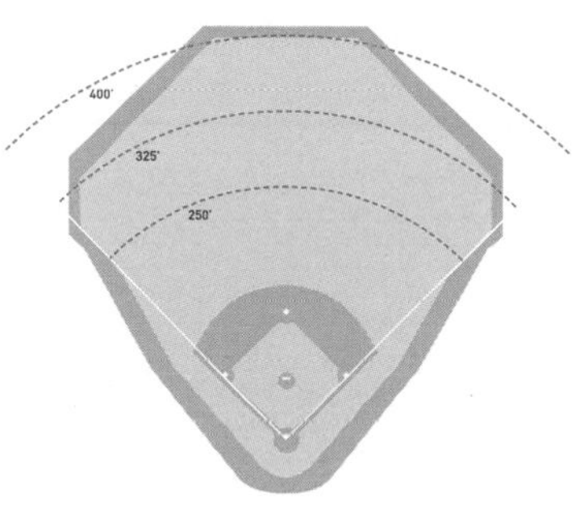

San Diego Padres

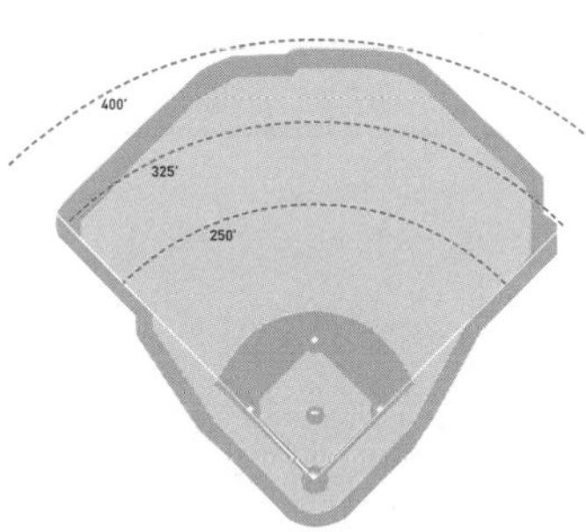

Colorado Rockies

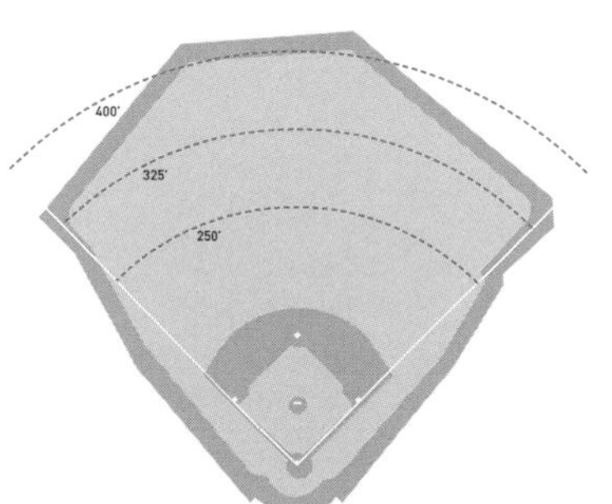

San Francisco Giants

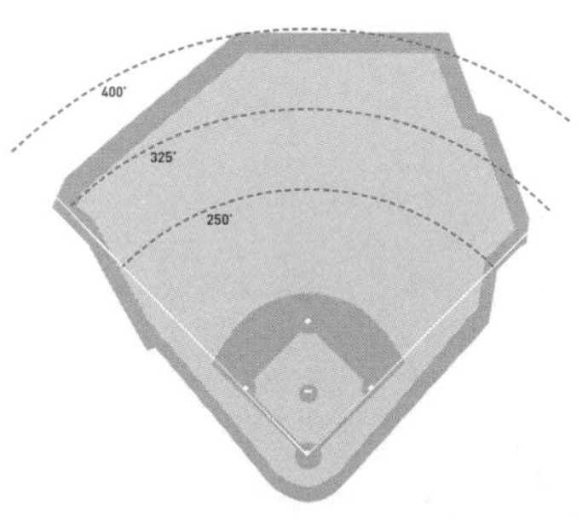

6 | Pitching

Because he handles the ball constantly, the pitcher is perhaps the most closely scrutinized player in the game.

The rules strictly specify the movements a pitcher is and is not allowed to make when throwing the ball from the pitcher's mound. This chapter covers a wide range of topics such as balks, ball tampering (it's frowned upon), and visits to the pitcher's mound by a coach or manager.

Pitching: contents

Pitching Positions: The Windup and Set (or Stretch) Positions

Overview: There are two legal pitching positions that can be used by a pitcher at any time in a game — the windup position and the set position.

Pitching Positions

The Windup Position

The delivery from the windup position is designed to give the pitcher optimum power.

The windup is typically used when there are no runners on base. It's a slow and deliberate delivery that would allow plenty of time for a runner on first or second base to steal a base.

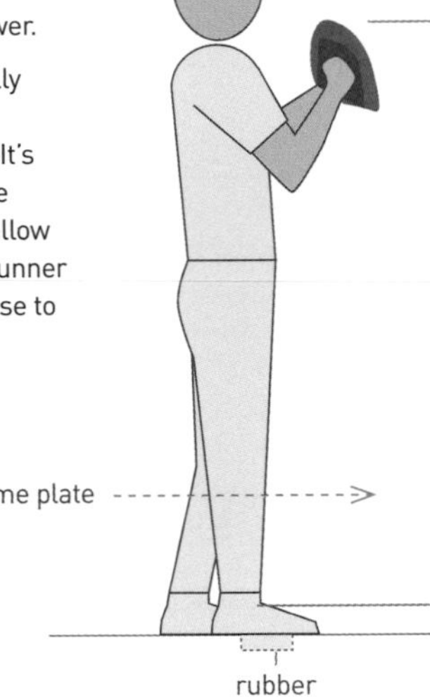

His head must be facing the batter.

The pitcher's hands may be joined or apart. If apart, the pitcher will generally join his hands during or just prior to starting his motion to pitch, getting his desired grip on the ball.

His pivot foot (the right foot for a right-handed pitcher, left foot for a left-handed pitcher) is on the rubber, his "free foot" can be to the side or behind the rubber. His body will be facing home plate.

The windup delivery and footwork

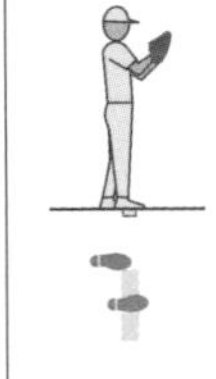

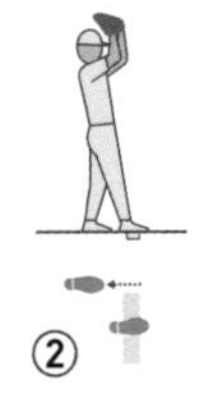

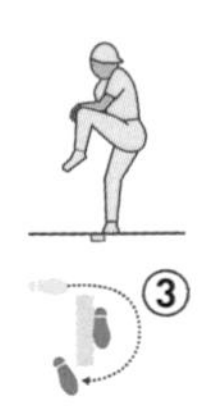

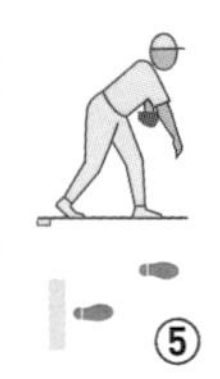

1. To start, both feet must be on the ground. His pivot foot must be on the rubber, and his other foot can be anywhere — usually just behind his pivot foot. This is the position in which the pitcher takes his signs.

2. As he begins the pitch, his free foot can move one step back.

3. The pitcher then lifts his leg around the pivot leg, and the pivot foot will turn to be parallel with the rubber for traction.

4. The pitcher will lunge forward into the pitch.

5. After releasing the ball, he will try to be in a position to field a hit ball.

Pitching with a runner on base

The pitcher's role becomes far more complicated when there is a runner on base. Not only must he try to put the batter out, he must prevent the runner from stealing a base or taking a big lead. Accordingly, the rules are more complex and constraining for a pitcher when there is a runner on base. He is not allowed to "deceive the runner" during his pitching sequence, or he will be charged with a balk (see page 62).

Pitching Positions

The Set Position

Pitchers use the set position to keep runners at bay by delivering the ball to the plate sooner and with less warning. The delivery is a quick lunge into the pitch, and the pitcher sacrifices some power.

The set position is used primarily when there are runners on base.

His head must be facing the batter.

He must move from a position where one hand is by his side or behind him to a position where both hands are in front of his body.

With his pivot foot in contact with the rubber, his free foot must be in front of the rubber. This puts his body in a sideways position.

The set delivery and footwork

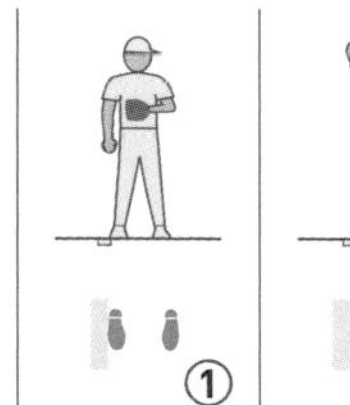

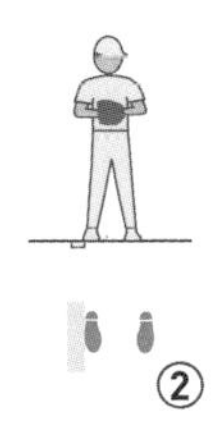

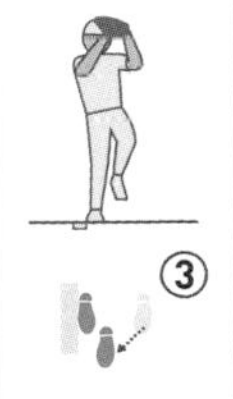

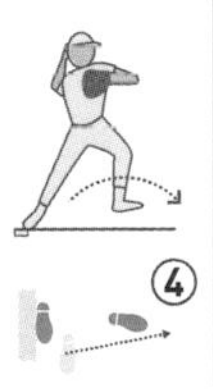

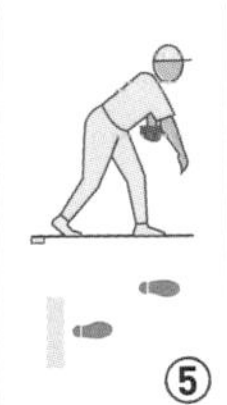

1. To start, both feet must be on the ground. His pivot foot must be in contact with the rubber, and his other foot must be in front of it. This is the position from which the pitcher takes his signs.

2. As he moves to the set position, his feet remain in the same position.

3. As he begins the pitch, he will lift his front foot up and back quickly into an abbreviated windup.

4. From here, the two deliveries are very similar — the pitcher will lunge forward into the pitch.

5. After releasing the ball, he will try to be in a position to field a hit ball.

The Pitching Sequence: Windup vs. Set

Overview: While the rules of baseball refer to the windup and set as alternate "positions," it's easier to understand them if you consider the entire sequence and delivery of each.

The windup position: home plate is toward the right →

1. Taking signs. The pitcher stands with his pivot foot on the rubber and his other foot on or slightly behind the rubber. He will be facing home plate.

2. The windup position. The pitcher may raise his glove in front of him to indicate he is ready to pitch. Any throwing motion after this will commit the pitcher to the pitch. From this point he can:

- step off the rubber
- commit to the pitch
- throw to a base

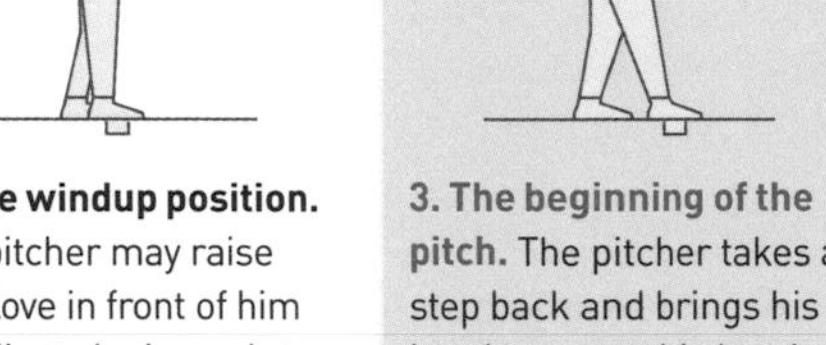

3. The beginning of the pitch. The pitcher takes a step back and brings his hands up over his head.

As soon as he begins this motion, the pitcher has committed to the pitch and must complete it. If not, a balk will be called.

The set position: home plate is toward the right →

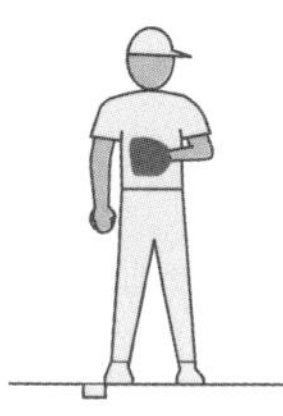

1. Taking signs. The pitcher stands with his back foot (the pivot foot) on the rubber, and one hand behind him or at his side. He will be facing first base if he is a left-hander, or third base if he is a right-hander.

2. Optional transition. The pitcher can make a quick motion, raising his hands up or even above his head as he moves into the set position.

3. The set position. The pitcher brings his hands in front of him with both hands on the ball. He must come to a complete stop in his motion. He can remain in this position indefinitely. From this point he can:

- step off the rubber
- throw to a base
- commit to the pitch

Comparison of the windup and set deliveries:

The windup is slow but powerful

- Pitcher commits to the pitch as soon as he begins his motion.
- A big slow step backward and then a powerful lunge forward into the pitch.

The set is quick and flexible

- Pitcher can decide to throw to a base or commit to the pitch at the last instant.
- Quick delivery of the ball.

4. The windup or pivot. The pitcher literally winds himself up to deliver as much power as he can, lifting his leg up and around his body.

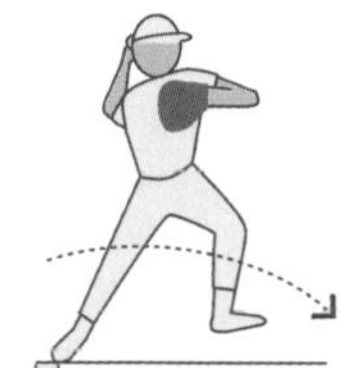

5. The stride. The pitcher lunges toward home plate as he releases the ball.

6. The follow-through. After the pitcher releases the ball, he is typically facing the batter, ready to field a hit.

4. The beginning of the pitch. The pitcher takes a step toward the plate.

At soon as he begins this motion, the pitcher has committed to the pitch and must complete it. If not, a balk will be called.

5. The stride. The pitcher lunges toward home plate as he releases the ball.

6. The follow-through. After the pitcher releases the ball, he is typically facing the batter, ready to field a hit.

The Balk

Overview: A balk is a penalty charged against a pitcher for illegally deceiving the base runner. Since there are twenty distinctly different ways to balk, it is among the most complex and misunderstood rules of the game.

Intent of the balk. The balk is meant to prevent the pitcher from illegally deceiving the base runner or the batter. It occurs most often when a pitcher tries to catch a runner off guard in order to prevent possibilities such as stealing a base or getting too much of a lead off a base.

Penalty. In all cases, the penalty for a balk is a single base awarded to all runners (but not the batter). This penalty is always charged to the pitcher.

Dead ball. For a balk called while the pitcher is throwing to a base, or while he is not involved in the act of pitching, the ball is dead immediately.

On a pitched balk, it is a delayed dead ball. This means that the umpire will wait to see if the batter gets a hit before calling the balk. If he gets a hit the balk will not be called.

Quick list: Twenty ways to balk

1. **Interrupt his pitching motion.**
2. **Fail to come to a complete stop during the set position.**
3. **Fail to step toward and ahead of a throw.**
4. **Fail to have both hands on the ball once he's in the set position.**
5. **Pitch while his pivot foot is not touching the rubber.**
6. **Pitch while his head is not facing the batter.**
7. **Fake a throw to first or third base.**
8. **With runners on first and third, step toward third without throwing.**
9. **Fake or complete a throw to an unoccupied base.**
10. **Commit to a pitch without completing the pitch.**
11. **Make a quick pitch.**
12. **Fake a pitch.**
13. **Drop the ball while on the rubber.**
14. **Disengage the rubber improperly.**
15. **Delay the game.**
16. **Come to the set position twice.**
17. **Change from one pitching position to the other without disengaging the rubber.**
18. **Pitch using a tampered ball.**

Balks caused by other players:

19. **Catcher or other player tries to block a runner attempting to score from third base.**
20. **Catcher is outside the catcher's box during an intentional walk.**

The Balk

Twenty Ways to Balk

1. Interrupt the pitching motion, perhaps the most common way to balk. After the set position, the motion must be continuous without jerks or stops.

2. Fail to come to a complete stop during the set position. There must be a noticeable pause in the pitcher's motion (see page 60).

3. Fail to step toward and ahead of a throw. The pitcher is required to take a clear and deliberate step in the direction he is about to throw the ball. The step must precede the throw (even if only by a split second).

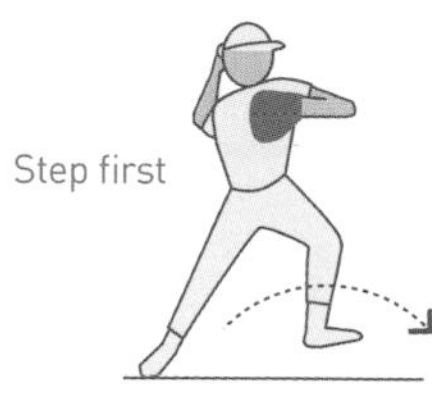
Step first

then throw

This rule applies to a throw to any base or a pitch to the plate.

This rule is often broken when the pitcher twirls toward a base and throws the ball in one fluid motion. Instead, he must spin, step, and throw. Without this rule it would be too easy to "pick a runner off" (catch the runner while he has stepped off his base).

4. Fail to have both hands on the ball once he's in the set position. If he takes one hand off the ball without pitching, it is a balk (see page 60).

Note: The pitcher is not required to have both hands on the ball while in the positions preceding the set position.

5. Pitch while his pivot foot is not touching the rubber. The pitcher's pivot foot must be touching the rubber during a legal pitching motion.

6. Pitch while his head is not facing the batter. If the pitcher pitches the ball without his head turned toward the batter, it is considered deceptive (and probably a bit dangerous).

7. Fake a throw to first or third base. The pitcher cannot begin a throwing motion to first or third without completing the throw.

8. With runners on first and third, step toward third without throwing, then throw to first to pick off the runner.

9. Fake or complete a throw to an unoccupied base, although it's okay to fake a throw to second if a runner is occupying the base, or the pitcher is making a play on a runner who may be approaching second base.

Note: If the bases are empty and the pitcher throws to a base, he can be charged with delaying the game.

10. Commit to a pitch without completing the pitch. From the set or windup position the pitcher cannot begin a motion to pitch without completing the pitch.

See page 60 for in-depth information about the entire pitching motion and "committing" to the pitch.

11. Make a quick pitch. Pitching before the batter is ready is considered an illegal deception. For example, the pitcher cannot step off the pitcher's rubber and then quickly step back on and pitch the ball, catching the batter unprepared.

Note: A quick pitch is illegal even if there are no base runners, at which time the penalty is a ball.

12. Fake a pitch. This type of balk can be called whether or not the pitcher has possession of the ball and whether or not he is touching the rubber.

Example: If the pitcher steps on the rubber without having possession of the ball, the umpire should interpret this as an intent to illegally deceive the runner.

13. Drop the ball while on the rubber. This includes a pitched ball that slips out of his hands and fails to cross a foul line.

14. Disengage the rubber improperly. When disengaging hands must be at his sides. He may not disengage after taking signs.

(continued...)

The Balk

Twenty Ways to Balk

continued

15. Delay the game, if the umpire believes that a pitcher is intentionally delaying the game.

16. Come to the set position twice.

17. Change from one pitching position to the other without disengaging the rubber.

18. Pitch using a tampered ball. A balk and an automatic ball will be charged — unless the manager of the team at bat chooses to accept the play that ensued. The pitcher will also be ejected and suspended from future games for this violation.

Balks caused by other players:

19. Catcher or other player tries to block a runner attempting to score from third base by stealing home, or during a squeeze play.

20. Catcher is outside the catcher's box during an intentional walk. A balk is called if an intentional ball is pitched when the catcher is outside of the catcher's box.

Note 1: With a runner on base, if the batter steps out of the batter's box, or otherwise unintentionally interrupts the pitcher after he has started his windup, the pitcher will be allowed to stop his pitching motion. (See page 85.)

Note 2: No member of the opposing team may cause a pitcher to balk. For example, if a bat boy yells "time," causing the pitcher to stop his pitch, the bat boy will be removed and the balk will be nullified.

The Strike Zone

The strike zone is an area over home plate. The width and depth is that of home plate, and the top and bottom of the strike zone is determined by the height and stance of the batter. If a legal pitch passes through any point in the strike zone, it's called a strike. If a pitch that isn't swung on doesn't pass through any point in the strike zone, it's called a ball.

The strike zone is defined by both the batter and home plate

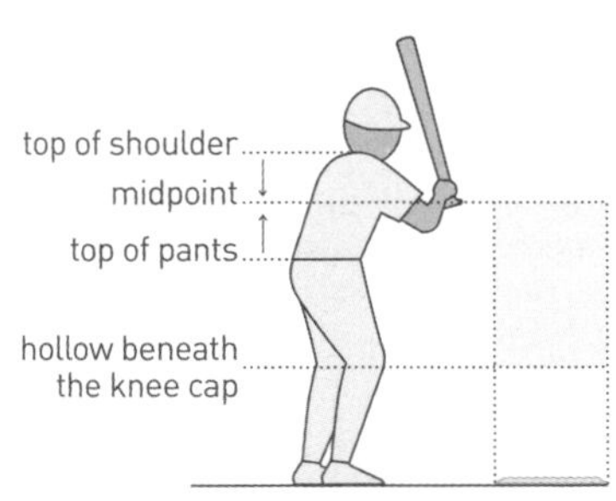

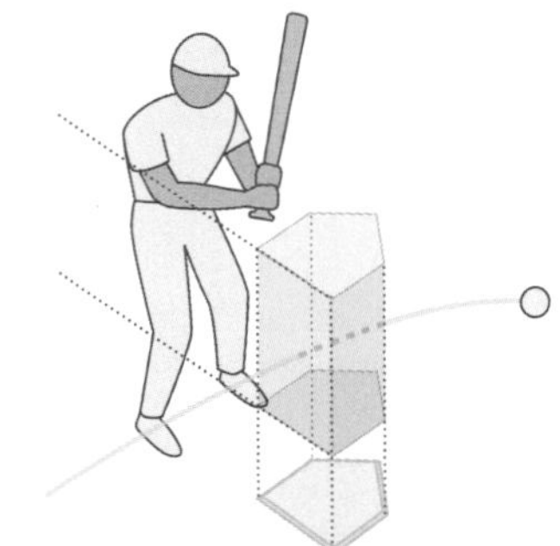

Note: For an extensive description of the strike zone, see page 80 in the Batting chapter.

Strikes and Balls

Overview: A pitched ball can result in a strike, a ball, a foul, or a hit. This page explains the rules that define whether a pitch, when not successfully hit, is declared a strike or a ball.

A strike is called when:

1. A pitch passes through the strike zone and...	the batter does not swing the bat.
	the ball touches the batter. (This is not considered a "hit by pitch.")
2. A pitch does *not* pass through the strike zone and...	the ball touches the batter as he attempts to hit it. (This is not considered a "hit by pitch.")
3. On any pitch (strike zone or not)...	the batter swings but misses.
	the batter bunts the ball into foul territory.
	the batter, with fewer than two strikes against him, hits a ball that is ruled a foul ball (unless it is caught for an out).
	the batter hits a foul tip. A "foul tip" occurs when the batter swings, the bat grazes the ball, the ball goes directly into the catcher's mitt and is caught.

A strike for misbehaving

A strike is also called when an umpire must penalize a batter for refusing to enter the batter's box.

In Minor League games, an umpire calls a strike if a batter leaves the batter's box without a good reason.

A ball is called when:

1. A pitch does *not* pass through the strike zone and...	the batter does not swing.
2. A ball can also be called as a penalty against the pitcher for four infractions:	the pitcher makes an illegal pitch (such as a quick pitch) when no runners are on base.
	the pitcher delays the game when, with no runners on base and the batter in position, he does not pitch within twelve seconds of receiving the ball. (With runners on base, this delay will result in a balk.)
	the pitcher touches his pitching hand to his mouth while on the pitcher's mound.
	the pitcher (or an unidentified player on his team) defaces or otherwise tampers with the ball. (The pitcher will be ejected and given a ten-game suspension.)

Wild Pitches and Throws by the Pitcher

Overview: Wild pitches and wild throws are those that are unable to be caught by the catcher or a fielder with "ordinary effort" because the ball is thrown too high, too low, or too wide.

The rules governing wild pitches vary depending on where the ball ends up, and whether the wild pitch occurred on the third strike or fourth ball. Wild throws by the pitcher are throws to fielders that are unable to be caught with ordinary effort. They can sometimes end up in the dugout, stands, or otherwise go out of play.

On a wild pitch:	the ball...	runners advance...
if the ball gets past the catcher but remains on the playing field....	**remains in play**	**at their own risk**
if the pitch goes into an area where the ball is dead, including the dugout, stands, and other areas that would make the ball unplayable....	**is dead**	**1 base**
if the ball deflects off the catcher into an area where the ball is dead....	**is dead**	**1 base**
if a pitch hits a runner attempting to score at home....	**is dead**	**1 base**
if a pitch (not the result of a foul tip) lodges in the umpire's or catcher's mask or equipment....	**is dead**	**1 base**

On a wild throw by the pitcher:

if a ball is thrown by the pitcher from his position on the rubber to a fielder, and the ball goes into an area where it is dead....	**is dead**	**1 base**
if the pitcher steps off of the pitcher's rubber before making a wild throw, he is acting as an infielder. The wild-throw rule for infielders applies....	**is dead**	**2 bases**

The third-strike rule

When the catcher does not catch a pitch on the third strike and no one is on first base, or there's a runner on first with two outs, the batter is not out and must attempt to run to first base.

When a wild pitch occurs on a third strike and results in any of the situations described in the above chart, the batter-runner is governed by the same rules as the other runners. He is awarded the same number of bases.

Example: If on a third strike a pitch gets past the catcher and becomes lodged in the umpire's mask, the batter advances to first base and all runners advance one base. See page 83 for more on the third-strike rule.

A batter hit by a wild pitch

A batter hit by a pitch is awarded first base. The ball is dead and runners advance only if they are forced to advance as a result of the batter going to first. (Also see "Hit by a Pitch" on page 90.)

Miscellaneous Pitching Rules

Taking hand signs

The official rule book states that pitchers "must take signs from the catcher while standing on the rubber." While in this position, he may actually take signs from any member of his team, although typically signs come from the catcher.

Penalty. Accepting hand signs when not standing on the pitcher's rubber will result in a warning from the umpire (it is not a balk). However, with repeated offenses, the umpire may choose to eject the pitcher from the game.

Note: After receiving his signs a pitcher may elect to disengage the pitcher's rubber (step off the plate) or continue with the pitching sequence.

The pitcher becomes an infielder when he steps off the rubber

A pitcher becomes an infielder if he disengages the rubber by stepping off with his pivot foot. When he is off of the rubber, the pitcher may throw to any other base just like any other infielder. In this situation a wild throw by the pitcher is treated like a wild throw by an infielder. That is, the batter and runners may be awarded two bases on a wild throw that goes out of play (as opposed to one base if the wild throw occurred while he was throwing from his pitching position).

Attempting to hit the batter with a pitch

The pitcher, and possibly the manager and the pitcher, may be ejected from the game if, in the umpire's judgment, the pitcher pitches with the intention of hitting the batter. The umpire has the option, on the first offense, to issue a warning. Alternatively both teams may officially receive this warning from the umpire before the start of the game.

Because throwing with the intention of hitting the batter is dangerous behavior, in addition to being ejected from the game, a League President may take further action to punish the offenders.

Pitcher's uniform and glove

The rules impose special restrictions on the pitcher's uniform to minimize visual distractions.

- No numbers, letters, or insignias on the sleeve of his undershirt.
- The pitcher's glove cannot be white or gray, since those colors can obscure the ball. All parts of the glove — the stitching, lacing, and web — must be uniform in color, and no other material with a varying color can be attached to the glove.
- As with other players, but especially the pitcher, glass buttons and any kind of shiny metal jewelry are not permitted.

A pitcher can be ejected from the game for the following:

- Having a foreign substance (or an altering object) in his possession.
- Throwing the ball with the intention of hitting the batter.
- Continuing to take signs while not in his position on the pitcher's rubber.
- Pitching with a tampered ball.
- Being an illegal substitute.
- Intentionally delaying the game by throwing the ball needlessly to other fielders when a batter is in position. (A warning and balk will be given first.)
- Intentionally walking a batter by having four balls called by repeatedly touching his mouth or lips then touching the ball.

Ball Tampering: Spitballs and More

Overview: Tampering with the ball is the act of wetting it, rubbing it with dirt or another foreign substance, discoloring it, or scuffing it, for the purpose of making it more difficult to hit. Simply put, the pitcher is not allowed to alter the ball in any way. If tampering is suspected, the umpire can demand to inspect the ball. He becomes the sole judge of whether a violation has occurred.

Intent of the rule. Tampering with the ball can affect the way the ball is thrown, its flight pattern, or otherwise make a pitched ball more difficult to hit. Ball tampering is therefore illegal.

Tampering | ## Types of Ball Tampering

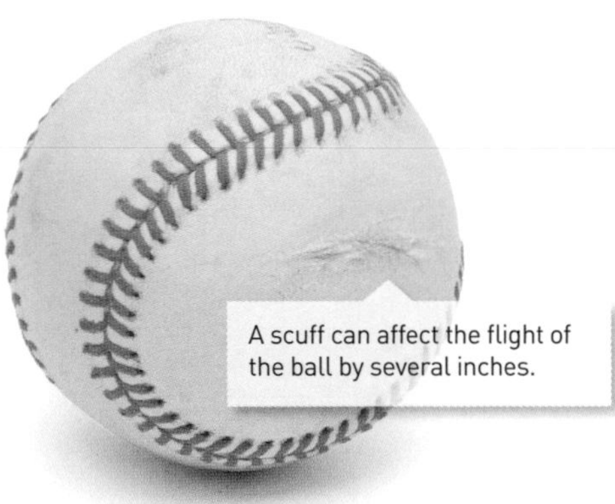

A scuff can affect the flight of the ball by several inches.

Illegal actions

The pitcher may not:

1. apply any "foreign substance" to the ball.

2. spit on the ball, his hand, or his glove.

3. rub the ball using his glove, body, or clothing (although he can rub the ball using his bare hands).

4. alter the ball in any way.

5. scuff the ball, or use what the official rule book terms the "emery ball."

6. touch his hand to his mouth (unless authorized by the umpire).

Illegal substances

The Official Baseball Rules ban specific substances from being carried onto the field. These include soil, rosin, paraffin, sandpaper, or emery paper. The rules go on, however, to cover themselves by adding any "other foreign substance" to the list of banned materials.

Penalty: The penalty against the pitcher for either tampering with the ball or carrying an illegal substance will be:

- immediate ejection from the game, and
- automatic suspension.

Minor League rules specify a ten-game suspension. In the Major Leagues the length of suspension is up to the commissioner.

Note 1: If a play continues after the violation is called, the offensive team's manager can elect to accept the play. He must notify the plate umpire immediately after the play is completed.

If the play is *not* accepted:

- With no runners on base, a ball is added to the count.
- With runners on base, the penalty is a balk and the pitch does not count.

Illegal candy

There is a dated mention in the official rules of the use of licorice as an illegal substance. It was used, at times, to discolor or mark the ball.

Note 2: In the case that the batter successfully reaches first base and no other runner is put out, the play will count. This is the case regardless of whether the batter reached first base on a hit, an error, a walk, a hit batter, or other means. But even with the play accepted the tampering violation will be charged against the pitcher.

Note 3: If a player other than the pitcher is identified as the offender, that player will be immediately ejected from the game. He will receive an automatic ten-game suspension.

However, if the pitcher pitches a ball that has been discolored or damaged and the umpire cannot identify the offender, the pitcher will be considered at fault.

Marked ball. A ball that has been discolored is illegal because it can be visually distracting or more difficult for the batter to see.

Scuffed ball. A scuff, scratch, or tear on the ball will affect its flight, creating greater aerodynamic drag on one side of the ball than the other. The ball will curve toward the scuffed side of the ball. The effect on the flight path can be slight, but even a small deviation can make a big difference.

Banned from either hand. Rules specifically mention tape, Band-Aids, Super Glue, and bracelets among the banned materials.

Spitballs. A spitball is a ball thrown after wetting the ball or the pitcher's fingers, using spit, sweat, Vaseline, or any other form of lubricant. Wetting makes it easier to throw the ball with little or no spin. A non-spinning ball can curve or drop more readily and can therefore be more difficult to hit.

Hand-to-mouth rule. Touching his mouth or lips is a less blatent form of ball wetting. A pitcher is not allowed to:

- touch the ball after touching his mouth or lips when standing on the mound, or
- touch his mouth or lips at all while in contact with the pitcher's rubber.

He must clearly dry his pitching hand before touching the ball or contacting the rubber.

Exception 1: In cold weather, if agreed upon by both managers prior to the start of the game, the umpire will allow pitchers to blow on their hands to warm them.

Exception 2: In cases where the pitch is completed and the batter reaches first base without any other runner being put out, the play will automatically count as if the violation had not occurred.

Penalty: On first violation the umpire will warn the pitcher and take the ball out of play. Any following violations will be a "ball." Further, the League President can impose a fine for a pitcher's repeated violations.

Balls that come apart. A ball that comes apart will stay in play until the end of that play.

The rosin bag

Pitchers are allowed to use a bag of rosin to help them get a good grip on the ball. The umpire-in-chief is responsible for making sure no one tampers with the rosin bag. He ensures the placement of an official rosin bag to be used by all pitchers during that game.

The rosin bag is placed on the back of the pitcher's mound, but if it's raining, the umpire may ask the pitchers to put the bag in their hip pocket. The pitcher can apply the rosin to his bare hands. No player is allowed to apply rosin directly to the ball, a glove, or any part of a player's uniform.

Pitcher Substitutions (Relief Pitchers)

The starting pitcher

Prior to the start of the game, each team is required to hand their batting order to the umpire-in-chief. The pitcher whose name appears on the batting order cannot be substituted until the first batter, or a substitute for that batter, either reaches first base or is put out. The only exception would be when a starting pitcher becomes injured or ill, and if, in the judgment of the umpire, he is no longer able to play.

Substitute pitchers

A substitute pitcher, also called a relief pitcher, may replace the current pitcher at any point in the game (provided the current pitcher has pitched through at least one batter's turn at bat). The pitcher will not be eligible to play once he is removed from the game. However, a pitcher can be switched to another position and return to the pitcher's position at a later time.

Substitute pitchers while a batter is still at bat

When a substitute pitcher replaces the current pitcher while a batter is still at bat, the substitute pitcher must pitch to that batter (or to a substitute for that batter) until the batter reaches first base or is put out, or until the inning is over. The only exception would be if the substitute pitcher becomes injured or ill, and if, in the judgment of the umpire, he is no longer able to play.

Improper substitutes for the pitcher

In the case of an improper substitution for the pitcher, the umpire shall require the proper pitcher to return to complete his turn at the pitcher's mound.

Even in situations where, by mistake, the umpire-in-chief announces the substitution of an improper pitcher, the mistake, if caught, should be corrected before the improper pitcher begins pitching.

However, any play that takes place while an improper pitcher is pitching will be legal and will stand. As soon as the improper pitcher delivers a pitch to the batter, or as soon as a runner is put out, the improper pitcher is no longer improper — he becomes the proper pitcher and continues his turn at the mound. At this point, the manager cannot remove that pitcher until the batter has completed his turn at bat, or until the end of the half-inning. The umpire is required to notify the manager of this ruling.

Pitchers are allowed up to eight warm-up pitches

The pitcher, either at the start of each inning or when substituting for another pitcher, may throw up to eight warm-up pitches to the catcher. The warm-up pitches should not exceed one minute of time. The umpire-in-chief may extend this in possible "emergency" cases, when the pitcher has not had adequate time to warm up prior to being called to the pitching mound.

Note: In televised games, the period in-between innings is determined by the time allotted for television commercials. The pitcher is generally allowed to use as much of this time for warm-up pitches as he wants.

Changing positions

Upon being substituted a pitcher may assume another playing position rather than be removed from the game. If he returns to the pitching position that same inning, he cannot change positions again that inning — that would require a second visit to him by the manager, resulting in his removal.

Note: Also see *When a pitcher crosses the line* on page 170.

Visits to the Pitcher's Mound

Visits to the pitcher's mound by a coach or manager

Simply stated, the coach or manager may visit the pitcher just once per inning. His "visit" to the pitcher starts when he crosses the foul line on his way to the mound, and ends when he leaves the eighteen-foot circle surrounding the pitcher's rubber.

Note: He may temporarily leave and return to the circle if it's just to notify the umpire about a substitution.

A coach or manager is allowed more than one visit to the mound if he is visiting more than one pitcher in the same inning. For instance, if the coach visits the pitcher's mound to remove a pitcher, and the manager visits the new pitcher that same inning, that will be considered one visit to the new pitcher.

If a pitcher is substituted during a batter's turn at bat, the coach or manager may not make a second visit to the pitcher's mound while that batter is still at bat, even though the visit is to the new pitcher.

The manager cannot use another player to communicate with the pitcher in order to avoid a second visit. For example, if the coach or manager visits the catcher, and before the next pitch or play takes place, the catcher visits the pitcher, it will be considered a visit by the manager.

Exceptions: The manager or coach may freely talk to the pitcher before the completion of his eighth warm-up throw, and before the pitcher's one-minute time limit for warming up, without this talk being charged as a visit. If the team at bat calls "time," a manager may also talk with the pitcher without that talk being counted as one of the visits — as long as the visit ends with the time out.

A second visit to a pitcher's mound

If a coach or manager visits the same pitcher for a second time in the same inning, that pitcher must be removed from the game, and a substitute pitcher must be named. There is no exception to this rule, even in the case when a pinch hitter has been substituted for a batter.

Penalty. If the manager persists in attempting to abuse this rule after being warned by the umpire, the manager will be immediately removed from the game. The pitcher will also be removed, at the conclusion of the current batter's turn at bat.

When this is the case the umpire should notify the manager that the pitcher is about to be removed from the game, so that a substitute pitcher can begin his warm-up. If the umpire feels it is justified, the new pitcher may be allowed to take more than the usual eight warm-up pitches when starting his turn at the mound.

A new pitcher resuming a suspended game

If a substitute pitcher hasn't ended an inning or put a batter on base, and the game is suspended, that substitute is not required to (but may) start the game when it is resumed. (This is the case even if the batter to which he was pitching did not complete a full turn at bat, therefore coming to bat when the game resumes.) However, if he does not start pitching in the resumed game he will be considered as being substituted and will not be allowed to play for the remainder of that game.

Ambidextrous Pitchers: Rules for any pitcher who can pitch with either hand

Overview: This is by no means a common occurrence. Finding a pitcher with the ability to use either hand to deliver equally great pitches is a rare event. Yet, it can happen.

The advantage of switch-pitching

The statistics show that batters consistently struggle against same-handed pitchers. For example, right-handed batters are less successful against right-handed pitchers. A pitcher who can throw with either hand can maintain that advantage by switching hands as necessary.

The rules for switch-pitching

MLB's Official Baseball Rules set requirements for pitchers who have the unusual ability (to say the least) to pitch in a Major League game with either hand. The rules for ambidextrous pitchers state:

- the pitcher must let the umpire-in-chief, the batter, and the runners know which hand he will be using to pitch. (This is a rather easy requirement, because he will do that simply by placing his glove on his non-pitching hand.)
- he must use that hand to pitch until that batter's turn at bat ends.

  Exception: The pitcher will be allowed to switch hands if his hand becomes injured. But if he switches for this reason he will not be permitted to pitch with that hand for the remainder of the game.
- he will be allowed to switch hands if a pinch-hitter substitutes for the batter.
- when switching pitching hands within an inning, he will not be permitted to take any warm-up pitches.

When a switch-hitter faces a switch-pitcher

Although ambidextrous hitting is also very difficult, it is a comparatively common skill. A versatile batter will switch hands in order to maintain an advantage over the pitcher.

The rule regarding ambidextrous pitching in this circumstance is simple. When a switch-hitter faces a switch-pitcher, the pitcher must choose first. The batter has the advantage of choosing hands after that.

Making a "mockery" of the game

In 1995, Greg Harris, a right-handed relief pitcher for the Montreal Expos, switched to his left hand against two batters in a game against the Cincinnati Reds.

After 15 years of pitching, he had never switch-pitched before that game. That was because he had played most of his career for the Boston Red Sox, where Lou Gorman, the general manager, didn't allow switch-pitching, saying "it would make a mockery of the game."

The Pat Venditte Rule

In 2008 Pat Venditte pitched an ambidextrous inning for the Staten Island Yankees in a Minor League game against the Brooklyn Cyclones. The last player he faced was Ralph Henriquez, a switch-hitter. Comedy and confusion ensued when every time Venditte switched pitching hands, Henriquez moved to the opposite side of the plate. It was a standoff until the umpires ruled that the batter must commit to one side of the plate before the pitcher was made to choose his pitching arm. A very angry Henriquez was subsequently struck out.

Weeks later, and because of the Venditte incident, the opposite ruling was adopted by Major League Baseball — the pitcher must commit first.

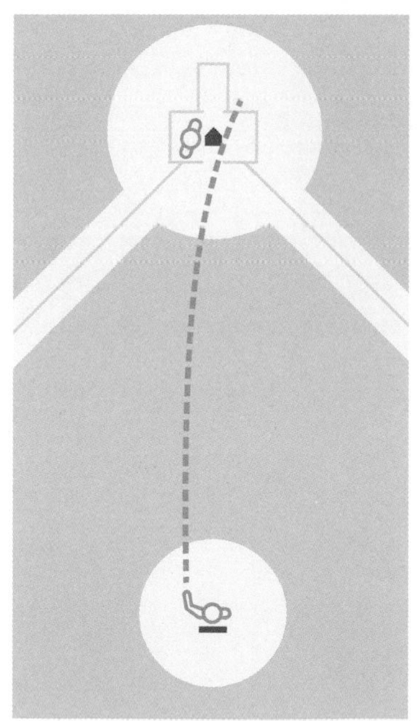

Righty or lefty... what's the diff?

There are varying opinions about why same-handed pitches are harder to hit. Here are a few popular theories:

- Curveballs and sliders move away from a same-handed hitter, toward the outside of the plate. Most hitters have more success with pitches to the inside of the plate.
- Many batters say it is more difficult to track a ball moving away from them.
- Some batters claim it is more difficult to see the ball as it leaves the hand — especially when coming from a pitcher with a side-arm delivery.

7 | Batting

Every offensive effort starts with a batter. It's where all the action begins in the game of baseball.

This chapter covers the rules concerning the batter, from the time he steps up to the plate, to the point when his turn at bat ends — either because he is out or because he became a runner. Included is a detailed description of the strike zone, the batter's box, and a list of every way a batter can get on base or be put out.

Batting: contents

Basics for the Batter

Overview: In order to understand many of the rules about batting, it will help to understand some terms and facts about the field. Here are a few basics.

Basics

Key Areas of the Field

The left and right foul poles: Rising above the outfield wall are the left and right field foul poles. They are an extension of the left and right foul lines and are there to help judge whether fly balls are fair or foul. Like the foul lines, the foul poles are actually in fair territory.

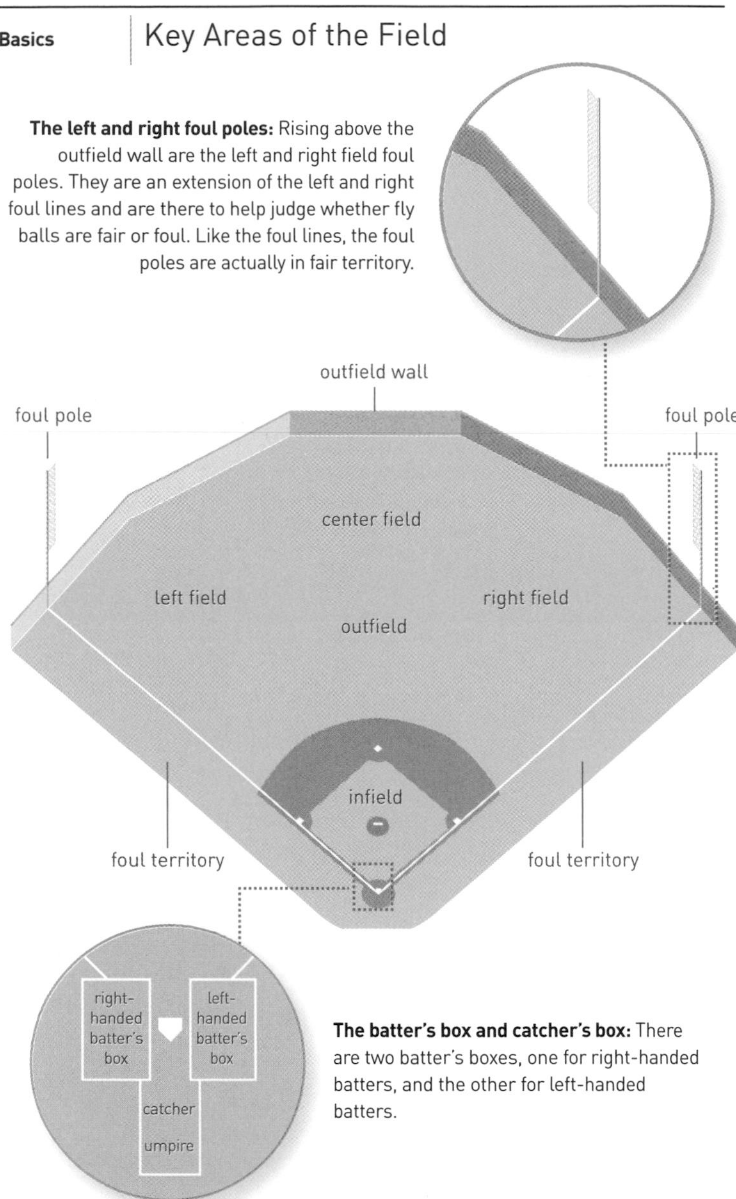

The batter's box and catcher's box: There are two batter's boxes, one for right-handed batters, and the other for left-handed batters.

Basics

Batting

At the end of a player's turn at bat, one of two things will happen:

1. The batter gets on base. See page 88 for all the ways a batter can get on base.

2. The batter is out. See page 98 for all the ways a batter can be out.

If another player is put out to end the inning

If a runner is put out for the third out before the batter ends his turn at bat, then that batter will be the first batter up for his team in the next inning. His new turn at bat will start a new count of balls and strikes.

Using the term "at-bat":

A completed turn as a batter is refered to as an at-bat. To the official scorer, however, not every plate appearance counts as an at-bat. See page 210.

Every legal pitch will result in a ball, a strike, a foul, or a hit.

A batter is out after receiving three strikes. See page 80 for information on strikes.

A batter walks after receiving four balls, freely advancing to first base (see page 79 for details about balls and walks).

Foul balls are strikes. A ball hit foul is counted as a strike against the batter, unless the batter already has two strikes (in which case the foul is ignored, and the batter continues with the same count of strikes and balls).

Like a fair ball, however, a foul fly ball can be caught by a fielder for an out.

See pages 78 and 79 for more information about fair and foul balls.

Basics

Bunting

A bunt is a type of hit designed to deaden the ball so it will slowly roll into the infield. While some batters attempt to bunt for a base hit, typically the intent is to sacrifice the batter so that a runner will be able to advance to the next base.

When a batter bunts, he hits the ball without swinging the bat. Instead he holds the bat stationary and lets the ball bounce off the bat. The official rules, however, have no guidelines about what constitutes a bunt.

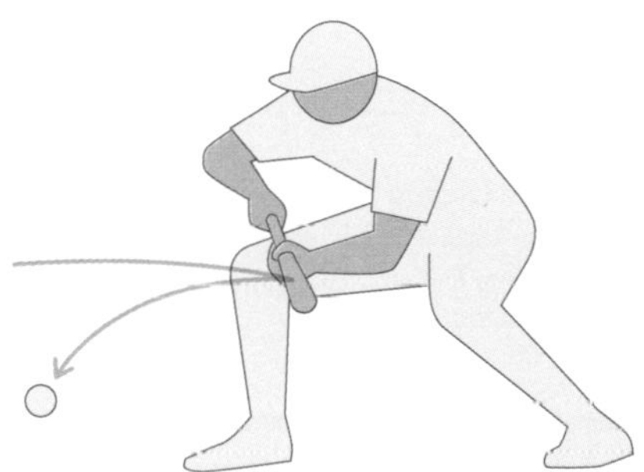

Bunting foul with two strikes is a strike — and an out.

The batter will be charged with a strike if he bunts the ball foul with two strikes against him. This will give him three strikes, and he will be out.

This is only true when bunting. Normally, if a batter fouls with two strikes, it is not counted as a strike. Because of this rule it is rare to see a batter attempt a bunt once he has two strikes.

Foul tips

A strike is called on a "foul tip," a situation in which the batter swings, the bat barely touches the ball, and it goes directly into the catcher's mitt to be caught. The ball must touch the catcher's hand or mitt first. If it's the third strike the batter is out.

Basics

Fair Balls

A fair ball is a ball hit into fair territory that is caught before it touches the ground, or that touches the ground and does not roll or bounce into foul territory before passing first or third base. If the ball bounces or rolls into foul territory after passing first or third base, it is still a fair ball.

If a fair ball touches the ground before being caught, the batter becomes a batter-runner and must run to first base. All other base runners may advance at the risk of being tagged or thrown out (in some cases they may be forced to advance).

If a fair ball is caught before it touches the ground, the batter is out. Other base runners may only advance if they tag their current bases after the ball has been caught (see "Tagging Up" on page 112 in the Running chapter).

Examples: **Fair balls**

1. If a batted ball hits first or third base, it's considered a fair ball even if it then bounces into foul territory.

2. If a batted ball hits the foul line, it is considered a fair ball — unless it goes into foul territory before passing first or third base.

3. When a fly ball hits the foul pole it will be called a fair ball (and therefore a home run).

4. If a batted ball lands in foul territory and then rolls fair before passing first or third base, it is a fair ball.

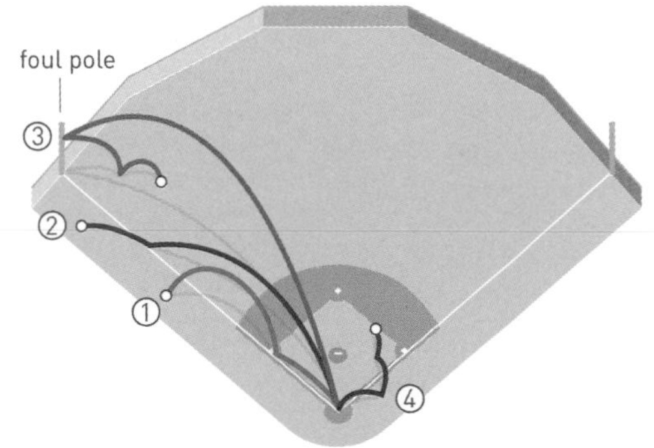

Examples: **Fair balls landing near home plate**

1. Home plate is in fair territory. If a batted ball bounces on home plate, it is a fair ball (at that point).

2. The foul lines extend through the batter's box, even though the white chalk lines are not drawn there. If a hit ball bounces within the batter's box, but inside the imaginary foul lines, it will be a fair ball.

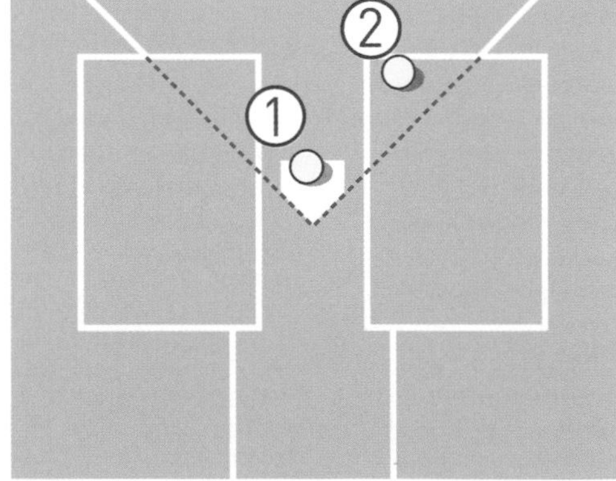

Basics

Foul Balls

A hit ball is foul when 1) a fly ball lands outside the foul lines in foul territory, or 2) it rolls or bounces into foul territory before passing first or third base.

- When a ball is hit foul the ball is dead. Runners may not advance or steal a base on a foul ball.
- If a ball hit into foul territory is caught before touching the ground, the batter is out, but the ball is still live. Runners will be allowed to tag up and advance (see "Tagging Up" on page 112 in the Running chapter).
- A foul is counted as a strike against the batter. However, a foul cannot result in a third strike. If the batter has two strikes against him, any foul balls he hits will simply be called dead — the count will remain at two strikes.

Exception: If, with two strikes already in the count, a bunted ball goes foul, the batter will be out (see "Bunting" on page 77).

Examples: Foul balls

1. If a ball hits the ground in the infield and bounces or rolls into foul territory before going past first or third base, it is a foul.

2. If a fly ball lands outside of either foul line, whether in the stands or in foul territory, it is a foul.

3. If a fly ball goes over the outfield wall to the outside of either foul pole, it is a foul.

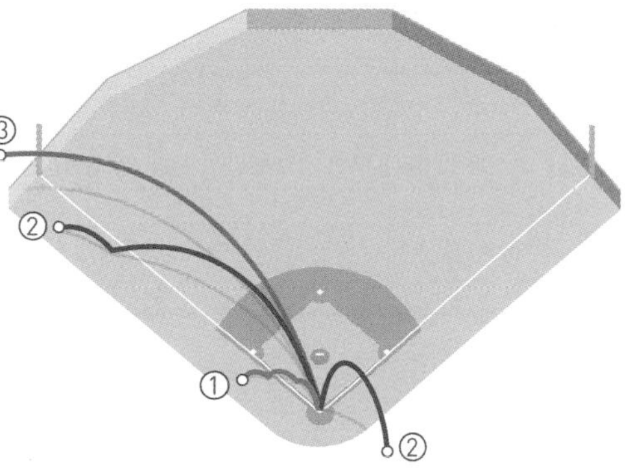

Basics

Balls and Walks (Base on Balls)

A *ball* is a pitch outside of the strike zone on which the batter does not swing. Once a batter receives four balls he is awarded first base. This is called a "walk" or a "base on balls."

- When a batter is walked, any other base runners that are forced to advance will also be allowed to advance.
- When a pitch is called as a ball, the ball is still in play and runners may attempt to steal a base. If a pitch is dropped by the catcher, runners may also try to advance at risk of being put out.
- After a fourth ball is called, the ball is still live. Runners can steal a base. Even the batter being walked can attempt to advance to second base, at risk of being put out.

Intentional walks

If a pitcher chooses to walk a batter intentionally (by throwing pitches far outside the strike zone — also called a "pitch out"), the batter must remain within the batter's box. He can swing at the pitch, but he is not allowed to step outside the batter's box in an attempt to hit the ball.

Strikes and the Strike Zone

Overview: Even the most indifferent spectator knows that it takes "three strikes and you're out." The concept of strikes and the strike zone is one of the most fundamental rules in baseball. This section will cover the complex (and somewhat ambiguous) rules regarding strikes.

Strikes

The Strike Zone

The strike zone defines whether a pitch is a ball or a strike. It is an area in space located above home plate. The size and location of the strike zone is determined by the width and depth of home plate, and by the height and stance of the batter. If a legal pitch passes through any part of the strike zone, it's called a strike. If a pitch on which the batter does not swing fails to pass through the strike zone, it's called a ball.

Note: It is widely accepted that the strike zone varies from one umpire to the next, and even from one pitcher to the next. For instance, if a pitcher is well known as a strikeout pitcher, he may get the benefit of more strike calls than a rookie throwing pitches in the same area.

Strikes

The Strike Zone Size and Location

For each batter the umpire must use his judgment to imagine the size and area the strike zone occupies in space. He does this by using visual reference points that define the boundaries of the strike zone, as specified in the official rules.

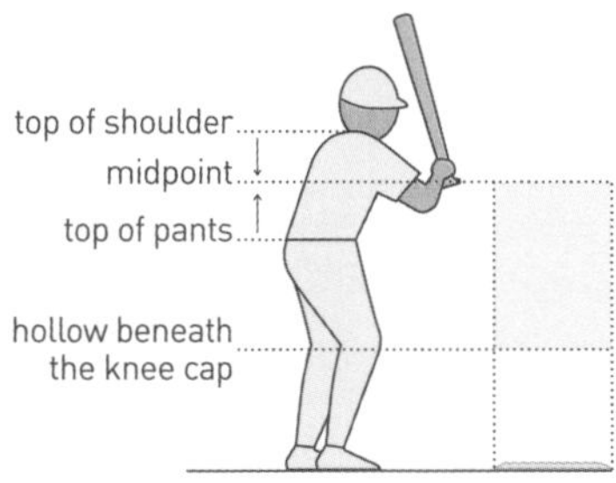

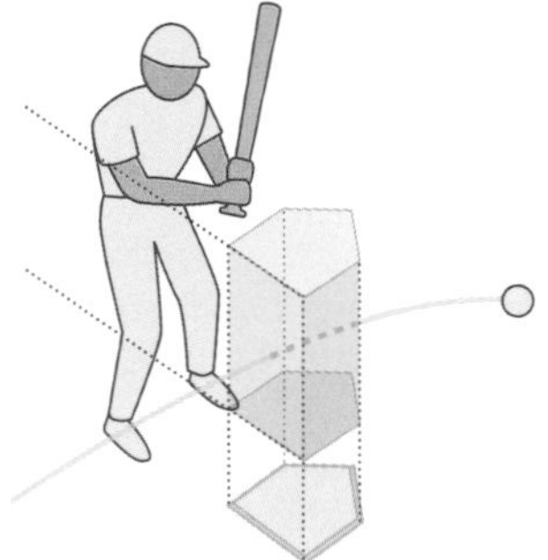

The width of the strike zone is determined by the width of home plate — it remains the same for every batter. The upper and lower boundaries, however, are defined by points on the batter's body. The lower boundary is at the back of the knees, where they bend (described in the rules as the "line at the hollow beneath the knee cap"). The upper boundary is defined as the halfway point between the waist and the shoulders (more or less at the letters spelling the team name on his chest).

The strike zone is a three-dimensional area the exact shape of home plate. If a ball passes through any point in the three-dimensional space, it will be called a strike.

Bouncing pitches

If a pitch hits the ground and then passes through the strike zone, it's a ball. If the bouncing ball hits the batter he will be awarded first base. If the batter swings and hits the ball, the bounce will be ignored and the swing will count.

Strikes

The Strike Zone and a Batter's Stance

The height of the strike zone depends on the stance of the batter during his normal swing. It becomes shorter if the batter crouches and taller if he is more upright.

Note: It doesn't matter how low the batter crouches as he is waiting for the pitch. The strike zone is determined during the batter's normal swing.

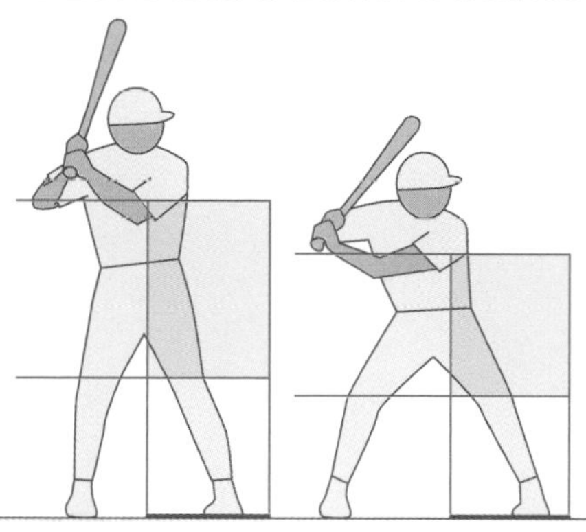

The strike zone and a batter's height

On August 19, 1951, Eddie Gaedel, a midget, was put into the St. Louis Browns lineup by manager Bill Veeck. At only three feet seven inches. Eddie Gaedel is an excellent example of how the strike zone is relative to a batter's height.

The strike zone for Eddie Gaedel was about a foot high — a difficult target for any pitcher. Gaedel was walked in his first and only at-bat.

To the right, Sammy Sosa and his strike zone is shown at the same scale as Eddie Gaedel's.

Strikes

Rules vs. Reality

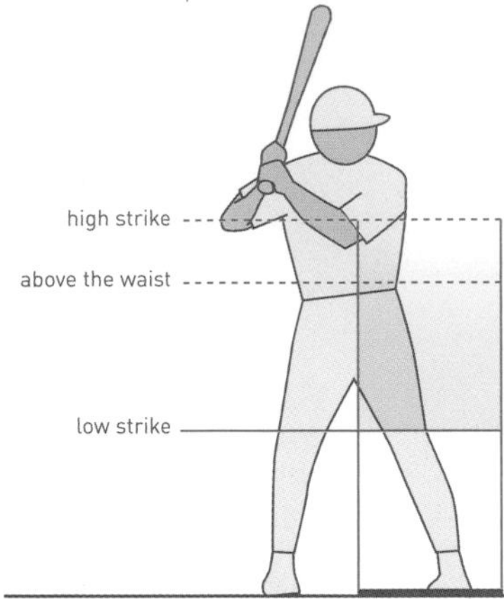

The official strike zone

The rules say the strike zone should extend from the knees to the midpoint between the batter's waist and shoulders.

The strike zone in actual use

Although the strike zone will vary slightly based on an umpire's judgment, Major League umpires tend not to call the "high strike" (meaning, they do not strictly interpret the rule). This is because they do not want to encourage high pitches, which are easier to hit. In fact, until a recent rule change encouraging higher strikes to be called, umpires typically used the top of the belt as the uppermost limit of the strike zone.

A tale of two strike zones

At one time, there was a difference between the strike zones called in the American League and the National League. This came about because of different chest protectors in use at the time. The American League umpires wore a bulky foam rubber "outside" chest protector (also called a "balloon protector") that prevented them from crouching very low. In the National League, the umpires wore a lighter "inside" chest protector that allowed them to crouch lower and call the lower end of the strike zone more accurately. As a result, the American League had a higher strike zone than the National League.

In the seventies, the American League adopted the inside protector. More recently, umpires from both leagues have joined to become a unified entity.

Now all umpires call pitches from a position known as "the slot." They crouch down and view the pitch between the catcher and batter, as shown in the diagram below.

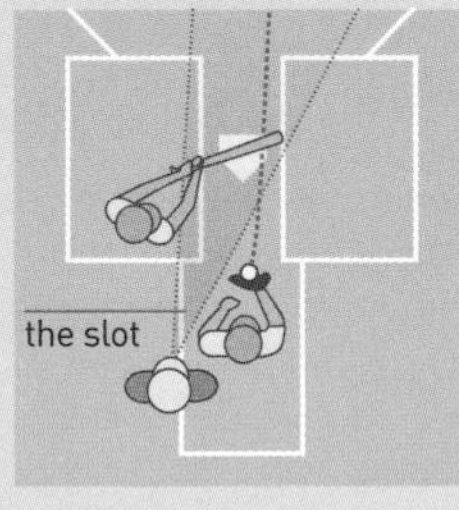

This photo shows umpire Emmett Ashford wearing a balloon protector. In 1954 he was the first black umpire to join professional baseball.

Strikes

The Third-Strike Rule

As everyone knows, after three strikes, the batter is always out. Well, almost always. There is a loophole. In certain cases, whether the batter swings or not, if the catcher misses a catch on the third strike, the batter is not out and must attempt to run to first base.

This rule applies when:

1. there is no runner on first base, or
2. there is a runner on first and two outs.

Note: Even though it may seem to be a disadvantage for the batter that the third-strike rule is not allowed if there is a runner on first base with fewer than two outs, this condition is actually in the offensive team's best interest. It prevents the defensive team from making an easy double play. In most cases, a missed or dropped third strike is picked up quickly by the catcher, who either throws the batter out easily at first base, or is able to tag the batter before he is able to get far from the batter's box. If a runner on first was forced to run to second because of a missed or dropped third strike, it would typically end in a double play. The catcher throws to second for the first out, and the second baseman throws to first base to make the second out.

If this condition were not in place, the catcher could be tempted to miss the catch intentionally to make a double play.

If the missed catch rolls out of play

If the batter swings and misses for his third strike, the catcher misses the catch, and the ball goes off the field and out of play (even if it bounced off the umpire), the batter will be awarded first base. Any base runners at the time of the play will also be awarded one base. The ball is dead.

Strikes

Check Swing: How Much Is Too Far?

If a batter stops the motion of his swing before pivoting too far, it will not count as a swing. This is called a "check swing" (or a "half-swing"), and the pitch will be called a strike or a ball according to the location of the pitch. This is a judgment call by the umpire. A check swing is not actually defined in the rules.

One indication of when a batter swings too far is if the head of his bat swings past the foul line or the front of home plate. Another indication is if the batter "breaks" his wrist, meaning he bends his wrist as he commits to the swing. (Also see page 152 in the Umpires chapter.)

Example: One way to judge a check swing

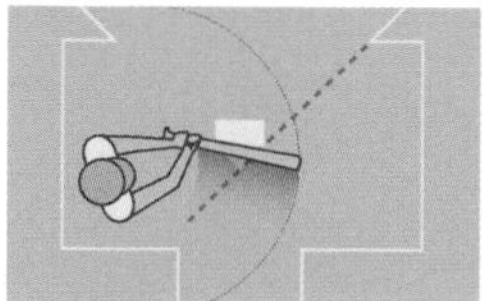

Check swing: If the batter is able to stop the swing before the head of the bat crosses the foul line, it is not considered a full swing.

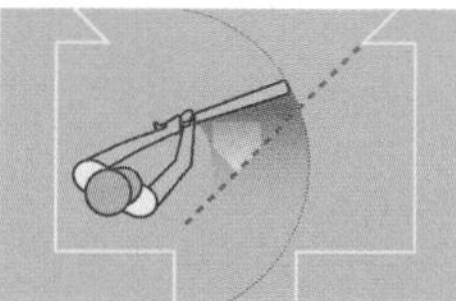

Full swing: If the head of the bat crosses the foul line, it is considered a full swing.

Appealing the call

Often the defensive team will disagree with the home plate umpire's judgment concerning whether a batter went too far with his swing. On a ball, the defensive team can appeal to the plate umpire if they feel that a batter swung far enough to be charged with a strike. The catcher can make the appeal by pointing at the appropriate umpire — the first base umpire if the batter is right-handed, or the third base umpire if the batter is left-handed. The plate umpire will consult with that umpire, who will have the final word because he was in the best position to see if the head of the bat passed the first or third baseline.

Illegal Bats

Overview: If a tampered bat is detected, the batter will be called out and ejected from the game. If the ball was hit, no runners will be allowed to advance, but any outs made on the play will stand.

One solid piece of wood

The bat must be carved from a solid piece of wood with no foreign materials added.

The handle

The handle area can be treated with any substance or material, but it must not extend more than eighteen inches from the bottom. Typically pine tar is used to improve the grip, applied to the bat with a rag.

Too much pine tar

If a bat is discovered to have pine tar above eighteen inches, it will be removed from the game without penalty to the batter. If the bat has already been used in the game, it will not be grounds for ejecting or even calling the batter out, and any play will stand. The bat can be used again after the excess material is removed.

See page 33 for complete bat specifications.

18 inch handle area

Tampering with a bat

There are several ways a batter might try to gain an advantage by modifying his bat. Perhaps the best known is corking, but the rules also mention bats that are filled, flattened, nailed, hollowed, grooved, or covered with wax.

How to cork a bat

It's a fairly simple process, and most any ball player could manage it if properly motivated.

A hole about one inch in diameter is drilled into the bat and filled with pieces of cork, rubber, or any light material. The hole is then plugged with wood filler so no one is the wiser — until the bat breaks.

The great corked-bat caper

In 1994 a corked bat belonging to Albert Belle was confiscated by the umpire. During the game, Jason Grimsley, Belle's teammate, crawled through the ceiling into the umpire's locker room to replace the corked bat with an unaltered bat. All of Belle's bats were corked, so Grimsley (thinking fast) used another teammate's bat. Unfortunately, the switch was noticed immediately, in part because the replacement bat bore the name of the other player.

Calling "Time"

Overview: The batter cannot just step out of the batter's box at his own discretion. Once the pitcher is in position the batter must stay in position, or request a time out from the plate umpire.

Note: Umpires tend to discourage batters from taking too many time outs and slowing the game down. They will often make exceptions based on special circumstances, such as adverse weather conditions or a pitcher taking too much time.

When a time out is not allowed

The pitcher goes through several steps in the pitching sequence. Once he has left the set or windup step in the sequence, the batter will not be granted a time out for any reason — even if he claims he has something in his eye, he missed a sign, or he provides any other excuse. Remember that the pitcher's motion is quick between taking signs and moving into the set or windup position (see page 58 in the Pitching chapter for details on the pitching motion). In some cases the umpire may allow a time out right up to the instant the pitcher gets to the set or windup step in the sequence.

If the batter steps away with no time out

If the batter steps away from the batter's box without being granted a time out, the pitcher can throw a pitch and the umpire will rule it a strike or a ball accordingly.

If the batter leaves the box and delays play he'll get a warning. If he does it twice, he'll get a penalty from the League President.

If a pitch is thrown during a time out

If the pitcher throws a pitch after a time out has been granted, the ball is ruled dead and the pitch will not count.

If a batter refuses to take his position

If the batter refuses to take his place in the batter's box, the umpire will call a strike and the ball will be dead. The batter will be allowed to return to the batter's box, but if his refusal continues he will be called out.

Note: With a runner on base, if the batter unintentionally interrupts the pitcher (for example, by stepping out of the batter's box) after the pitcher has started his windup, the pitcher will be allowed to stop his pitching motion without throwing the ball. A balk will not be called against him. (See "The Balk" on page 62.)

When is it too late for a batter to call time out?

Too late to call time out

While the pitcher is taking signs, and until the point that the pitcher commits to the pitch, the batter will usually be allowed to call time out.

After the pitcher leaves the set or windup position, the batter will not be granted a time out.

The Batter's Box

Overview: The batter's box is an area next to home plate indicated by white chalk lines. The batter must stand in the box when batting. Rules concerning the exact position of his feet within the box depend on whether the batter is waiting for the pitch, swinging the bat, or running after hitting the ball.

The batter's box

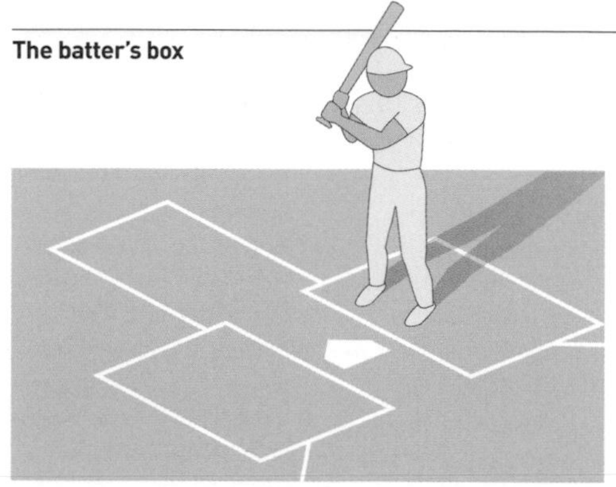

The batter's box is actually two identical boxes on each side of home plate. One box is for right-handed batters and the other is for left-handers.

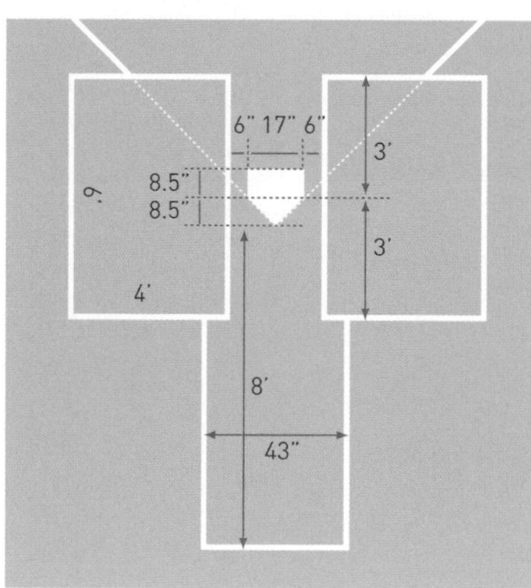

Dimensions

At four by six feet, the box is big enough for a full swinging movement by the batter. The area behind the box designated for the catcher and umpire is far enough away from the batter to avoid hitting the catcher during the swing.

Note: The box is actually defined by the outer edges of the white chalk lines. In some ballparks the lines nearest to home plate are not drawn.

Batter's Box

Waiting, Swinging, and Running

There are three basic stages of batting: waiting for the pitch, swinging the bat at the ball, and running once the ball has been hit. For each of these stages there are specific rules that dictate where the batter's feet should be positioned within the batter's box.

Waiting for the pitch

Legal: His foot is on the line but not across the line.

Illegal: His foot is crossing the outer edge of the line.

Before the pitch is thrown, the batter must stand completely within the box. His feet may touch the white chalk line but should never cross the outer edge of the line.

Penalty: The batter may be warned to change to a legal position. If the batter makes contact with the ball while in an illegal position, he will be out.

Swinging the bat at the ball

Legal: At least some portion of his foot is still within the box or touching the line.

Illegal: His foot is completely past the outer edge of the line and therefore out of the box.

The batter may step partly across the outer edge of the line while making contact with the ball during his swing, but his foot must be touching the line. He must never step completely outside of the line.

Penalty: If he makes contact with the ball while one foot is completely outside of the box, the batter is out and the ball is dead.

Running: touched by a hit ball

Foul: If a hit ball touches the batter when he has at least one foot still on the ground inside the box, the hit is called a foul, and the ball is dead.

Out: If a hit ball touches the batter when both feet are outside the box, or if one foot is in the air and the other is outside the box, the batter is out and the ball is dead.

If a hit ball comes into contact with the batter as he leaves the batter's box, the umpire's call will depend on the position of the batter's feet when the contact was made.

Getting on Base

Overview: A batter can reach a base either by becoming a runner (at the risk of being put out) or by being awarded bases. There are two ways he can be allowed to run. There are eighteen ways he can be awarded bases.

On Base

Ways a Batter Becomes a Runner

1. The batter hits the ball into fair territory. If a hit ball touches the ground in fair territory before being caught by a fielder, the batter becomes a runner and must run to first base.

2. The catcher drops or misses a third strike. Under certain conditions, if the catcher misses the pitch on a third strike, on a pitch where the batter made no contact with the ball, the batter becomes a runner and must run to first base (see "The Third-Strike Rule" on page 83).

On Base

Ways a Batter Can Be Awarded First Base

1. The pitcher has thrown four balls. Once the pitcher throws four balls, the batter is entitled to a *walk* (also called a "base on balls"). He will be allowed to advance to first base without risk.

2. The batter is hit by a pitch. When a batter is hit by a pitch he will be awarded first base. The ball will be dead and other runners will not be allowed to advance (unless forced) — even if the ball deflects off the batter in such a way that the catcher is unable to catch the ball.

Important: There are three conditions for awarding first base under this rule:

a. The pitch must not be in the strike zone.

b. The batter must not be swinging at the ball.

c. The batter must attempt to get out of the way.

See page 90 for more about being hit by a pitch.

3. The catcher interferes with the batter. If a catcher interferes with a batter while he is trying to hit a pitch, the batter will be awarded first base.

4. On the third strike, the pitch goes out of play. If on a third strike, the ball is not caught by the catcher and gets stuck in the catcher's or umpire's mask, or it rolls or is deflected into the dugout or off the field, the batter will be allowed to advance to first base.

5. An umpire or a runner is touched by a hit ball. The batter will be awarded first base if a fair batted ball touches an umpire before it touches a fielder. The same is true if the ball touches a runner before it touches a fielder — but in this case, while the batter is awarded first, the runner will be called out. This is the call even if the runner was touching his base when the ball touched him.

Note: If an umpire or runner is touched by the ball after it has been in contact with a fielder, the ball simply remains in play.

6. A fielder obstructs the batter-runner. If not in possession of the ball, a fielder may not obstruct a batter-runner (or any other runner) or cause him to miss touching his base. If this occurs the fielder will be charged with obstruction and the batter-runner (or the affected runner) will be considered to have reached the base.

7. A fielder touches a pitched ball with his cap. If a fielder intentionally uses his cap, mask, or any other detached part of his uniform or equipment to touch a *pitched* ball, the batter and all runners will be awarded one base. The ball will remain in play.

On Base

Ways a Batter Can Be Awarded Second Base

8. A fielder throws his glove to stop a thrown ball. If a fielder intentionally throws his glove, cap, or any piece of equipment at a *thrown* ball and hits the ball, the batter and all runners are awarded two bases. The ball remains in play.

9. A fielder uses his cap to catch a thrown ball. If a fielder uses his cap, uniform, or anything but his hand or glove to catch a *thrown* ball, and touches the ball, all runners are awarded two bases. The ball remains in play.

On Base

Awarded Second Base: Ground Rule Doubles

If a fair ball bounces or rolls completely out of play, the umpire will rule the ball dead, and all base runners (including the batter) will be awarded two bases. This rule is in the best interest of the defense because it puts a limit on the number of bases a runner can advance.

Examples: Ground rule doubles

10. A fair ball bounces over the outfield wall.

11. A fair ball bounces out of play, going into the stands, the dugout, or anywhere out of play.

12. A fair ball gets stuck somewhere, or goes through or under a wall, or lodges in a fence or vines.

13. A fair ball is deflected. After touching the ground, a fielder deflects the ball over the outfield wall or any other area where it is out of play.

14. A fair ball is kicked or deflected into the stands or dugout. If deflected into the stands or dugout, regardless of whether the ball touched the ground first, two bases will be awarded.

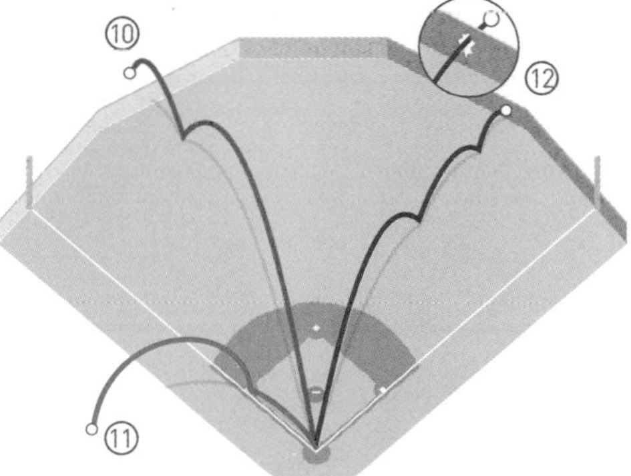

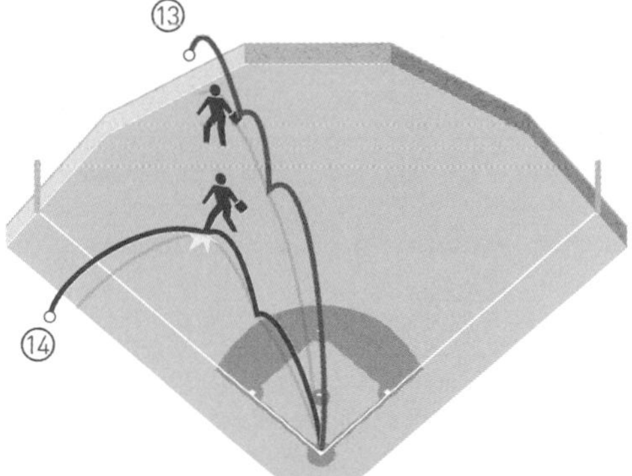

Note: If a ballpark has an outfield wall in fair territory that is less than 250 feet from home plate, any hit ball that flies, bounces, or is deflected over it will be a ground rule double and not a home run.

On Base

Ways a Batter Can Be Awarded Third Base

15. **Fielder throws his glove to stop a batted ball.** If a fielder throws his glove, cap, or any piece of equipment at a *batted* ball, and it touches the ball, all runners (including a batter-runner) are awarded three bases. The ball remains in play.

16. **Fielder tries to catch a batted ball with his cap.** If a fielder tries to catch a *batted* ball with his cap, shirt, or anything but his hand or glove, the batter and all other runners will be awarded three bases at the end of playing action.

Note: Even though these last two points seem like bad behavior on the part of the fielder, there is no consequence whatsoever — including no awarded bases — if the ball is not touched.

On Base

Ways a Batter Can Be Awarded a Home Run

17. **Batter hits a home run.** A ball that is hit over the outfield fence, between the left and right foul poles, earns the batter a home run. If the ball hits either of the foul poles, it is still considered fair and will qualify as a home run.

18. **Deflected home run.** If, without touching the ground, a fair ball bounces off a player and over the outfield fence in fair territory, it will be a home run.

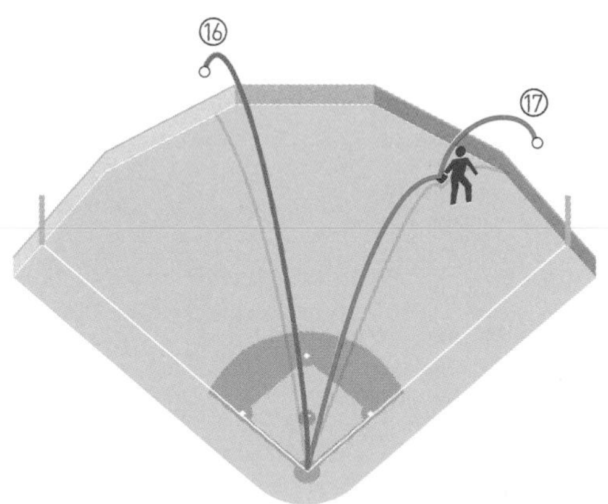

Hit by a Pitch

When a batter is hit by a pitch he will be awarded first base. The ball will be dead and no other runners will be allowed to advance (unless forced) — even if the ball deflects off the batter in such a way that the catcher is unable to catch the ball.

Important: There are three conditions for awarding first base under this rule:

a. **The pitch must not be in the strike zone.** When a pitch is in the strike zone it's the batter's responsibility to get out of the way of the ball. When a batter is hit by a strike, there will be no bases awarded and the pitch will be called a strike.

b. **The batter must not be swinging at the ball.** If the batter was hit while he was swinging at the pitch, there will be no bases awarded. The pitch will be called a strike, the same as if the batter swung without making contact with the ball.

c. **The batter must attempt to get out of the way.** If in the judgment of the umpire, a batter made no attempt to dodge the oncoming pitch, there will be no bases awarded. The pitch will simply be called a strike or ball, as appropriate.

The Batting Order

Overview: The manager of each team determines the sequence in which his nine players will come to bat. This is called the "batting order" (also referred to as "the lineup"). This section discusses the batting order and what happens if a batter bats out of turn.

Batting Order

Presenting the Batting Order

The batting order is determined before the start of the game.

Players must come to bat in the sequence specified in the team's batting order. Five minutes prior to the start of the game, the home team hands two identical copies of the batting order to the umpire-in-chief. Next, the visiting team does the same. The umpire-in-chief checks to make sure each of the duplicates are, in fact, identical. He then gives each team a copy of the opposing team's batting order, keeping one copy of each for himself.

At this point the batting order becomes official and the sequence cannot be altered.

Starting the game

The visiting team is the first team to bat. The first player listed in the visiting team's batting order takes his place in the batter's box. With this action, the umpire calls "play" and the game begins.

Likewise, the first player on the home team's batting order shall be the first batter for that team.

At the beginning of each subsequent inning, the starting batter is the player whose name appears after the player who last completed his turn at bat in the previous inning.

Substitutions

If during the game a substitute player takes the place of a player, the substitute must bat in that player's position in the batting order.

Errors in the batting order should be corrected immediately.

Teams are not liable for obvious errors in the batting orders handed to the umpire. If a batting order contains fewer than nine names, or if two players with identical last names appear on the list and are not differentiated, the mistake should simply be corrected before the umpire calls "play." If these problems are discovered after the start of the game, they should be corrected at that time.

(See page 28 for additional information on presenting the batting order.)

Batting Order

Batting Out of Turn: Improper Batters

A batter who bats out of turn in the batting order is considered an "improper batter." The umpire, if he is the first to notice that a batter is out of order, shall not call this violation on his own. He must wait until the players or managers on either team take action.

The course of action taken depends on whether the violation is corrected by the batter's team, or if and when it is called to the attention of the umpire in an appeal by the defensive team.

Batting Order

Three Ways to Deal with an Improper Batter

An improper batter will be handled differently depending on the circumstances. The actions taken depend on when the improper batter is called to the attention of the umpire. The umpire can be notified by the offensive team, or by the defensive team in an appeal:

1. before the end of the improper batter's turn at bat.

2. after the improper batter completes his turn at bat.

3. after a pitch has been thrown to the next batter or any other play has been made.

The repercussions of each are explained below.

1. Before the end of the improper batter's turn at bat

There is no penalty if the defensive team makes an appeal or if the offensive team corrects their mistake while the improper batter is still at bat. The proper batter simply switches places with the improper batter. Play will continue exactly where it left off, and any strikes and balls incurred by the improper batter will be applied toward the proper batter's count.

2. After the improper batter completes his turn at bat

The defensive team can make an appeal after the improper batter completes his turn at bat, but must do so before another play is attempted or before a pitch is made to the next batter. On the appeal, the batter who missed his turn at bat (not the improper batter) will be declared out for violating the batting sequence. Any plays or advances made as the result of the improper batter's performance will be nullified. Outs, if any, will not count and all runners will return to their positions as if the improper batter had not come to bat. The next proper batter will come to the plate (even if that means that the previously improper batter must bat again).

Any advances or plays that were not the result of the improper batter's turn at bat, such as runners advancing due to a stolen base, a balk, or a wild pitch, will stand. See the examples on the following page.

3. After a pitch has been thrown to the next batter, or after any other play has been made

If the defensive team appeals to the umpire about the batting-out-of-turn violation after a pitch or play has been made, it is too late for any action to be taken. Once a play takes place, the "improper batter" has become the "proper batter" and the game continues as if no mistake had been made. Anything that occurred as a result of the improper batter's turn at bat (hits, outs, runs , etc.) is now considered legal.

Since the improper batter's turn at bat is now considered legal, the batting order jumps to the batter following the improper batter in the lineup. In other words, the next proper batter is the person whose name appears on the batting order following the out-of-turn batter's name. Any batter who was skipped simply misses his turn at bat.

Batting Order

Improper Batter Examples

Example 1: Improper batter

Batter 1 is due up next in the batting order, but batter 2 bats in his place and hits a double.

Batter 3 comes to the plate and waits for the first pitch.

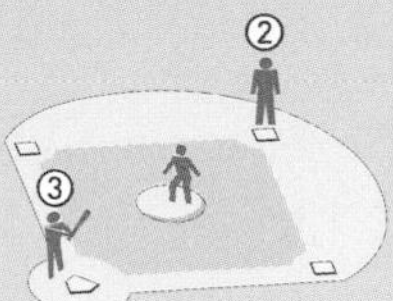

If the appeal is made...

1. Before the next pitch or play:

- batter 1 is called out because he was the batter who missed his turn.
- batter 2's hit doesn't count.
- batter 2 is the next batter because he comes after the last proper batter on record.

2. After the next pitch is made to batter 3, or after a play is attempted:

- batter 3 is now the proper batter because as soon as the next pitch or play was made batter 2 became a proper batter. Batter 1 missed his turn.
- batter 2 stays on second.

Example 2: Improper batter

With batter 1 on third base and batter 3 on first, batter 5 bats out of turn.

On a wild pitch with batter 5 at bat, batter 1 scores from third while batter 3 advances to second.

Batter 5 grounds out, sending batter 3 to third.

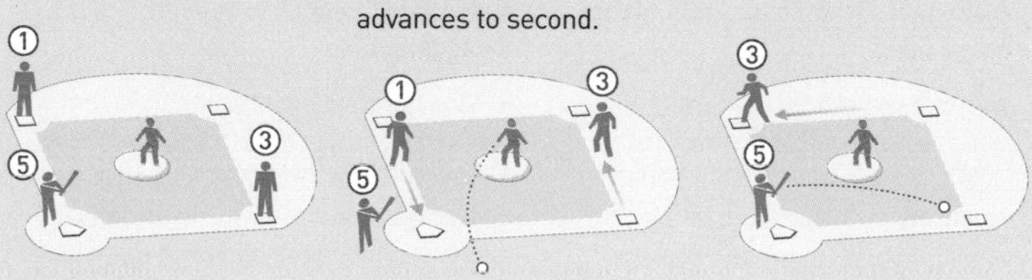

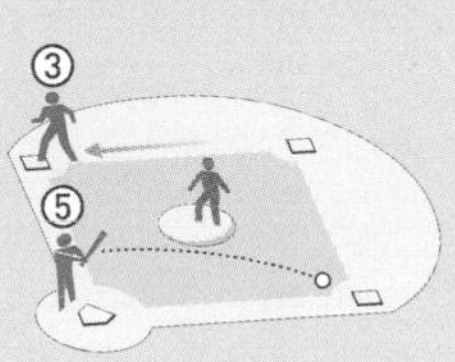

If the appeal is made...

1. Before the next pitch or play:

- batter 1's run and batter 3's advance to second count, because they were the result of a defensive error (the wild pitch) rather than the actions of the improper batter.
- but, batter 3 goes back to second because his advance to third was the result of the improper batter's batting.
- batter 4 is called out for missing his turn at bat. Batter 5's out is nullified.
- batter 5 is now the proper batter, coming to the plate again to start a new at-bat.

2. After the next pitch is made to batter 6, or after a play is attempted:

- batter 1's run counts.
- batter 3 stays on third.
- batter 5's turn at bat is considered to have been proper (he grounded out).
- batter 6 is a proper batter.
- batter 4 missed his turn, but is not out.

(continued...)

Batting Order

Improper Batter Examples continued

Example 3: Improper batter

Bases are loaded with two outs. Batter 8 bats, but it was batter 6's turn.

Batter 8 hits a triple, sending three runs home.

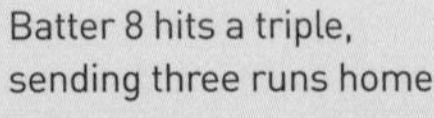

Batter 7 steps up to the plate.

If the appeal is made...

1. **Before the next pitch or play:**

- batter 6 is called out because he was the batter who missed his turn.
- batter 8's triple doesn't count.
- batter 7 is the next batter because he comes after the last proper batter on record.

2. **After a pitch is made to batter 7, or after a play is attempted:**

- batter 8's triple counts, and three runs are scored.
- batter 9 is now the proper batter because as soon as that next pitch or play was made, batter 7 became a proper batter. (Batter 6 missed his turn, but is not out.)

2b. Continuing, let's look at two scenarios:

Scenario 1: Batter 8 is thrown out, picked off at third base, ending the half-inning.

Batter 9 will still be the next proper batter when his team comes to bat again, because the pitch to batter 7 made batter 7, and batter 8's triple, legal.

Scenario 2: Batter 7 flies out, ending the half-inning. A pitch is delivered to the opposing team.

Batter 8 will be the next proper batter when his team comes to bat again, not batter 9. Because there was no appeal, batter 7's time at bat was legalized with the first pitch to the opposing team's batter.

If a proper batter is already on base

If things get really out of hand, it's conceivable that several improper batters could follow each other in succession. As a result, the next proper batter could even be on base at the time that an appeal is finally made. In this event, the batting order will skip to the next available batter.

Example 4: Improper batter

Batter 4 bats out of turn and is walked. Batter 1 comes to bat.

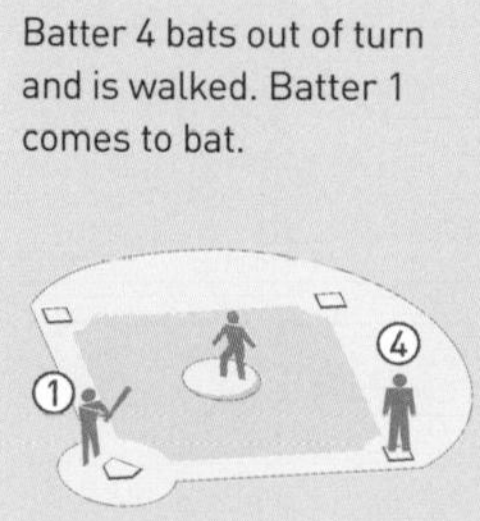

Batter 1 flies out.

Batter 2 comes to bat.

What happens next...

1: An appeal is made before a pitch is delivered to batter 1.

- batter 1 is called out because he was the batter who missed his turn.
- batter 4's walk doesn't count.
- batter 2 is the next batter because he comes after the last proper batter .

2: No appeal is made, a pitch is delivered to batter 1.

- batter 4's walk counts.
- batter 5 becomes the next proper batter. Batter 5 can replace batter 1 while batter 1 is still at the plate, but doesn't.

In this case...

2b. With no appeal having been made, batter 1, who was an improper batter, flies out. Batter 2 comes to bat. To continue, let's look at two scenarios:

Scenario 1: An appeal is made before a pitch is made to batter 2.

- batter 5 is out, and batter 6 is the next proper batter.

Scenario 2: No appeal is made, and a pitch is made to batter 2.

- batter 1's out counts, and batter 2 is the next proper batter.
- batter 2 is walked, sending batter 4 from first base to second. Batter 3 becomes the proper batter.
- batter 3 hits a line drive that is caught for an out.
- batter 4 is now the proper batter, but he is on second base. Batter 5 now becomes the proper batter.

Note: If the proper batter is already a runner, he is skipped in the batting sequence.

Offensive Interference by the Batter

Overview: Offensive interference is an act by a batter or runner to disrupt a fielder making a play. In many cases the umpire must believe the act to be intentional in order to make the call.

Interference

Types of Interference by a Batter

Interfering with the catcher

The batter will be called out for interference if he steps outside of the batter's box to intentionally interfere with the catcher receiving or throwing the ball. That is not to say that it's okay to interfere while inside the box, but because of the distance between the batter and catcher, if the batter was able to interfere with the catcher while still in the batter's box, the catcher would be too close to home plate.

Example: Interference will be called if the batter blocks the catcher's attempt to throw to a base when trying to put out a runner stealing a base.

Penalty: On the call of interference the batter will be out and the ball will be dead, therefore no runners will be allowed to advance.

Pop fouls

The batter will be called out if he interferes with the catcher's attempt to catch a pop foul.

Hitting the catcher during the swing

It is not considered interference if the batter, when swinging his bat, swings completely around and unintentionally hits or hinders the catcher. As long as the batter remained within the batter's box, the pitch will simply be called a strike (even if the bat came completely around and hit the ball on the backswing).

If the catcher is hit by the bat and he is still able to complete a play, that play will stand. Otherwise, "time" is called and runners return to their bases.

This prevents the batter from interfering with the catcher to help a runner. Because time is called, a runner attempting to steal a base during the play will be unable to benefit from the batter's actions — he must return.

Throwing the bat or equipment

If, when swinging, the entire (unbroken) bat slips and flies into fair territory, hitting or otherwise interfering with a fielder, interference will be charged against the batter.

The batter will also be charged with interference if he throws his helmet or any other object into the path of a hit or thrown ball (whether he hits it or not), or toward a fielder with the intention of interfering with a play.

If the bat breaks and a piece of the bat hits the ball or a fielder, the batter will not be charged with interference. Since this happened unintentionally, the ball remains in play.

Running outside the running lane

If the ball is being fielded at first base following a hit, once the batter has run more than half the distance between home and first base he may not step to the left of the foul line or step more than three feet to the right of the foul line. Stepping on the foul line is okay.

If the umpire believes the batter has stepped beyond these boundaries and in so doing interfered with a fielder making a play, the batter will be called out for interference.

Exception: The batter-runner is permitted to step outside these boundaries to avoid interfering with the fielder's play.

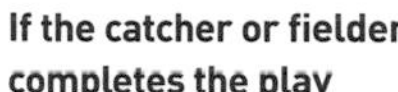

If the catcher or fielder completes the play

If the batter interferes with the catcher or any other fielder making a play, but a runner is put out on the play despite the batter's actions, then the interference will be ignored and the batter will not be out.

Example: A runner attempts to steal second base. The batter interferes with the catcher while he is trying to make a throw to put the runner out. If the catcher successfully makes the throw and the runner is put out, the interference is nullified.

The batter and the runner can be called out due to interference by the runner

If, after a hit, a runner already on base intentionally interferes with a fielder trying to make a play on the hit or a thrown ball, both the batter and the runner will be called out.

This harsh two-out penalty discourages a runner from attempting to prevent a likely double play.

Example 1: A batter bunts the ball and a runner on first intentionally interferes with the play. The ball is dead. The batter-runner and the runner closest to home will be called out.

Note: If there are already two outs and the batter interferes when a runner is trying to score from third base, the batter (not the runner) will be the player called out.

Example 2: During a possible double play, a runner from first base slides into the second baseman, preventing him from throwing the ball to first base in time to put the batter out.

Runners attempt this move frequently and are given a lot of leeway by the umpire. However, if the action is flagrant enough, both the batter and the runner will be called out.

Defensive Interference Against the Batter

Interference by the catcher against the batter

If a catcher (or any other fielder) is judged by the umpire to have hindered the batter in any way during his swing, the catcher or fielder will be charged with interference.

If the batter hits the ball in spite of the interference, his manager will wait to see the outcome.

Note 1: The manager of the offensive team may decide to reject the call of interference if he feels it is to his team's advantage. It becomes his choice whether to accept the awarded bases or accept the results of the completed play.

Penalty: If interference is called, the batter will be awarded first base. The ball is dead and base runners who are forced to advance or were stealing a base will advance.

Example: With a runner on third base and one out, the batter hits the ball, but the catcher interfered with the batter during the swing. The batter is thrown out at first, but the runner from third scores at home. The manager may accept the interference penalty, which puts the batter on first base but requires the runner to return to third base. Or he may choose to reject the call of interference, in which case the batter will be out but the runner on third will have scored a run.

Note 2: In cases in which defensive interference occurs but the batter successfully reaches first base and all the other runners successfully advance at least one base, the interference will be automatically ignored, since it will be judged to have had no effect.

Before the pitch

Before a pitch is delivered, if the catcher interferes with the batter interference will not be called. The umpire will call "time." The pitcher and batter will start again.

Making an Out

Overview: At the end of every at-bat, one of two things will happen — the batter will safely reach a base, or he will be out.

Making an Out

Ways a Batter Can Be Out

Out as a result of a pitcher, catcher, or fielder's action:

1. **A fly ball is caught** in either fair or foul territory, before it touches the ground.

2. **Three strikes.** The batter is out as soon as he receives his third strike (unless the third strike is dropped by the catcher — page 83).

Note: With 0 or 1 out, a pitch into the strike zone that is not swung at, or missed by the batter's swing, will be a strike even if the catcher drops it.

3. **First base is tagged.** When the batter hits the ball he is forced to run to first base. A fielder in possession of the ball can tag first base before the batter reaches it for an out.

4. **The batter is tagged.** After hitting the ball, the batter-runner is out if tagged by a fielder in possession of the ball before the batter-runner is able to reach his base.

5. **The Infield Fly Rule is called** resulting in an automatic out for the batter while the hit is still in the air (averting an easy double play).

6. **An infielder intentionally drops a fly ball.** With a runner on first base (with or without runners on second or third), and 0 or 1 out, if an umpire believes that an infielder touched then intentionally dropped a fair fly ball he will call the batter out and the ball dead. (The hit can be a fly ball or a line drive.)

Note 1: The Infield Fly Rule will take precedence over this rule. One difference — on the Infield Fly Rule the ball remains in play.

Note 2: This rule and the Infield Fly Rule both protect the offense, preventing the defense from making an easy double play (see page 124).

Out as a result of a batter's action:

7. **He bunts foul with two strikes.** With two strikes in the count, a bunted ball that goes foul is counted as a third strike, putting the batter out (page 77).

8. **A hit touches the batter.** If after he has left the batter's box a fair ball touches the batter before touching a fielder, the batter will be called out (see page 87).

9. **The batter alters the path of a hit ball.** If the batter intentionally interferes with a hit ball in a way that alters its path, he's out. For instance, if he kicks a slow ground ball that he hit along the first base line.

10. **The batter intentionally throws his helmet and hits the ball.** If the batter intentionally throws his helmet at the ball, and it makes contact, he will be called out.

11. **The bat hits the ball twice.** If the batter hits the ball twice (for instance, by releasing the bat and hitting the ball again on fair territory) he will be called out. The ball is dead.

Exception: If the batter has no control over the second hit, a foul will be called.

If the bat misbehaves

If a piece of a broken bat contacts a ball hit in fair territory, play will continue. If this happens in foul territory then the hit is, of course, a foul. Play also continues if the broken piece hits a runner or fielder — interference will not be called. Interference will be called if the entire bat flies into fair or foul territory and hinders a fielder, intentionally or not.

12. The batter runs outside the running lane. When more than halfway to first base and with the fielders attempting to make a play at first base, the batter must not step to the left of the foul line and must stay within a three-foot distance from the right of the foul line, unless he is trying to avoid interfering with a fielder or the play (pages 96 and 114).

13. The batter leaves the dirt batting circle on a dropped third strike rather then run to first, not realizing the "third-strike rule" situation.

14. The batter steps outside of the batter's box. If the batter hits the ball while one or both feet are outside the batter's box, he will be out (page 87).

15. The batter switches between the right and left batter's box. If the batter switches from one side of home plate to the other while the pitcher is in pitching position, he will be called out (page 181).

16. The batter interferes with the catcher. If the batter steps out of the batter's box to intentionally interfere with the catcher, he will be called out (page 96).

17. The batter is caught with a tampered bat. If the umpire believes the batter is using an illegal bat, he will call the batter out (page 84).

18. The batter refuses to advance to first base after being walked. If the pitcher throws four balls (four pitches outside the strike zone) the batter is awarded first base. He must "accept" that award.

19. The batter refuses to come to the batter's box. If there are two strikes against him, a third strike will be automatically called.

20. The batter misses his turn at bat. If the defensive team notices that the batter missed his turn, and makes an appeal to the umpire, the batter who missed his turn will be out. The appeal, however, must be made after the improper batter completes his turn at bat, but before another play is attempted or before a pitch is made to a new batter.

Out as a result of a teammate's action:

21. A runner interferes with a fielder. If a runner intentionally interferes with a fielder trying to catch a thrown ball or make a throw to complete a play, the batter will be called out — even though he wasn't involved in the interference (pages 97 and 135).

Note: The goal is to help prevent intentional collisions. For instance, it prevents a runner from deviating from his baseline to crash into a fielder for the purpose of thwarting a double play. Such action would definitely qualify as unsportsmanlike conduct. However, to quote Major League Baseball's rule book: "Obviously this is an umpire's judgment play."

22. A member of the team interferes with a fielder. If someone else on the team (not one of the runners — a coach, for instance) intentionally interferes with a fielder trying to catch or throw the ball, the batter will be called out.

23. If with two outs and two strikes in the count, a runner stealing home is hit by the pitch. For this situation to apply there needs to be two outs, and two strikes against the batter, and it needs to be a legal pitch. (The pitcher, for instance, can't just throw the ball at the runner). "Strike three" will be called, putting the batter out, and the run will not count.

Note: If there are fewer than two outs when this occurs, the batter will be out with the umpire calling "strike three," but the run will count. The ball will be dead.

If the ball hits the batter's helmet

If a thrown or hit ball touches a batting helmet on fair territory, it will be ignored – play continues. If a batted ball hits a helmet of any other foreign object in foul territory, it's a foul and the ball will be dead. If the umpire believes a runner dropped or threw his helmet to intentionally hit the ball, the runner is out, the ball dead, and other runners go back to their last legal base.

The Designated Hitter

Overview: The designated hitter rule allows a player who has no fielding duties to bat in place of the pitcher. The rule has been adopted by the American League but not by the National League.

History

In 1973, the New York Yankees became the first team to use a designated hitter (often referred to as the "DH").

The rule was implemented to liven up the game and has been controversial since its inception. Opponents of the rule feel that it eliminates some of the strategic complexities that make the game so interesting. They suggest that fans who need to see players score a few more points for excitement should try another sport — maybe football.

American League managers are not required to use a designated hitter, but to do so they need to name him in the batting order at the start of the game.

The rule

The designated hitter bats in place of the starting pitcher and any substitute pitcher for his team throughout the game. He is not required to participate as a fielder.

The designated hitter named in the batting order must come to bat at least once in a game, unless the opposing team changes pitchers.

During the game, the manager can replace the designated hitter with a pinch hitter (the term for a substitute batter), but the DH must come to bat at least once.

Once a designated hitter has been replaced by a substitute, he may not play in the game in any position.

Similarly, if the designated hitter is replaced by a pinch runner, that new runner becomes the designated hitter.

The person identified as the designated hitter must always bat in the same place in the batting order. Multiple substitutions cannot be made that will alter the DH position in the batting order.

Can the DH play the field?

A designated hitter may take a fielding position during the game, replacing another fielder, but the pitcher must then bat in the replaced fielder's position in the batting order.

Not a pinch hitter

Although a designated hitter hits in place of the pitcher, he should not be confused with a pinch hitter. A designated hitter is part of the lineup from the start of the game. A pinch hitter is a substitute, replacing another player in his turn at bat — the player he replaces is considered substituted and is thus out of the game.

If the designated hitter isn't identified in the batting order

The designated hitter, if one is to be used, must be identified in the batting order. If ten players are listed and the designated hitter isn't indicated, various things can happen.

Before the game starts: If one of the umpires or managers notices the omission prior to the call of "play," the umpire will simply ask the manager and correct it.

After the game starts: If the opposing team's manager notifies the umpire about the omission after play has started, then the pitcher will be placed in the batting order, taking another player's place. That player will be considered to have been substituted, and will be removed from the game. The team will have lost the right to use a designated hitter for the remainder of the game. Whose place will the pitcher take?

- if the team has already taken their defensive positions, the pitcher must bat in place of the player named in the batting order who has not taken a position on the field.
- if the team has not yet taken their defensive positions, the team's manager must decide whose place in the batting order the pitcher will take.

Note: Any plays that took place before the umpire was alerted to the designated hitter omission shall count.

A team can lose their right to use a designated hitter

Certain actions can result in the termination of a team's designated hitter role for the remainder of the game. A team will no longer be allowed to use a designated hitter for any of the following reasons:

- the pitcher is no longer a pitcher, meaning, if during the game the pitcher is moved to a different fielding position.
- a pinch hitter stands in for any player's time at bat, and then comes into the game as a pitcher.
- the pitcher comes to bat (pinch hits) in place of the designated hitter.
- the pitcher runs (pinch runs) in place of the designated hitter.
- the designated hitter takes a position on the field.
- the pitcher is substituted by a defensive player.

Note: The designated hitter is the only player for whom the pitcher can pinch-hit or pinch-run — but in doing so the designated hitter will be considered replaced, terminating the DH role.

When an American League team and National League team get together

In the World Series or an exhibition game: The rules of the home team will preside.

In the All-Star Game: Designated hitters will be used only when both leagues agree.

The designated hitter in the bullpen

Unless he is catching in the bullpen, the designated hitter isn't allowed in.

8 Running

The goal of the runner is to advance around the bases until he reaches home plate to score a run for his team. It may sound simple, but many things can happen as he makes his way around the bases.

This chapter discusses the rules concerning base running, including information about force plays, obstruction, missing a base, and other topics.

Running: contents

Basics for the Runner

Overview: A runner's objective is to get from one base to the next without being put out. Specifications for the base paths are shown below.

The base paths are six feet wide. The bases are ninety feet apart. Just outside of first and third bases are the base coaches' boxes. The base coaches are allowed to signal advice to runners and batters as long as they don't interfere with the play.

Dimensions of the base paths

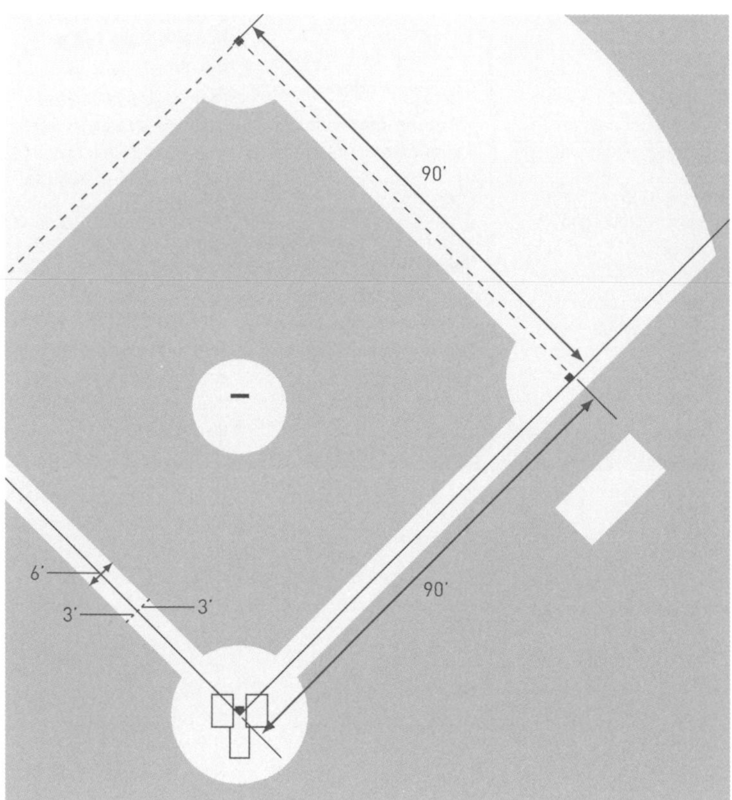

Note: The official rules refer to a batter on his way to first base as a "batter-runner." This somewhat awkward term is used in this chapter, and throughout the book, to distinguish a batter who has just become a runner from the other runners.

Twelve Ways a Runner Can Be Put Out

Overview: Once a batter has successfully reached a base, he becomes a runner. Here are twelve ways a runner can be put out.

1. Tagged out by a fielder. A runner can be tagged out by a fielder with the ball, provided the ball is in play and the runner is not touching his base.

2. Fielder tags a base on a force play. When a runner is forced to advance to a base, he can be put out without being tagged. Instead, a fielder with possession of the ball can simply tag the base he is running to. See "Force Plays" on page 106.

3. Misses a base. If a runner misses a base, and continues to advance to the next base, the defensive team can tag the runner or the base he missed. They can also appeal after the play is over.

4. Fails to "tag up" before advancing after a fly ball is caught. Runners are allowed to advance on a hit (fair or foul) that is caught for an out, but they must touch their base after the catch is made before attempting to advance. If they fail to do so, the defensive team can appeal once the play is over. The appeal is made by tagging the original base. The appeal must be made before another play takes place. See page 112.

5. Runs outside the baseline. If to avoid being tagged a runner runs more than three feet away from his baseline, he will be called out (unless he is trying to avoid interfering with a fielder making a play). See page 114 for the definition of "baseline."

6. Passes another runner. A runner is out if he passes a runner ahead of him on the bases.

7. Touched by a batted ball. A runner is out if a ball hit into fair territory touches him before it passes or is touched by a fielder. When this happens:

- the batter is awarded first base,
- the ball is dead, and
- no other runners score or advance unless they are forced to advance.

See page 115.

Exception: Different rules apply if the hit is an infield fly. See page 124.

8. Abandons the bases. If a runner leaves his base, abandoning his attempt to (eventually) reach subsequent bases, the umpire can rule him out. This is not an appeal play. This situation may occur by mistake. For example, if a runner mistakenly believes he was put out, or thinks the half-inning is over, and he heads toward the dugout, by walking away from the base he can be called out. See page 111, "Abandoning the Bases."

9. Does not immediately return to first base. Even though a runner is allowed to run or slide past first base, the runner must immediately return to first base or else he can be put out. See page 111, "Overrunning First Base."

10. Interferes with a thrown ball or a fielder. The runner must never intentionally interfere with a thrown ball or interfere with a fielder making a play on a ball. See "Interference by a Runner" on page 132.

11. Batter interferes. A runner can be called out when a batter interferes with the play at home plate while a runner is attempting to score. See page 133.

12. Runs the bases in reverse. A runner will be called out if, after successfully reaching a base, he runs the bases in reverse order. This rather odd rule is intended to prevent the runner from intentionally tricking or distracting a fielder. This action must be intentional and does not apply to a runner who runs back to a previous base because he mistakenly believes a ball was caught or because he was deceived by a fielder.

Force Plays: When a Runner Is Forced to Advance

Overview: When a batter becomes a runner and attempts to reach first base, he forces runners immediately ahead of him to advance as well.

Rules of a force play: Under normal circumstances, a runner must be tagged to be put out. However, when a runner is forced to advance, a fielder needs only to tag the base that the runner is attempting to reach in order to put him out.

The cause of a force play

The "forced run" takes place when a runner must vacate a base in order to make room for a batter-runner or another runner immediately behind him.

The force begins with a batter who is attempting to reach first base. If a batter gets a hit, he has no other option but to advance to first base. He is forced to run. Because he is forced, the fielders need only to tag first base to retire the batter-runner.

If there is a runner occupying first base when the batter gets a hit, that runner must also advance in order to make room for the forced batter. This has a domino effect — all runners occupying a base immediately in front of another forced runner must also advance.

A force occurs only when the runner has no choice but to advance.

For example, if a runner attempts to steal second base, he will not force a runner ahead of him to advance. This is because the runner trying to steal the base is not forced to steal, so he can't force a runner ahead of him.

Example: A basic force play – the force double play

1. **With a runner on first base**, the batter hits the ball sharply toward second base. Both batter and runner must advance.

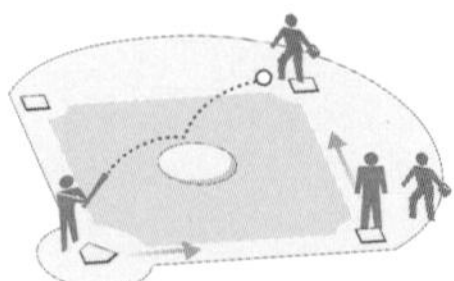

The force play is on. Both runners are forced to run, and either one can be put out if a fielder tags the runner's base before he reaches it.

2. **The second baseman tags second base** to retire the lead runner.

The lead runner is out. Since he is forced by the batter-runner, he is out if the fielder tags the base before he reaches it.

3. **The second baseman throws the ball** to the first baseman who tags first base before the batter reaches it.

The batter is out. Because he is a forced runner, the batter is out when the first baseman tags first base. This very common play is called a "force double play."

Force Plays

Force Plays Can Be Removed

The force play is off when the runner behind him is put out

When two or more runners are being forced, it is because the lead runner needs to make room for the runner behind him. The force play is removed when the runner immediately behind a forced runner is put out. There is no longer any need to make room, so the runner is no longer forced to advance.

A force situation is over when his base is reached

The force situation is over as soon as the runner touches the base to which he was forced. For instance, if a batter reaches first base safely and chooses to continue to second base, the force play is off after he passes first base. The runner has the option to remain on first base, therefore he is not forced to advance to second.

However, if the same runner (for whatever reason) retreats back past first base toward home plate, the force play is back in effect as soon as he recrosses first base.

Example: The force play is removed when the runner behind is put out.

1. With a runner on first base, the batter hits the ball toward the pitcher. Both the batter and the runner must run.

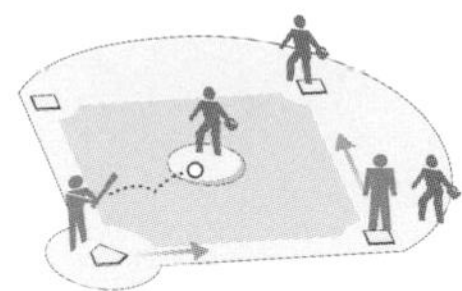

The force play is on. The batter and the runner are forced to run, and either one can be put out if a fielder tags his base before he reaches it.

2. The pitcher throws the ball to the first baseman who steps on first base to put out the batter-runner.

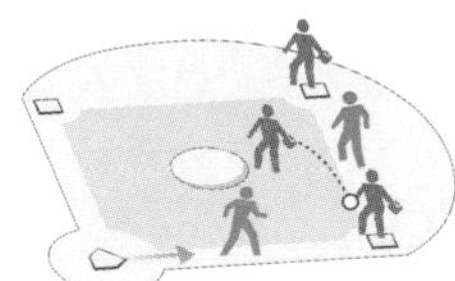

The force at second is off The batter-runner is out because he is a forced runner. As soon as he is out, the lead runner is no longer forced to advance to second.

3. The first baseman throws the ball to the second baseman who tags second base. The runner slides into second without being tagged.

The runner is safe. Since there is no longer a force play in effect on the lead runner, he must be tagged to be put out.

A reverse force double play

The situation above is called a reverse force double play because the force is removed from the lead runner as soon as the batter-runner is put out. In our example, however, the reverse force double play was not completed.

(continued...)

Force Plays

Force Plays Can Be Removed continued

Example: The force play is removed as soon as the runner passes the base.

1. With a runner on first base, the batter gets a hit to deep left field. Both the batter and the runner must advance.

The force play is on. The batter and the runner are forced to run, and either one can be put out if a fielder tags his base before he reaches it.

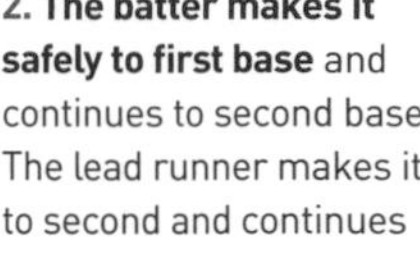

2. The batter makes it safely to first base and continues to second base. The lead runner makes it to second and continues toward third base.

The force play is off. As soon as the runners pass the bases to which they are forced, the force plays are removed.

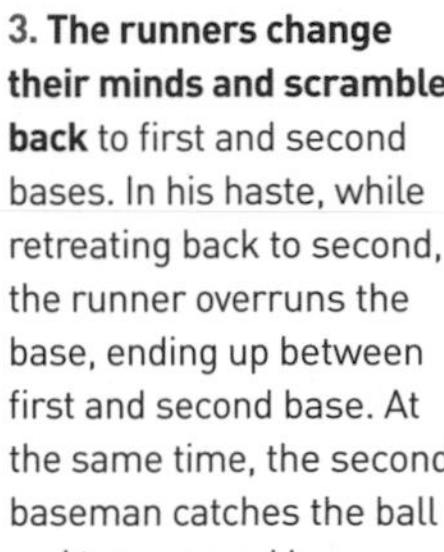

3. The runners change their minds and scramble back to first and second bases. In his haste, while retreating back to second, the runner overruns the base, ending up between first and second base. At the same time, the second baseman catches the ball and tags second base.

The force play is back on, and the lead runner is out. As soon as the runner recrosses second base, the base to which he was originally forced, the force play is again in effect. At this point, the second baseman only needs to tag second base to put out the lead runner.

Force Plays

Forced by an Awarded Base

Forced by a walk or any awarded bases

When a batter or runner is awarded a base, runners directly in front of him will also be allowed to advance without risk of being put out. They are, in effect, forced to advance by the runner or batter who was awarded the base or bases.

If a runner advances beyond his awarded base, he can be put out if the ball is still live.

For instance, a batter gets a base on balls, forcing a runner on first base to freely advance to second. The lead runner carelessly walks past second base toward third base. The alert pitcher throws the ball to the second baseman who tags the runner for an out.

Since the runner moved past the base to which he was allowed to advance, he is no longer protected by the awarded base.

Base-Running Mistakes

Overview: This section is about the many ways the offensive team can be penalized when a runner makes a mistake. It includes mishaps such as passing another runner, missing a base, or failing to tag up.

Mistakes |

Missing a Base

Bases must be touched in order

While running the bases, a runner must touch all the bases he passes in order. If he fails to touch one of the bases, the defensive team can put him out by either tagging the runner or by tagging the base that was missed.

The runner can also be called out after the play is over by making an appeal. The appeal is made by tagging the runner or by tagging the missed base.

Going back to retouch a missed base

The runner may return to retouch a base that he missed under the following circumstances:

- **During a play** he may return to retouch a missed base, but as he returns, he must touch each base in reverse order.
- **When the ball is dead** he can only return to a missed base if he has not yet reached the next base. For example, if a runner misses second base during a home run trot around the bases, he can no longer return to retouch second base once he steps on third base. He can be called out by appeal.

Note: A runner may no longer return to a missed base after a runner behind him scores. For instance, if a runner fails to touch home plate, and a runner behind him reaches home plate before he can retouch it, the first runner may no longer return to touch home plate. He can be called out by appeal.

Example: Missing a base

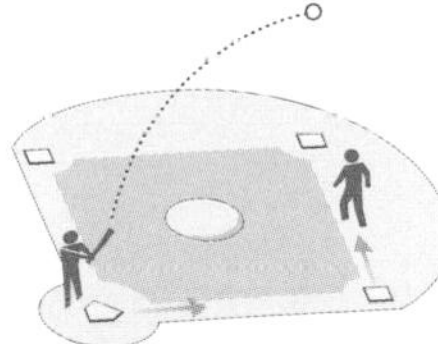

With a runner on first base, the batter hits a fly ball deep into the outfield. Thinking the ball will not be caught, the runner runs past second toward third base.

The left fielder catches the ball for an out, and the runner must return to first base before being tagged.

The runner makes it back to first base, but failed to touch second base on his return.

The defensive team may put out the runner by tagging him or by tagging second base (the base he missed).

Note: If a runner misses home plate, he may attempt to retouch it before a fielder tags him. If, however, the runner begins to walk from the base toward the dugout (either believing or bluffing that he touched the base safely), the fielder with the ball can tag home plate to make the out, even though it is not a force situation.

Mistakes

Missing or Passing an Awarded Base

Missing an awarded base

When a runner is awarded bases, he still must touch the bases in order — even if the ball is dead.

Example: A runner who is awarded third base can be put out on appeal if he fails to touch second base on his way to third.

Moving past the awarded base

When a runner is awarded bases he is allowed to advance to those bases without risk of being put out. However, while the ball is in play, if a runner overruns the base to which he is awarded, he may be put out. He will lose his immunity as soon as he moves past the base.

Example: A batter walks with a runner on first base. The runner on first base is entitled to advance to second base. After reaching second base, the runner thoughtlessly steps off the base toward third, and the alert second baseman tags him with the ball. Even though he was awarded second base without liability to be put out, the runner can be tagged out as soon as he passes that base.

Mistakes

Failing to Tag Up Before Advancing

If a batter hits a fair or foul ball that is caught for an out, following the catch a runner can touch his original base and then attempt to advance to the next base.

Therefore the runner can either wait at the base until the fielder catches the ball, or he can retouch the base after the ball is caught.

Sometimes a runner will leave the base too early, or fail to retouch the base after the catch. If the runner fails to tag up, he can be put out during the play when a fielder holding the ball tags him or his original base.

See a full description of "Tagging Up" on page 112.

Mistakes

Appeal Plays and "Fourth Outs"

An appeal play can result in a "fourth out." If a third out is made but at the same time a violation by another runner takes place that results in an appeal, the out called as a result of the appeal counts as the third out. In cases where two separate appeal plays take place but only one is needed to end the half-inning, the defense can choose to accept the out that is to its advantage.

Example: With two outs, the batter gets a hit, and two base runners advance to home plate. The first runner misses the base but the second runner touches it. An instant later, the batter-runner is thrown out at second for the third out. At this point, both runs count. However, after the play, the first runner is called out by appeal, and his run no longer counts. Since the first runner's out ended the inning, the second run will no longer count either. See "Scoring with Two Outs" on page 113.

Mistakes — Abandoning the Bases

It is in the team's best interest for a runner to try to make it safely to the next base. In fact, it is against the rules to give up this attempt and walk away.

If a base runner leaves the bases before the end of the inning or before being called out, he will be called out by the umpire for "abandoning his effort to touch the next base."

Typically this infraction will be made by a runner who is somehow confused and thinks that he is out or that the inning is over, and leaves his base to return to the dugout.

This is a judgment call by the umpire, and no appeal is necessary by the defensive team. Before the call is made, the runner must walk far enough from the base to indicate to the umpire that he is abandoning further effort.

Mistakes — Overrunning First Base

When a batter-runner is attempting to reach first base, typically his momentum will take him several steps past the base. This is called overrunning first base, and the runner is allowed to do so without risk of being put out, except under the following circumstances:

The batter-runner fails to return to first base immediately

The batter-runner is required to return to first immediately after overrunning the base. If he fails to retouch first base quickly enough in the umpire's judgment (and doesn't call time out), a fielder will be allowed to tag him out.

The batter-runner moves toward second base

A legal "overrun" must be in the same direction as his run to the base. It is not considered "overrunning" or "oversliding" if the batter-runner rounds first base toward second. If the umpire judges him to be intentionally moving toward second base he can be tagged out.

Mistakes — Passing a Runner or Sharing One Base

Passing a runner

This rule is very simple. A runner who passes a runner in front of him will be called out. The runner who was in front will be allowed to continue his attempt to advance.

Two runners occupying the same base

If two runners end up on the same base, it is the lead runner who has the right to be on the base. The runner who is following him will be called out.

This is because the lead runner is not considered to have given up his right to the base until he has been either put out or until he has successfully reached the next base.

Passing a runner on a game-winning home run

On a game-winning home run, if a runner passes a runner in front of him before the winning run touches home plate, the passing runner is out. If there were already two outs, the inning ends and only the runs that scored before he passed the runner will be counted. If there were fewer than two outs, he is out but the play will continue.

Tagging Up: Advancing on a Caught Batted Ball

Overview: Runners are allowed to advance even when a batted ball is caught for an out. Before attempting to advance, the runner must retouch his base after the fielder touches the ball.

A runner can advance, at risk of being tagged out, after a hit ball has been caught for an out. This principle is the basis for a "sacrifice fly" — where a batter hits a fly ball to the outfield. Even though the batter will be out if the ball is caught, a runner can tag up and advance to the next base.

The rule. The runner must touch his original base after the hit ball is touched by the fielder. That means he can wait on his base and begin running once the fielder touches the ball, or he can retouch the base at any time after the fielder touches the ball before advancing to the next base.

Example: Tagging up

1. The ball is hit. The runner stays on his base and readies himself to run.

2. The ball is caught. The runner must touch his original base after the hit ball is first touched by the fielder.

3. The runner is allowed to advance. The runner will try to leave the base as quickly as possible after the ball is touched by the fielder.

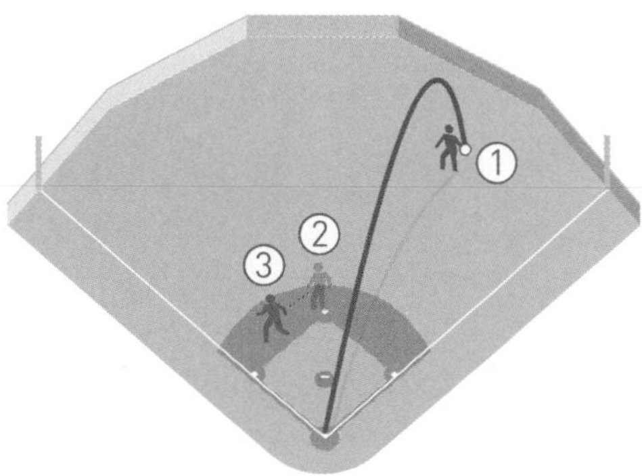

Note: On a high fly ball, the runner will act like a track sprinter waiting for the pistol to signal the start of a race. He will begin running the instant the ball is touched.

Tagging Up |

Failing to Tag Up

Sometimes a runner can be caught off the base, or will have begun his run thinking that the ball will not be caught. If a fair ball is caught for an out, a runner must retouch his base before he attempts to advance.

If a runner fails to tag up, he can be put out in the following ways:

Tagging the runner. A runner who fails to retouch his original base can be tagged out at any time during a live play.

Tagging the original base. If a runner needs to retouch his original base, it is treated like a force play in which the runner has no choice but to reach the base. As in the case of a force play, the runner can be put out when a fielder tags the base in question.

By appeal. If the defensive team feels that a runner left his base before a fly ball was caught, they can make an appeal after the play is over by throwing the ball to his original base or by tagging the runner.

Example: Failing to tag up

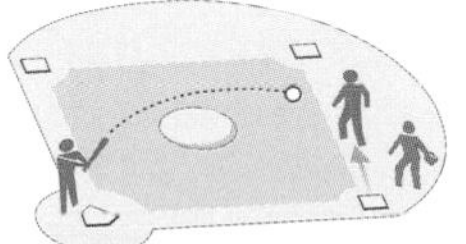

A batter hits a line drive, and a runner on first base, thinking the ball will go over the first baseman's head for a hit, begins running as soon as the ball leaves the bat.

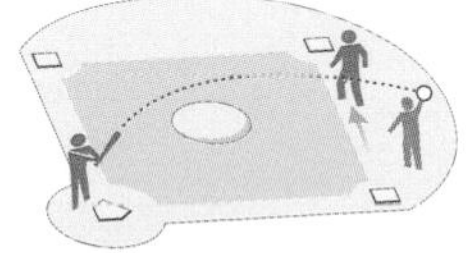

The hit is caught by the leaping first baseman as the runner approaches second base.

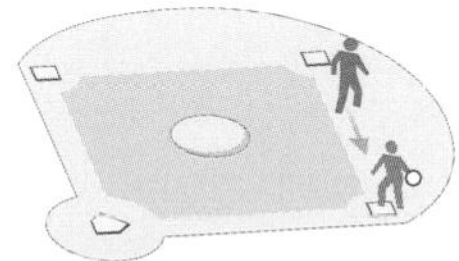

At this point, the runner must return to first base. He may not proceed to second because he didn't touch first base after the catch. The first baseman tags first base and the runner is out.

A touch is close enough

The rule book states that runners may not advance until the fielder actually catches the ball, and a catch is officially defined as having controlled possession of the ball.

However, in a tag-up situation the runners are allowed to advance as soon as the fielder touches the ball, even if the fielder juggles or bobbles the ball before gaining full control.

This prevents the fielder from intentionally juggling the ball while walking toward the infield in order to keep the runners on their bases.

Scoring with Two Outs

Overview: A run scored during a play in which the third out is made may or may not count, depending on the circumstances.

When the run does not count

The run will not count if a runner crosses home plate on a play in which the third out is made, under any one of the following circumstances:

- the batter-runner is called out before he reaches first base.
- a runner is forced out.
- a runner in front of the scoring run missed one of the bases.
- the third out occurs before the scoring runner touches home.

The winning run

With the bases loaded, if the winning run is made because a batter is awarded a base (by being walked or hit by a pitch for instance), the game will not end until:

- the batter touches first base.
- the runner at third touches home plate.

If one or both runners take too much time to touch their bases (perhaps because they are too busy celebrating) the umpire will call the culprit out and resume the game.

Exception: If the fans mob the field and prevent the runners from reaching their bases, the umpire will ignore the infraction. The run will be scored.

Running Outside the Baseline

Overview: Under normal circumstances, it is not against the rules for a runner to stray outside his baseline. He is only penalized if he does so intentionally to avoid a tag or to interfere with a play.

Avoiding a tag

The official rules were rewritten in 2007 to state that the baseline is not a fixed line on the field. It is determined by the runner's position.

Umpires consider the baseline to be a straight line between the runner and the base he is trying to reach. This line is established at the moment a fielder first begins his tag attempt.

A runner must not stray more than three feet to either side of that line when trying to avoid a tag.

Penalty: The runner will be called out.

Exception: It is okay (and may even be necessary) to run outside the baseline to avoid interfering with a fielder who is actively making a play on a batted ball.

A runner determines his own baseline

The baseline is defined as a straight line between the runner's position at the instant a tag is first attempted, and the base.

Interfering with a play at first base

Normally a runner is allowed to use the entire six-foot width of his baseline, but the rules are a little more constraining for a batter-runner on his way to first base.

While a play is being attempted at first base, after the batter-runner has passed more than half the distance to first base, he must stay within an area three feet to the right of the foul line, and he must not cross to the left of the foul line.

Penalty: The ball is dead, and the batter-runner will be called out.

Interfering with a double play

Interference is called when a runner, in the umpire's judgment, does not try to touch the base and hinders a fielder attempting a double play. See the example on page 135.

Running to first base. While running to first base, the batter-runner must stay out of the way of a play being made at first — after reaching the halfway point he must be outside of the foul line.

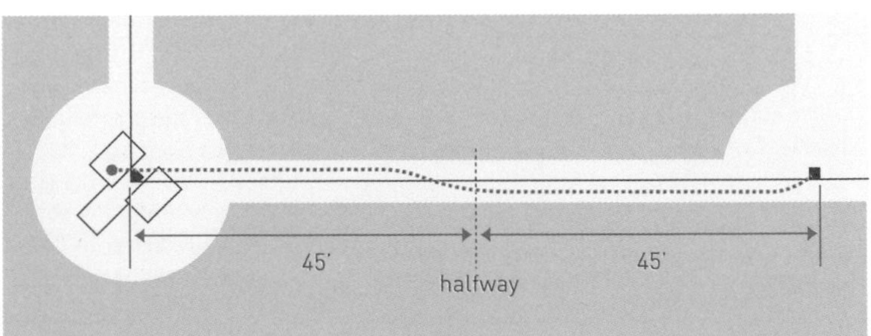

Touched by a Batted Ball

Overview: If a batted ball hits a runner or umpire, it could hinder or prevent a fielder from making a play. The rules address this situation differently depending on the circumstances under which the player or umpire is touched by the ball.

Explanation: The actions taken under this rule depend on whether the runner or umpire is touched before or after the ball gets past a fielder.

If the contact is made before passing a fielder, then the ball is dead and the umpire must address the incident. This is the case whether the runner was touching his base or not.

If the ball makes contact after a fielder has already missed the ball and has let it get by him, then the play will continue as if the incident did not occur.

Like many rules in baseball, it isn't quite that simple. There are a few more circumstances to consider. Refer to the specific examples and circumstances below.

A runner is touched by a hit before it passes a fielder.

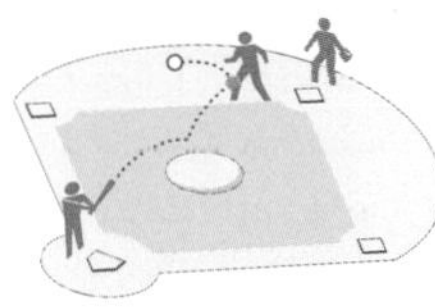

Example: A ball is hit hard and grazes the runner, who has a lead off second base (or is touching second base), before any fielder can attempt to catch the ball.

What happens: The runner is out, and the batter will be awarded first base.

The ball is dead, and no other runners score or advance unless they are forced to advance by the batter.

Note: In the rare event that two runners are touched by the same fair ball, the first runner will be the one called out. The ball becomes instantly dead after touching the first runner.

Exception: If a runner on his base is touched by a fly ball hit to the infield, the batter is out, not the runner. If he is not on his base when the fly ball touches him, the batter and the runner are both out.

A runner is touched by a hit that gets past a fielder.

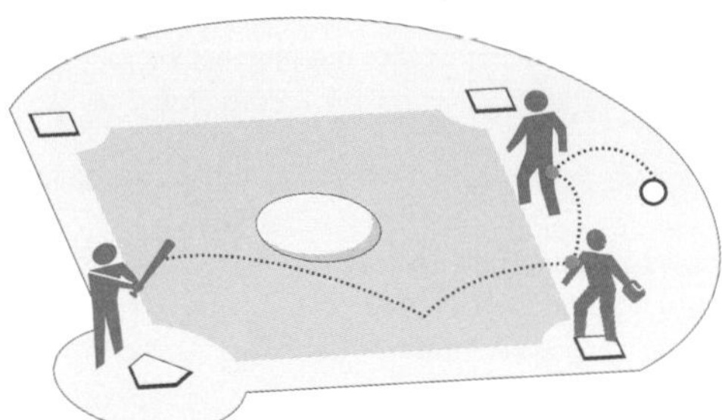

Explanation: There is no penalty if a fair ball deflects off or gets past a fielder as he attempts to catch it and it touches a runner immediately behind him.

In this case the play continues as if nothing happened.

Example: A ball is hit hard toward the first baseman with a runner on his way to second. The ball deflects off the first baseman and touches the runner.

What happens: The ball remains in play as if the incident did not occur. All runners, including the batter, will continue to advance at risk.

Note: If, however, the umpire decides that the runner purposely kicked or deflected the ball, the runner will be called out for interference.

(continued...)

Touched by a Batted Ball

continued

A runner is touched by a batted ball while in front of a fielder making a play.

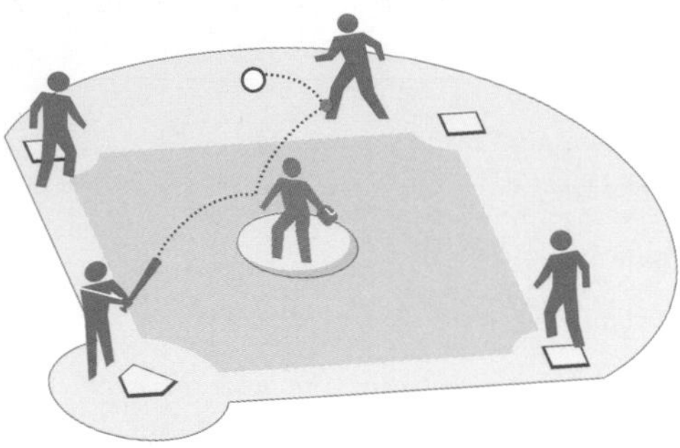

Explanation: When the ball touches the runner, the ball is dead, and no other runners score or advance unless they are forced to advance by the batter. The runner on first base advances because he was forced by the batter. The runner on third base stays put because he was not forced by the batter.

Example: While the bases are loaded (a runner on every base), the batter hits a ground ball that gets past the pitcher and glances off the runner between second and third base.

What happens: The ball is dead, and the runner touched by the ball is out. The batter will be awarded first base. The runner on first base will be awarded second base. The runner on third base will not be allowed to advance.

Note: The runner is safe and play continues if, before touching the runner, the hit ball:

- gets past any fielder except the pitcher.
- touches any fielder including the pitcher.

A batted ball is deflected by a fielder, bounces off a runner, and is then caught by another fielder.

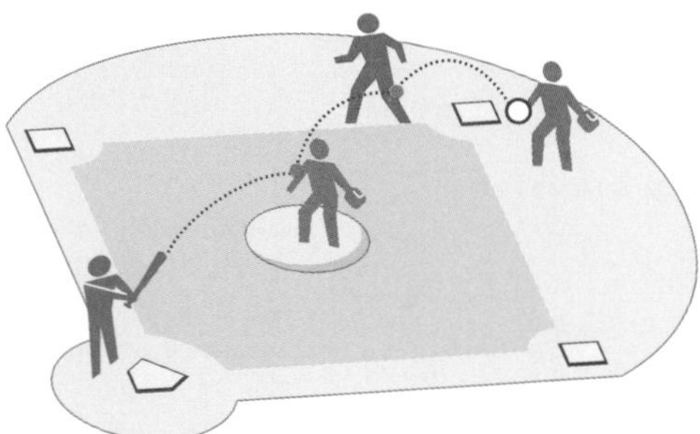

Explanation: Once the ball bounces off the runner, it is treated as if it had touched the ground, so it is no longer a fly ball.

Note: If the umpire decides that the runner purposely kicked or deflected the ball, the runner will be called out on interference.

Example: A ball is hit to the pitcher who deflects the ball toward a runner going to second base. The ball bounces off the runner into the hands of the second baseman, without yet touching the ground.

What happens: The catch doesn't count. The ball remains in play as if the incident did not occur.

All runners (including the batter) will continue to advance at risk.

Touched By a Batted Ball

If an Umpire Is Touched by a Batted Ball

With a few exceptions, these rules are very similar to those addressing a runner who is touched by a batted ball. Many of the diagrams found in the previous section could help to clarify the following circumstances.

Touched by a hit before it passes a fielder

If a fair ball touches an umpire before it touches or passes by a fielder:

- the ball is dead.
- the batter advances to first base.
- no other runners score or advance unless they are forced to advance by the batter.

Touched by a hit that gets past a fielder — except the pitcher

The ball is in play if a fair ball touches an umpire after having passed through, or close to, a fielder who was trying to stop the ball. The pitcher is not included in this case.

The play continues as if the incident didn't occur.

Touched by a hit that gets past the pitcher

There are two conditions by which this will happen:

If the ball does not touch the pitcher, bouncing over or continuing past the pitcher, and the ball touches an umpire:

- the ball is dead.
- the batter is awarded first base.

If the ball does touch the pitcher, gets past him, and then touches the umpire:

- the play continues as if the incident didn't occur.

9 | Fielding

A baseball defense is composed of nine fielders who will do anything (within the rules) to prevent the offense from scoring. This chapter discusses the ways a fielder can stop a batter's or a runner's advance. It also discusses violations committed by fielders that can have the opposite effect — runners can be awarded bases.

Fielding: contents

Basics for the Fielder

Overview: A fielder's job is to put out three offensive players before their team can score a run. Fielders hope to prevent batters from reaching first base and prevent runners from advancing to their next base. All nine defensive players, including the pitcher and catcher, are considered fielders.

Note: The pitcher is, technically, one of the nine fielders. There are enough rules on pitching, however, for the pitcher to merit his own chapter. The rules regarding the catcher and the other seven fielders (and just a few references to rules concerning the pitcher) are covered here.

Positions of the nine fielders

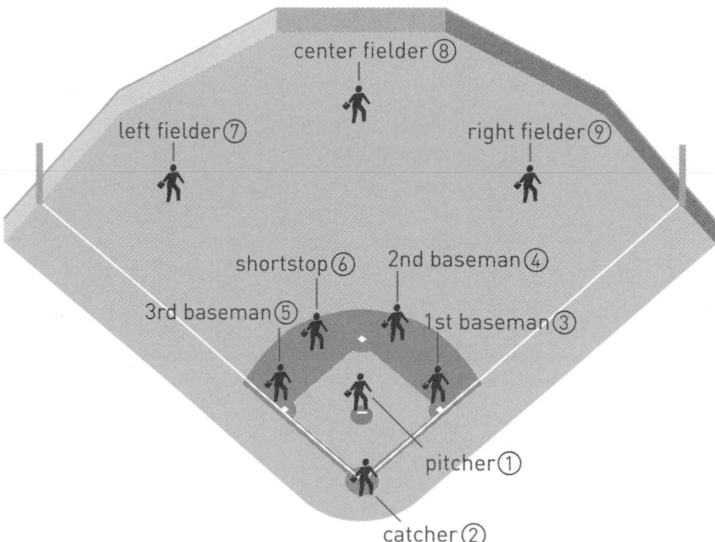

Note: Fielding positions are sometimes referred to by number, shown here circled. These are not official rule book designations, but are shown here for reference.

Distance of a typical throw from outfielder to infielder to home plate.

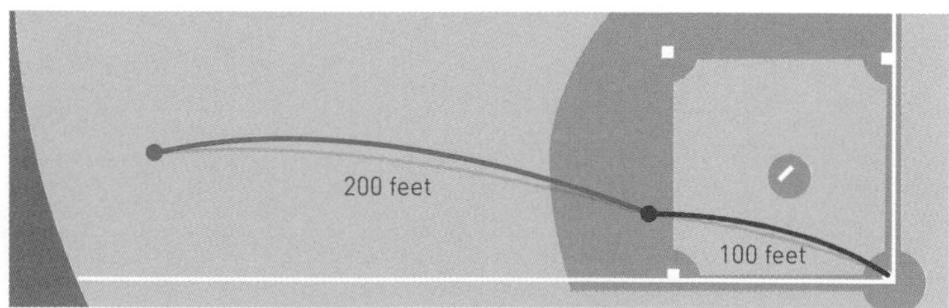

Basics

Fielding

Fielders must be in fair territory when the umpire calls "play."

The nine fielders are:

- pitcher
- catcher
- first baseman
- second baseman
- shortstop
- third baseman
- right fielder
- center fielder
- left fielder

At the start of the game, and anytime the umpire calls "play" during the game, the catcher must be in his position in the catcher's box behind home plate, and the pitcher will be in his position on the pitcher's mound. The other seven fielders must be positioned in fair territory.

While the fielders are each assigned specific locations on the field, the pitcher and the catcher are the only fielders required by the rules to be in specific locations — and this is only required at the time of the pitch. The other seven fielders may position themselves anywhere in fair territory. The seven "standard" positions, shown in the diagram at left, are universally accepted, assuring that both the infield and outfield are adequately covered, but they are not required by the rules.

Exception: No fielder can position himself between the pitcher and the catcher, blocking the batter's view of the pitch. Fielders must also stay out of the way of base runners unless they are in the act of making a play. See "Obstructing a Runner" on page 136.

The Pitcher: Some rules pertaining to fielders are different for the pitcher.

Most rules covered in this chapter pertain to all nine fielders. However, while the pitcher is technically a fielder, when performing his role as a pitcher some rules are different.

An example is the rule regarding **wild throws**. If a pitcher makes a wild throw, to first base for instance, and that throw goes into the stands or elsewhere out of play, the batter and all runners will be allowed to advance one base (awarded one base). If a fielder does the same, the batter and all runners will be awarded two bases each, not one.

A pitcher "stops" being a pitcher, and is treated like another fielder when:

1. the pitcher disengages from the pitcher's rubber, or

2. the pitcher completes his pitch.

When pitching, the pitcher must assume his legal pitching position. Early in his pitching sequence the pitcher may decide to step off of the pitcher's rubber, "disengaging" the rubber. If he does, he is governed by the rules regarding fielders.

This means that immediately following the pitch, the pitcher may cover any location on the field just like any other fielder. Once he stops being a pitcher, all fielder's rules apply (see the Pitching chapter, page 56).

The Catcher: The catcher is not confined to the catcher's box.

The only time the catcher is required to be in the catcher's box is when the umpire calls "play." Otherwise, to catch a pitch or to make a play, his position is not restricted. He can be anywhere on the field.

Exception: When the pitcher is intentionally delivering a base on balls (a "walk") the catcher must have both feet within the catcher's box at the time the ball leaves the pitcher's hand. If he fails to do this, or if the pitcher makes his pitch before the catcher has a chance to position his feet inside the catcher's box, the pitcher will be charged with a balk.

Awarded Bases Due to a Fielder

Overview: Sometimes a fielder's attempt to prevent a runner from advancing can have the opposite effect. Following is a list of ways a runner can be awarded bases due to actions of a fielder.

Awarded Bases

One Base Is Awarded...

1. **if a fielder falls into the dugout or stands after catching a fly ball,** the batter will be out and all runners will be awarded one base. The ball is dead.

Note: If the fielder remains standing after making the catch, the batter will be out, the ball remains live and no bases will be awarded.

2. **if the catcher or a fielder interferes with a batter while a runner is stealing a base,** all runners will be awarded one base.

3. **if a fielder touches a pitched ball with his cap.** If a fielder intentionally uses his cap, mask, or any other detached part of his uniform or equipment to touch a pitched ball, the batter and all runners will be awarded one base. The ball remains in play.

Awarded Bases

Two Bases Are Awarded...

1. **if a fielder intentionally touches a thrown ball with his cap** or any piece of his uniform or equipment detached from his body — for instance, if he tries to catch a thrown ball with his cap. The batter and all runners advance two bases. The ball remains in play.

2. **if a fielder intentionally throws his glove or cap at a thrown ball** or throws any piece of his uniform or equipment at a thrown ball, and it contacts the ball, the batter and all runners will be awarded two bases. The ball remains in play, allowing runners to further advance at their own risk.

Note: In instances where the ball is touched by a detached glove, cap, piece of uniform, or equipment unintentionally, the bases will not be awarded. For instance, if a fielder is running to make a catch, he jumps while reaching up, his glove flies off of his hand from the momentum of his arm's movement, and the glove touches the ball, it would be considered unintentional — bases would not be awarded.

3. **if a fair ball deflects off of a fielder and goes out of play.** If the deflected ball goes into the stands along the first or third base foul line, or if the ball goes under or through or becomes stuck in a fence, scoreboard, shrubbery, or vines, two bases are awarded.

4. **if a fielder makes a wild throw and the ball goes out of play.** If the throw puts the ball in the stands or into the bench or dugout, or if the throw goes over, under, or through or becomes stuck in a fence, two bases are awarded. The ball is dead. If the wild throw was made on the first play by an infielder after the ball was hit, the two bases will be awarded according to the position of the runners at the time of the pitch. Otherwise, the two bases will be awarded according to the position of the batter and runners at the time the ball left the fielder's hand.

Note: In some cases this will make it impossible to award each runner two bases, since two runners may be between the same two bases. For example, it is possible for two runners to be between second and third base when the wild throw takes place. If this occurs, one of the runners will be awarded only one base, since two runners cannot occupy the same base and no runner can advance more than two bases under this rule.

Awarded Bases

Three Bases Are Awarded...

1. if a fielder intentionally touches a batted, fair ball with his cap or any piece of his uniform or equipment detached from his body — for instance, if he tries to catch a batted ball with his cap and it touches the ball. All runners advance to home to score, and the batter advances three bases. The ball remains in play.

2. if a fielder intentionally throws his glove or cap at a batted, fair ball or throws any piece of his uniform or equipment at a batted, fair ball, and it contacts the ball, all runners advance to home to score. The batter advances to third base. The ball remains in play.

Awarded bases

Home Runs Are Awarded...

1. if a fly ball is deflected by a fielder and goes into the stands or over a fence in fair territory, the batter and all runners advance to home to score.

Example: A center fielder runs to the wall to make a catch that would have hit the wall. In reaching up to make the catch, the ball bounces off of his glove and goes over the fence. The batter is awarded a home run.

2. if a fly ball that would have been a home run is deflected. If, in the umpire's judgment, a hit would have gone into the stands or over a fence in fair territory for a home run, but it was deflected because a fielder threw his glove, cap, or any piece of his uniform or equipment at it, the batter and all runners advance to home to score.

Many uses for the term "tag"

Tag has several uses. **1.** A batter or runner tags his base when he touches it — usually with his foot, but sometimes also with his hand if sliding headfirst into the base. Any body part can be used to tag the base. **2.** It also refers to a fielder, with the ball in his possession, touching a base. (Without the ball, a fielder touching a base means nothing.) **3.** Lastly, a fielder can tag the batter or runner himself. With the ball in his hand or in his glove, the fielder can use that hand or glove to touch the batter or runner as he is running to first, running between bases, or caught off base.

If a Fielder Enters the Stands or Dugout

A fielder is permitted to reach but not step into the stands or dugout to make a catch. A catch may be completed in the stands or dugout, but the fielder's first touch must occur with one or both feet on or over the playing surface, and with no foot touching the ground inside the stands or dugout.

- **If the fielder falls into the stands or dugout** after making the catch, the ball is dead and runners are awarded one base.
- **If the fielder remains standing** after making the catch, the ball remains in play. Runners may tag up (by touching their original base) and advance, but at their own risk.

The Infield Fly Rule

Overview: Among the most misunderstood rules in the game, the Infield Fly Rule allows the umpire to call a batter out while the ball is still in the air.

When the Infield Fly Rule can be called. The Infield Fly Rule can only be applied when all three conditions are met:

- runners on first and second bases, or the bases loaded
- fewer than two outs
- a high fly ball (not a bunt or line drive) that can be easily caught by an infielder.

Intent of the rule. While it may not seem so at first, this rule is in the favor of the offensive team. It prevents the defensive team from intentionally dropping a fly ball in order to force the runners into an easy double play.

The result. The batter is out and the ball remains in play.

The umpire calls an infield fly when...

The batter hits an infield fly that seems likely to be caught. The batter begins to run toward first base, but the runners will wait to see if the ball will be caught (see "Tagging Up" on page 112). As soon as the umpire sees that the infielder is likely to catch the ball, he will call "infield fly, batter's out."

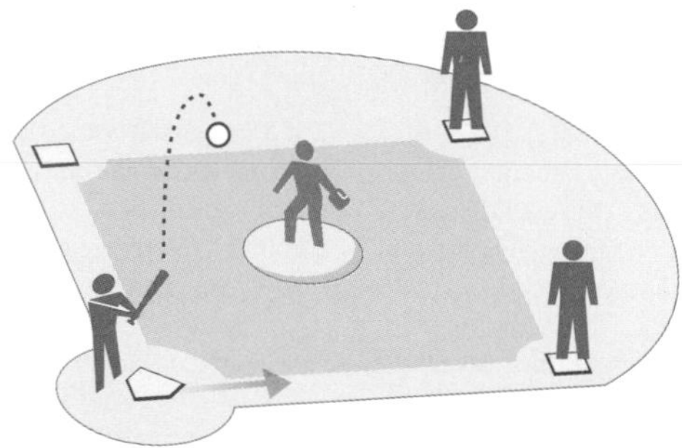

Offensive team: one out

Interference and the Infield Fly Rule

If during an infield fly a runner interferes with a fielder, the runner and the batter will both be called out if the ball is judged to be in fair territory. If it is a foul ball, caught or not caught, the runner will be called out but not the batter.

A closely related rule

If with fewer than two outs and a runner on first base (with or without runners on second or third), an umpire judges that an infielder intentionally dropped a fly ball after touching it, he will call the batter out after the ball is dropped. This is similar to the Infield Fly Rule, but requires the following four conditions:

- the ball must be touched first
- the out is called after the ball is dropped
- it requires only a runner on first base
- the hit in this case can be a high fly or a line drive

Infield Fly Rule

If the Infield Fly Rule Did Not Exist...

Like many rules in baseball, the Infield Fly Rule was put in place to discourage unsportsmanlike actions — players should play the game as intended. To best understand how this applies to the Infield Fly Rule, it helps to see what could happen if the rule did not exist.

If the Infield Fly Rule were not called, the following double play could occur....

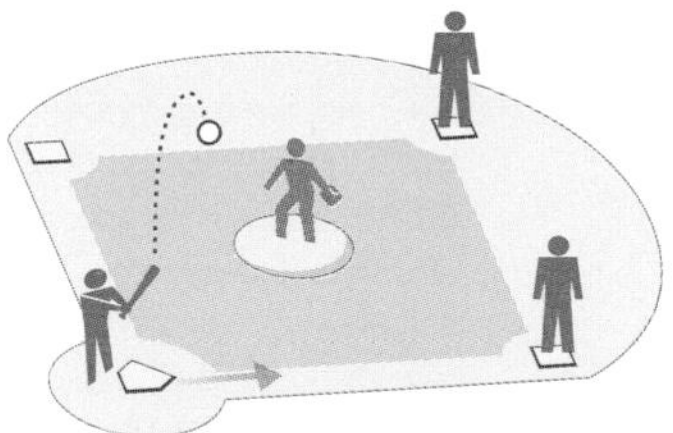

1. With runners on first and second (or first, second, and third), the batter hits a high fly ball that will land in the infield. Runners will remain on their bases, expecting the ball to be caught.

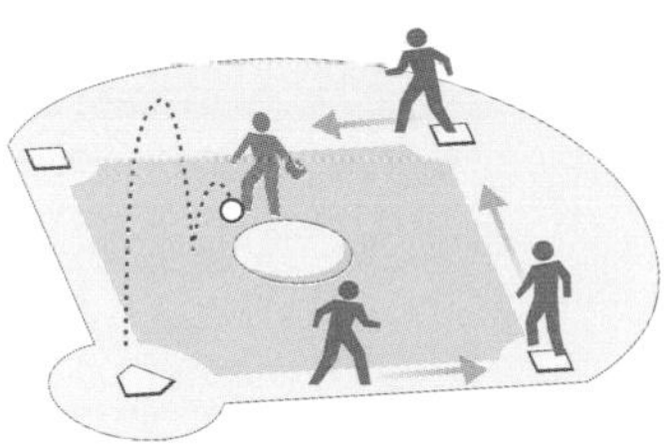

2. The fielder intentionally drops the infield fly. This now forces the runners to advance to their next base (see "Force Plays" on page 106).

3. With all runners in motion, and the ball in close proximity to the bases, the fielder quickly picks up the ball and throws it to third, where it then is thrown to second for an easy double play.

Offensive team: two outs

Note: If the Infield Fly Rule is called and the fielder legitimately misses the catch, the batter is still out and the ball remains in play.

Note: The Infield Fly Rule is not in effect with just a runner on first base because, with the ball lingering in the air and that runner staying close to first to see what happens, if the batter makes a strong effort he will typically have time to reach first base safely. Therefore the play will usually result in only one out.

Fielder's Choice

Overview: The term "fielder's choice" describes a play in which a fielder must choose between two or more runners, putting one of them out instead of the other.

The rules of baseball use the term fielder's choice to account for a number of situations:

1. A fielder's throw to anywhere other than first base. In this case fielder's choice refers to the decision by a fielder handling a ground ball to throw to a base other than first base, to make a play on a runner other than the batter. (The batter may subsequently be put out on a double play.)

2. The batter's advance to first base, or beyond. In this case the batter actually reaches first base or beyond, following a fielder's decision to throw in an attempt to make a play on a runner other than the batter.

3. Any runner's advance. Similar to the above, the term accounts for an advance by any runner to one or more bases, following a fielder's decision to put out a different runner. (It does not apply to runners advancing due to a stolen base or due to an error.)

4. A decision by a fielder to allow a runner to steal a base. Although not usual, in some situations the defensive team member may decide that it's okay to let a runner steal a base. Fielder's choice in this case refers to that decision.

Note: Definitions 2, 3, and 4 are typically used by the official scorekeeper.

Outs

Overview: For a fielder, some outs are more difficult than others. A fielder can actively put a batter or a runner out, or he can be credited with an "automatic" out by the official scorer.

Ways a fielder can put out a batter or a runner.

The fielder's job is to prevent a batter or runner from scoring at home plate. He does this by putting out the batter or runner, preventing runners from stealing a base, or by preventing runners from advancing whenever a ball is hit by the batter.

A fielder puts out a batter or a runner in three ways.

1. The fielder catches a fly ball hit by the batter in fair or foul territory, on a fly or a line drive (meaning he catches it before the ball has touched the ground).

2. The fielder tags a base. With the ball in his possession, the runner will be out when the fielder tags a base to which the runner is forced to advance before the runner reaches it. This includes a batter-runner who is trying to reach first base.

3. The fielder tags a runner with the ball while a runner is between bases. A fielder can put the runner out as long as the ball is in play and the runner is not touching his legal base. This includes batters running to first base.

Exception: Batters who overrun first base typically cannot be tagged out after they touch first base. See page 111 in the Running chapter.

Automatic Outs: Credits for Fielders

Overview: The official scorer, in certain cases, makes judgments about which fielder receives credit for plays that result in an automatic out.

The catcher receives credit for an automatic out on the *batter* when:

1. **the batter illegally bats the ball.** For instance, if the batter uses a bat that has been tampered with.
2. **the batter bunts the ball foul on the third strike.**
3. **the batter is touched by the ball he batted.**
4. **the batter interferes with the catcher.**
5. **the batter misses his proper turn at bat.**
6. **the batter refuses to advance to first base after receiving a base on balls,** (also called a "walk").

See the Batting chapter for more details on these rules, with examples.

The catcher receives credit for an automatic out on the *runner* when:

7. **a forced runner on third neglects to advance to home** to score the winning run. In the case of a winning run a forced runner on third is required to advance. If he doesn't, the umpire will call the runner out — the game will not be ended.

The fielder receives credit for an automatic out on the *batter* when:

1. **a batter is called out by the Infield Fly Rule** and the infield fly is not caught. The fielder who, according to the official scorer, could have made the catch receives credit for the out.

This rule can lead to an odd situation. The fielder in this case could have legitimately dropped the catch, which would normally be a error. Because of the Infield Fly Rule, however, he will be automatically credited with an out.

2. **the batter is called out because of interference by a runner.** In a double play situation, if the runner interferes with a fielder throwing the ball or catching a thrown ball, the first baseman receives credit for the batter's automatic out. If the interfered-with fielder was throwing the ball at the time of the interference, that fielder will receive credit for an assist.

The fielder receives credit for an automatic out on the *runner* when:

3. **a runner is touched by a batted ball.** The fielder closest to the ball receives credit for the out.
4. **a runner is called out for running out of the baseline to avoid being tagged.** The fielder whom the runner avoided receives credit for the out.
5. **a runner is called out for running past the runner in front of him.** The fielder who was nearest the runner when he passed the runner in front of him receives credit for the out.
6. **a runner is called out for running the bases in reverse order,** with the intent of confusing the fielders. The fielder who was covering the base from which the runner began the reverse run receives credit for the out.
7. **a runner is called out for interfering with a fielder.** The fielder with whom he interfered receives credit for the out. However, if the fielder was making a throw when the interference occurred, the fielder who was receiving the throw receives credit for the out. The fielder making the throw receives credit for an "assist."

10 Interference, Obstruction, and Collisions

Calls of interference (getting in the way of a fielder) and obstruction (getting in the way of a runner) are made often. The rules give either fielders or runners the right-of-way, depending on the circumstances. In some cases, however, contact can be unavoidable, just the nature of the game.

Interference, Obstruction, and Collisions: contents

Interference and Obstruction

Overview: Interference occurs when a runner or batter gets in the way of a fielder who is trying to make a play. Obstruction occurs when a fielder gets in the way of a runner who is trying to advance or return to a base.

Interference

Typically, interference occurs when an offensive team's player hinders a fielder's attempt at making a play. Other members of the fielder's team, an umpire, or a spectator may also be the cause.

Exception: The term "catcher's interference" is used when a catcher interferes with a batter — the only instance of defensive interference.

The act of interference could include physical contact with the fielder or the ball, or an attempt to confuse or distract a fielder who is making a play.

Obstruction

Obstruction occurs when a fielder illegally blocks or impedes a runner's advance during a play.

It must impact the play

For either interference or obstruction to be called, the umpire must determine whether the outcome of the play was affected by the action. No obstruction will be called if the umpire feels that the runner would have been out anyway. Likewise, no interference will be called if the fielder could not have made the play regardless of the interference.

Example: A runner on his way to third base goes out of his way to shove the shortstop. The ball is thrown by the right fielder to the third baseman, but the throw arrives too late and the runner is safe.

Although this was a blatant act, in this case, there is no interference because the shortstop was not part of the play. The runner's shove had no effect on the outcome, so the play stands. However, after the play is completed, the umpire may warn or even eject the runner from the game for his conduct.

The penalty is designed to correct the outcome

After a call of interference or obstruction, the umpire will take steps to minimize the impact that the illegal action had on the play.

An obstructed runner who was prevented from reaching a base will be awarded that base. A runner who reached a base will be called out if, due to interference, a fielder was prevented from completing a play at that base. If a fielder is prevented from completing a double play due to interference, both the runner and the batter will be called out — as if the double play had been successful.

Who Has Right-of-Way

Overview: For a call of interference or obstruction, the umpire must decide if the fielder or the runner had the right-of-way.

Right-of-way for a batted ball

The fielder always has right-of-way while making a play on a batted ball.

Example: Interference. A fielder dives in front of a runner in an attempt to catch a batted ball. The runner collides with the fielder, who misses the catch. Interference is called against the runner.

Right-of-way for a thrown ball

In most situations the runner owns the base path. A fielder has the right to be in the base path only if it is necessary in order for him to successfully field the ball. If the umpire judges him to be there unnecessarily, he will be charged with obstruction.

Example: Obstruction. A fielder dives into the path of a runner to catch a ball. He misses the ball and does not immediately move to get out of the runner's way. The runner collides with the fielder and is unable to reach his base as a result. Obstruction is called against the fielder, and the runner is awarded the base.

What if they're both right?

When the runner and the fielder both have the right to be in the base path, all bets are off! If a collision occurs, there will be no penalty called against either player, unless the umpire feels that one of the players intentionally or unnecessarily caused an otherwise avoidable collision.

Because of the danger involved in the worst of these situations, there are more specific guidelines as to what constitutes an "avoidable" collision in the case of a catcher making a play at home plate (see collisions at home plate page 138).

Collision at home plate

During the 1951 World Series, the umpire changed his call to safe when Alvin Dark of the Giants collided with Yogi Berra of the Yankees, causing him to drop the ball. Since both had a right to the base path, neither obstruction nor interference was called.

Since then, the rules regarding collisions at home plate have changed (see page 138).

Interference by a Runner, and Others

Overview: When a runner interferes with a fielder or a ball in play, he will be called out. A runner and the batter will both be called out if the interference was judged to have prevented a double play.

The runner is out:

- if a runner interferes with a fielder making a play on a batted ball, whether intentional or not.

  Exception: If a runner is touching a base when he interferes with the fielder, the umpire must determine that the interference was intentional before making the call.

- if a runner interferes with or is touched by a batted ball before it touches or goes past a fielder. In this case, it doesn't matter if the incident was intentional or not.
- if a batted ball gets past a fielder (whether or not he touched it), and the runner intentionally kicks or deflects the ball. See "Touched by a Batted Ball" on pages 115 and 116.
- if a runner intentionally interferes with a batted ball by throwing his helmet, bat, or any object at or in the path of the ball.
- if a runner intentionally interferes with a thrown ball.
- if a runner runs outside the base path to interfere with a play, on a thrown or batted ball. See "Running Outside the Baseline" on page 114.

Note 1: If a runner is hit by a thrown ball and it was not his fault, the ball simply remains in play, no penalty.

Note 2: If there is contact between the batter-runner and the catcher, while the batter-runner is on his way to first base and the catcher is fielding the hit ball, the umpire will rarely call interference unless the infraction is blatant or extreme.

The ball is dead, and no runners may advance.

When there are other runners who are not involved with the interference, they will be made to return to the last base they touched before the interference occurred (referred to as the "time of interference").

Exception: If the interference occurs before the batter-runner reaches first base, all runners will return to the base they occupied before the pitch was made.

If the runner or catcher didn't mean to do it

If the umpire believes that the runner's interference was not intentional or the batter did not hinder the fielder's play, he will award the batter first base.

Interfering with the catcher on the third strike

If the batter or runner impedes the catcher fielding the ball after a third strike has been thrown:

- the batter will be called out
- the ball will be dead
- runners go back to the bases they occupied at the time of the pitch

Note: Interference will not be called if the ball bounces off of the catcher or umpire and it simply touches the batter — unless the batter then does something deliberate to interfere with the catcher.

Note: When two or more fielders are attempting to field a ball, interference will only be called if it is committed against the fielder who the umpire thinks is entitled to the ball.

Example: Two fielders are trying to catch a ground ball. At the last second, one of them abandons his attempt and steps out of the way but directly in front of a runner. Even if the ball is dropped, there will be no call of interference because the contact was on the fielder who was not "entitled" to the ball. In fact, that fielder could be called for obstruction.

Interference

By a Coach or Teammate

There are several situations in which a runner will be called out due to the actions of his teammates, including a coach or the batter.

Interference by a teammate

All members of the offensive team are required to stay clear of a fielder in the act of fielding the ball. This includes team members on the sidelines, who must move away if a fielder needs that space.

As penalty for a team member or members not avoiding the fielder, the batter or runner involved in the play will be called out.

Teammates cannot gather around a base.

A runner's teammates are not permitted to gather near a base to which the runner is advancing for the purpose of distracting or confusing a fielder attempting to make a play. As a penalty the runner will be called out due to interference by his teammates.

A coach cannot touch a runner.

The first base coach or third base coach must never touch a runner to assist him in any way, unless it's to simply exchange equipment. As a penalty the runner will be called out.

Example: A runner is rounding third base and is planning on continuing to home plate. The third base coach sees that a throw being made to home is likely to put him out at the plate. The coach cannot grab or hold the runner in an effort to make him stop on third.

A coach interferes with a fielder.

A coach must never leave the coach's box in order to affect a fielder's throw or a play on the ball — he'll be removed from the game.

Batter interference at home plate

With fewer than two outs and a runner on third base, the batter must not intentionally hinder a fielder making a play at home plate. If he does, the runner will be called out even though it was the batter's fault. The idea is to penalize the offensive team by removing the more valuable player — the runner at third base.

If this occurs when there are already two outs, the batter, not the runner, will be charged with the third out.

Interference by a batter or runner who has been put out

A batter or runner who has just been put out must not interfere with a subsequent attempt to put out a second runner, for example, by trying to confuse or physically interfere with a fielder. If he does, the second runner will also be called out due to his teammate's action.

Note: It is not considered interference if the batter or runner who has just been put out continues to advance to the next base — for instance, if he did not realize he had been put out. This does not constitute an attempt to confuse the fielders or hinder a play.

Did he do it on purpose?

When it comes to interference by a non-player, the umpire must decide whether or not the interference was intentional.

Example: A first base coach rolls to the ground to avoid a thrown ball. The first baseman trips over the coach while trying to retrieve the ball. During the ensuing confusion, the batter-runner makes it all the way to third base.

It would be tempting for the umpire to automatically call interference on the coach, but if he feels that the coach was honestly trying to avoid the ball and never intended to get in the way of the fielder, he must not call interference. The play must stand.

Interference

By an Umpire or a Spectator

In certain situations an umpire or spectator may interfere with a live ball or with a fielder attempting to make a play. The following describes the effect these different types of interference have on a base runner.

If an umpire interferes with a catcher making a play

If an umpire gets in the way of a catcher attempting to pick off a runner or prevent a stolen base, the ball is dead and all runners must return to their bases. If the catcher is able to throw out the runner despite the interference, the interference will be disregarded.

If an umpire interferes with a catcher returning the ball to the pitcher

The ball will be dead, which means no runners can advance, no runs can score, and no runners can be put out.

If an umpire is touched by a fair ball before it passes a fielder

In this case:

- the batter will be awarded first base.
- the ball is dead.
- no other runners score or advance unless they are forced to advance by the batter.

See "Touched by a Batted Ball" on page 117 for more information.

Spectator interference

It is considered spectator interference if a spectator reaches out of the stands, or if he falls or steps out of the stands onto the playing field, and interferes with the fielder or touches a live ball.

If this occurs:

- the ball is dead.
- the umpire will take actions, such as calling runners out or awarding bases, to minimize or nullify the impact of the spectator's interference.

See "Spectator Interference" on page 192 for more information.

Caught on video

Some fans will go to great lengths to get a souvenir, like this guy interfering at Wrigley Field, June 2015. He leaned way over the wall while attempting a bare-handed catch — his left hand was busy holding his eight-month-old baby.

Interference on a Double Play

Overview: It is considered a good base-running strategy to veer toward a fielder at second base who is attempting to turn a double play. Even if unnecessary contact is made, umpires tend to give ample leeway to the runner (despite the risk to the fielder).

Runner interferes with a throw on a double play

The rules state that a runner must not intentionally and unnecessarily interfere with a fielder as he is attempting to make a double play.

Although it may seem contradictory, it is common and acceptable in this circumstance for a runner to slide toward the fielder rather than directly toward the base. Even though the intention is clearly to interfere with the fielder, a penalty will rarely be called as long as the runner stays within the base path — still in reach of the base.

If the runner is charged with interference, both he and the batter will be called out.

Example: Interference on a double play

Typically an umpire will not call interference unless the runner has strayed so far from the base that he can no longer reach it with his hand or foot as he slides by.

Note: The runner is not allowed to try to block the throw by raising his hands or putting his body in the way of the throw.

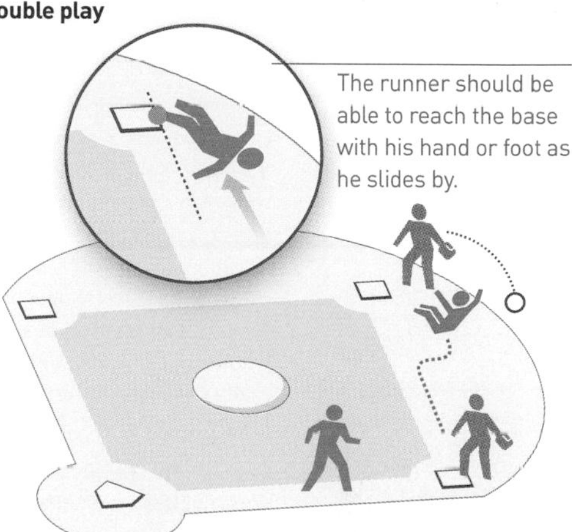

Runner or batter interferes with a batted ball on a double play

Both the runner and the batter will be out if either of them intentionally interferes with a batted ball or a fielder attempting to field a batted ball during a possible double play.

If the runner interferes:

- the runner and the batter are out.
- the ball is dead.
- no other runners will be allowed to advance on the play.

If the batter interferes:

- the batter and the runner closest to home plate are out.
- the ball is dead.
- no other runners will be allowed to advance on the play.

Note: The rule states that the batter and the runner closest to home should be called out in this case, even if the double play would have been made on another runner. The idea is to penalize the offense by removing the more valuable runner — the one closest to scoring.

Obstructing a Runner

Overview: Obstruction occurs when a fielder who does not have possession of the ball or is not actively fielding the ball impedes a runner who is trying to advance or retreat on the bases.

Obstruction of a runner

Baselines belong to the runners, not the fielders. Runners, including a batter on his way to first base, have right-of-way. Blocking the path of a runner or blocking the runner himself, without possession of the ball, is considered obstruction. The umpire signals obstruction by pointing to the source of the infraction and yelling "That's obstruction!"

Like interference, obstruction is a judgment call by the umpire. If there's contact between a runner and a fielder, the umpire must determine whether or not the fielder had a right to be in that particular spot at the time of contact.

If the fielder is making a play on a batted ball, he has right-of-way.

If the fielder is not actively making a play on a ball, the runner has right-of-way in the baseline.

What defines "the act of making a play"

If a fielder is about to catch a ball, and the ball is moving toward him at a speed and direction that requires him to be at a certain location on the field, then the fielder is "in the act of making a play." He has a right to be in that location.

Obstruction must have an impact on the play.

In order to qualify as obstruction the contact must have had an impact on the play. If the runner is obstructed but he makes it safely to the base he would have reached had the obstruction not occurred, then the incident will be ignored.

Contact is not always obstruction or interference.

There are only a few circumstances in which a fielder might block a runner in the base paths, and only one of these situations constitutes obstruction. The following is a list of circumstances where contact could be made between runner and fielder.

Obstruction. The fielder does not have possession of the ball and is not actively fielding the ball. This is the only instance when the fielder will be called for obstruction due to contact with the runner.

Intent is important

If the umpire believes a member of the defensive team made an attempt to get out of the runner's way, even if he obstructed the runner anyway, he will not be charged with obstruction.

No obstruction. The fielder is trying to field a *batted* ball. In this case, the fielder has right of way, and the runner may be charged with interference if contact is made.

No obstruction. The fielder is trying to field a *thrown* ball. The fielder has a right to be in the path of the runner if the umpire feels he must be there in order to field a thrown ball. However, the runner also has a right to the baseline and is not required to get out of the fielder's way. Even if there is a major collision, neither obstruction nor interference will be called unless the umpire judges one of the players to have unnecessarily impeded the other.

No obstruction. With possession of the ball, the fielder is trying to tag a runner. As in the case of a fielder trying to catch a thrown ball, both the runner and the fielder have a right to be in the same location. Neither obstruction nor interference will be called unless the umpire judges one of the players to have unnecessarily impeded the other.

If a fielder obstructs a runner while a play is being made on the obstructed runner:

- the runner or runners are awarded the bases that the umpire believes the runners would have reached had the obstruction not occurred. The obstructed runner must be awarded at least one base in advance of his position when he was obstructed.
- the ball is dead when the call is made.

If a wild throw was in flight before the obstruction call was made, the wild-throw rules will prevail. This can be to the advantage of the team at bat, since wild-throw rules award one or two bases to each runner.

Rules concerning wild throws by fielders are discussed on page 122. For wild throws by a pitcher, see page 66.

If a fielder obstructs a runner when no play is being made on the obstructed runner:

- the umpire will let the play proceed.
- when the play is completed, the umpire will call obstruction (by signaling "time").
- the runner or runners are awarded the bases that the umpire believes the runners would have reached had the obstruction not occurred.

Gone too far?

In cases where, before the ball was dead, an obstructed runner advanced to a base beyond the base he would have been awarded, and in doing so he was put out, the out will be upheld.

Obstruction at home plate:

If a catcher or other fielder without the ball in his possession obstructs a runner from third base when he is:

- attempting to score by stealing home, or
- attempting to score in a squeeze play (a play in which the batter bunts in an attempt to allow a runner on third to score),

or, with a runner from third stealing home or in a squeeze play:

- if the catcher or a fielder touches the batter or his bat,

a balk will be charged against the pitcher and all runners advance one base. The batter will be awarded first base. The ball is dead.

All members of the offensive team, including all players and coaches, must try to get out of the fielder's way.

In cases where a fielder is making a play on a ball that is batted or thrown, all members of the offensive team must try to get out of the way. This includes players, coaches, and anyone in the dugout.

Penalty: The penalty against the offensive team for failing to try to get out of the way is "interference." The umpire will call out the batter or runner on whom the play was being made.

Obstruction called on a fielder who has right-of-way

In rare situations an umpire may call obstruction on a fielder who is making a play and has the right-of-way, if the fielder unnecessarily impedes the runner.

The violation would have to be obvious and flagrant to earn the call. For instance, the fielder would have to intentionally punch, trip, or kick the runner.

Obstructing

Immediate vs. Delayed Dead Ball

An immediate dead ball

When a runner is obstructed while fielders are attempting to put him out, or when the batter is obstructed before he reaches first base, the umpire will call obstruction immediately. The ball will be dead the instant the call is made.

A delayed dead ball

If there is no play being made on the obstructed runner, and the batter-runner has already reached first base at the time of obstruction, the umpire will allow the play to continue until all action stops. This is known as a delayed dead ball.

When the play is complete, the umpire will decide if the obstruction had any impact on the outcome of the play. If the runner is obstructed, but all runners make it safely to the bases they would have reached had the obstruction not occurred, the obstruction will be ignored.

If the umpire believes that the obstruction prevented any of the runners from safely advancing, he will award bases to runners in an effort to nullify the effects of the obstruction.

Note: If during a play in which obstruction has been called, a runner advances beyond the base that he was awarded due to the obstruction, he does so at risk and can be tagged out.

Collisions at Home Plate

Overview: In the past it was an accepted strategy for a runner to charge into the catcher at home plate in an attempt to make him drop the ball. Exciting, but also dangerous for the catcher! Major League Baseball made rule changes intended to minimize the risk.

The old rule: anything goes on the base paths

When both a runner and a fielder had right-of-way (see "Who Has Right-of-Way" on page 131) neither would be called for an infraction, despite a resulting collision. If the fielder lost possession of the ball during a collision at a base, the runner would be called safe because the fielder was unable to make the tag.

This led to an obvious strategy — charge into the fielder or catcher with as much force as possible in order to dislodge the ball. The rule (or lack of a rule) resulted in some spectacular collisions, especially at home plate.

The new rule

There are key differences in the new rule that apply to both the runner and the catcher.

The runner will be called out if a collision is judged to have been avoidable — even if the fielder drops the ball.

The catcher is at fault, and the runner will be safe, if the catcher blocked his path to the plate unnecessarily — unless the catcher had possession of the ball or his being in the path was unavoidable in order for him to successfully field the ball.

The rule is not designed to eliminate contact — just minimize the danger.

A direct path to the plate

The runner must not deviate from a direct path to the base or initiate an avoidable collision. Essentially, this means the umpire must judge whether the runner went out of his way to make contact or did not avoid unnecessary contact — for instance, by not sliding into home.

Example: A runner veers outside the baseline to collide with a fielder making a catch. As a result the fielder drops the ball. The runner will be called out for interference.

A legal slide

Even if the runner has not deviated from the base path, he may still be guilty of interference if he slides too aggressively into the catcher. If, for instance, the runner begins his slide just before contact (often referred to as a late slide), he will still be upright enough to make direct body-to-body contact with the fielder. A late or hard slide can look more like a tackle than an attempt to avoid a tag.

Here are the rules for a legal slide:

- In a feetfirst slide, the runner's bottom and legs must touch the ground before he makes contact with the catcher.
- In a headfirst slide, the runner's body must touch the ground before contact with the fielder.

In short, the intent of a slide should be to avoid a tag rather than to collide with a fielder.

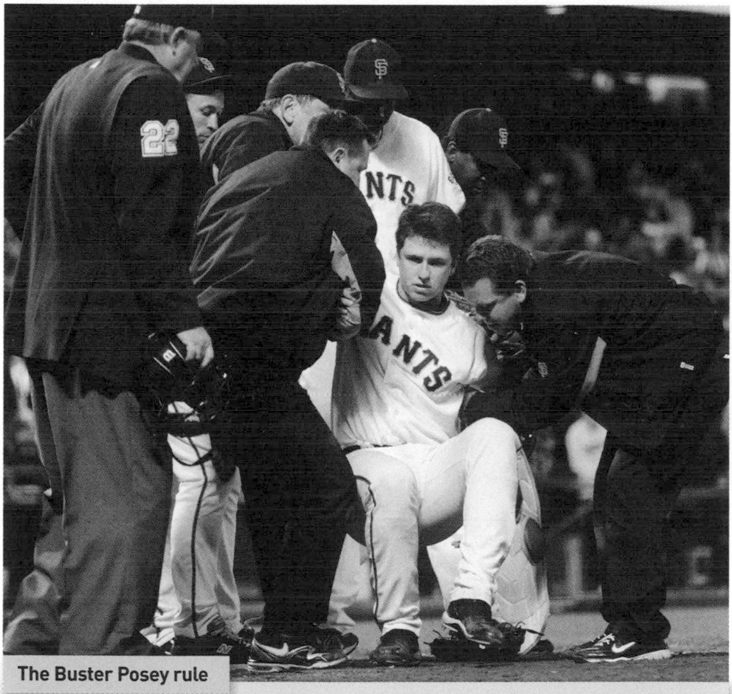

The Buster Posey rule

New rules on collisions were a direct result of San Francisco Giants catcher Buster Posey's leg injury, suffered in a violent collision when Florida Marlins' Scott Cousins slammed into him at home plate, May 2011.

11 | Umpires

Umpires are the official representatives of Major League Baseball. In addition to officiating, they are responsible for upholding the dignity of the game.

A typical game is overseen by an umpire-in-chief and three field umpires.

Umpires have tasks to perform before, during, and after the game. Their responsibilities range from checking the batting orders to ejecting players after a brawl. Here are their tasks as identified in the official rules.

Umpires: contents

Basics for Umpires

Overview: Umpires are appointed by the League President, who is responsible for assigning one or more umpires to officiate at each game. Umpires are representatives of the league, and the sport of baseball itself. Their job is to uphold the rules of the game. Additionally, umpires are responsible for maintaining proper conduct on the field throughout the game.

While the official rules of baseball cover many aspects of the game, each umpire has the authority to rule over situations not mentioned in the official rules. Members of either team, including players, coaches, managers, and team officers, must not do anything to prevent an umpire from performing his job. The umpire may enforce penalties, as appropriate.

An umpire's first rule

The first and most important rule for umpires, important enough to be printed in all capital letters in the official rules of baseball, states: BE IN POSITION TO SEE EVERY PLAY. This, of course, is mandatory if an umpire is to call a play correctly. It will also reduce objections and arguments from players who may otherwise not believe the umpire was in a good position to see what actually happened.

Positions of the umpires

A typical umpiring team consists of the umpire-in-chief, positioned at home plate (also referred to as the "plate umpire") and three field umpires. The three field umpires are responsible for specific areas of the field just like defensive players. Like fielders, umpires will shift positions depending on the circumstances. They try to be in the spot that will let them see the play correctly without getting in the way of the action.

Examples: Typical umpire positions

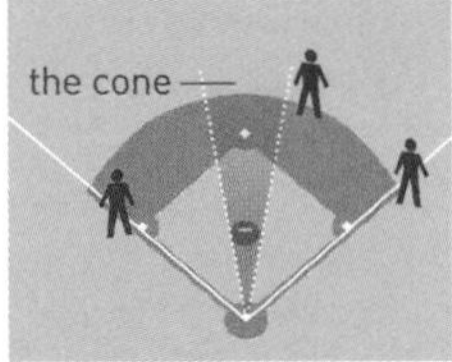

Stay out of the way: The second base umpire will often position himself behind second base but outside of the batter's line of vision to keep from distracting him — just to the side of an area known as "the cone." This gives the umpire a clear view of the pitcher. If the batter is left-handed the umpire will stay on the first base side of the cone. If the batter is right-handed the umpire will shift to the third base side of the cone.

Move to the best spot to see the play: If there is a runner on first base, the first base umpire will move closer to first base, and the umpire that was behind second will shift below second base. This will provide each of them with a better view of the action.

Instructions to the Umpires

Overview: Once they have entered the field, umpires are instructed to follow a strict code of conduct. While the players and other team members are certainly part of baseball, the rules below ensure that umpires proudly represent the sport.

Umpires are given instructions in addition to the one requiring them to be in the best position to see a play. These additional instructions can be divided into things umpires *must* do, things umpires *must not* do, and things umpires should *avoid*.

An umpire *must*

- remember that making a correct call is his first responsibility, more important than *umpire dignity*. (Conveniently, the term *umpire dignity* is not defined.)
- remain active and alert.
- keep the game going.
- keep his eye on the ball, even at the expense of missing other action on the field. The instructions state that it is more important to know the status of the ball than to see whether or not a runner missed touching a base.
- after calling a player out, watch for dropped balls.
- keep his uniform in proper condition.
- remain courteous to officers of the teams.
- be patient, use good judgment, maintain self-control, and not lose his temper.
- treat each team equally, not judge plays differently for the visiting or home team.
- be courteous, impartial, and firm. By doing so, umpires will gain respect.
- develop a set of simple signals with the other umpires to indicate when an incorrect call has been made, so that the erroneous call can be corrected.
- carry a rule book. Umpires are encouraged to consult the rule book when necessary, even if it delays the game. The point is that it is better to delay the game to confirm that a ruling is correct, than to have the game protested later, possibly requiring a replay of the game.

Note: While this last point about carrying a rule book is stated in the official rules, it is totally ignored. No self-respecting Major League umpire would ever be caught fumbling through a rule book in the middle of a game.

An umpire *must not*

- hold conversations with the players.
- enter the coaching box or hold a conversation with the coach.
- make calls too rapidly, or turn away from the action too soon when a fielder throws the ball in an attempt at a double play.
- begin to signal "safe" or "out" until the play at that base is complete.
- "compensate" for a bad call, if one is made, by trying to "even up" later in the game. Each call on a play must be made as it is seen.
- be fazed by criticism about a call.

On that last point:

If sure about a call, an umpire should not be intimidated by players' appeals to ask for second opinions from other umpires.

If not sure about a call, an umpire must consult with other umpires. However, he should not over-rely on this measure. His first responsibility is to call the play correctly. He should request assistance from other umpires only when help is required to ensure a correct call.

Umpires *must avoid*

The official rules call for the umpires to "avoid" two things: visiting a team's offices, and "thoughtless familiarity" with a team's staff.

The Umpire-in-Chief and the Field Umpires

Overview: The rules call for one or more umpires to be appointed by the League President to officiate at each game. Four umpires are standard practice at a game. Any number over one, of course, sets up the possibility of disagreement between umpires. Here is how the rules handle it.

Games with only one umpire

If there is only one umpire officiating at a game, he takes complete responsibility for administering the rules.

While he will usually take a position behind the catcher, he is allowed to take any position on the field that will provide him with the best vantage point. For instance, if there are runners on base, he may elect to stand behind the pitcher.

Games with two or more umpires

When two or more umpires are assigned to a game, one umpire will be appointed umpire-in-chief. The other umpires become field umpires. A field umpire's authority equals that of the umpire-in-chief, with the exception of game forfeits, terminating a game, and a few other calls — those can only be called by the umpire-in-chief.

That said, the umpire-in-chief and the field umpires work as a team and have specific responsibilities delegated to them.

Umpire-in-chief

The umpire-in-chief is also called the plate umpire, since he stands behind home plate. The umpire-in-chief's responsibilities include:

- ultimate responsibility for the game's conduct.
- passing the batting order to the official scorer, including any changes.
- calling pitches as either balls or strikes.
- decisions concerning the batter.
- decisions concerning forfeits of the game (a forfeit ends the game, giving one team an automatic win).
- announcing time limits before the start of the game (if any have been established).
- announcing any special ground rules he deems appropriate.

Field umpires

Field umpires may position themselves anywhere on the field. They choose their positions according to where they believe they will have the best vantage point for upcoming plays. Typically this means that in addition to the umpire-in-chief, one umpire each will be positioned at first, second, and third bases. A field umpire's job is to assist the umpire-in-chief, since it is often impossible for a single umpire to simultaneously monitor every action taking place on the field.

Field umpires are usually in the best location to rule on plays made at the bases — therefore they typically make these calls. However, any umpire can make a call, and field umpires share authority equally with the umpire-in-chief in making calls on plays at the bases.

Responsibilities shared between the umpire-in-chief and the field umpires

The following responsibilities are shared between all umpires:

- calling foul or fair balls,
- decisions concerning the rules of the game,
- enforcement of the rules of baseball, including those regarding conduct and discipline,
- calling "time," balks, illegal pitches, and ball tampering.

The Umpire

Umpires' Responsibilities Before the Game

Umpires have responsibilities before the game begins:

- **Identify the managers.** Although typically not an issue, the rules require that, at least thirty minutes prior to the game's scheduled start time, each team identify their manager to either the League President or to the umpire-in-chief.
- **Monitor the equipment.** The umpire must make sure the bats, uniforms, and all other equipment meet the requirements of the rules.
- **Get the baseballs ready.** The home team is responsible for supplying the umpire with baseballs for the game. The baseballs need to meet the requirements for size, weight, and construction (see page 32). The balls are delivered in sealed packages that contain the signature of the president of the league. A clubhouse attendant will break the seal, inspect each ball, then "prepare" the balls — removing the shine on the ball by rubbing each ball with a special mud. (See "Preparing the Baseballs" on page 26.)
- **Spare baseballs.** The umpire must make sure that the home team has at least one dozen extra regulation baseballs on hand, in case their use is required.
- **Keep two baseballs in his possession.** In addition to the ball that is put into play, the umpire holds at least two (and usually four) alternate baseballs to place into the game when needed.
- **Check the playing field.** Check that all lines are clearly marked with paint, nontoxic/non-burning chalk, or other white material.

See the chapter Before the Game Starts on page 22.

Rosin bag

At the beginning of play, the umpire-in-chief will ensure that the home team places an official rosin bag behind the pitcher's rubber for the pitchers' use. The rosin bag must indeed only contain rosin, not other foreign substances.

The pitcher can only apply the rosin directly onto his hands — not his glove or other parts of his uniform. Balls hitting the bag remain in play.

In poor weather the umpire may ask the pitcher to keep the rosin bag in his pocket.

The Umpire

Disagreements Among Umpires

When umpires make simultaneous, conflicting calls

While no umpire may question or criticize another umpire's decision (unless specifically asked by that umpire for assistance), situations may arise where two umpires make conflicting calls simultaneously. When this occurs, the umpire-in-chief will immediately call the umpires together for a conference (players and managers will not take part). The umpire-in-chief will determine which call will be upheld, basing that decision on the opinion of the umpire most likely to have had the best view of the play — therefore the umpire most likely to be correct. The play will continue based on this final decision.

As an alternative, the rules stipulate that the League President may designate an umpire other than the umpire-in-chief to take responsibility in making this determination.

The Umpire

Putting the Ball in Play

Beginning the game

The umpire (or umpires) will enter the field five minutes prior to the start of the game, proceeding to home plate, where:

- the home team's manager hands two identical copies of the home team's batting order to the umpire-in-chief.
- on receiving the home team's batting order, the home team's manager transfers authority of the field to the umpire-in-chief.

  This means, in part, that the umpire-in-chief now has the authority to suspend or postpone a game due to poor weather or unfit conditions of the field, and determine when and if a game will be resumed.
- the visiting team's manager hands two identical copies of the visiting team's batting order to the umpire.
- the umpire checks the copies to make sure they are identical, and looks for obvious mistakes.
- on delivering the lists to the umpire the batting order is established for the entire game, and changes in the batting order, through substitutions, for instance, can only be made as provided by the rules (see page 169).
- upon confirming that the lists are identical and with no mistakes detected, the umpire retains one copy of each list and hands the opposing team's list to each manager.

Note: A manager may delegate the exchange of batting orders to one of his team members.

Doubleheaders and beginning the second game

The second game of a doubleheader will start twenty minutes after the conclusion of the first game. The umpire-in-chief acts as the timekeeper. He may extend this interval to thirty minutes, but must notify both managers about the time extension at the end of game one.

Exception: If there is a special event scheduled to take place between two games of a doubleheader, the interval may be extended. This must be approved in advance by the League President. The umpire-in-chief must notify both managers of the effect the special event will have on the start time of the second game.

The umpire-in-chief must start the second game as long as weather, time restrictions, and field conditions make starting the game possible.

In cases in which the first game of a doubleheader is delayed, the first game played that day will be considered the first game of the doubleheader, regardless of that game's actual start time.

However, if a game from a previous day was rescheduled, creating a doubleheader, the first game played that day will be the regularly scheduled game, and the rescheduled game will become the second game of the doubleheader.

Note: Mistakes in the batting order. While the list handed to the umpire establishes the batting order for the game, the teams are not bound by obvious unintentional errors or omissions in the list. For instance, if the list contains only eight names instead of nine, or if it lists two players with the same name without identifying which player was intended, the error should simply be corrected. The teams' managers or captains should be notified of the error and the team will be allowed to correct it prior to the start of the game.

Putting the ball in play

The umpire-in-chief (also called the *plate umpire*) starts the game by calling "play."

Throughout the game, whenever a ball is dead, play resumes with the call of "play" by the plate umpire.

If a foul ball is not caught, the ball is dead. The umpire must wait until all runners have retouched their bases before putting the ball back in play.

In any case, the umpire should only call "play" when the pitcher, with the ball in his possession, has assumed his position on the pitcher's rubber. The catcher must be in position and the seven other fielders are required to be on the field, in fair territory, when the ball is put into play.

Putting new baseballs into play

Spare baseballs held by the plate umpire will be put into play when:

- a ball is batted out of the field.
- the current ball is no longer suitable for use (i.e., it has become discolored or damaged). See page 68.
- the pitcher asks that a new ball be put into play.

New balls are only put into the game after a play has ended and the current ball is dead. Even when a batter hits a home run, rules state that a new ball is not to be provided to the pitcher or the catcher until all runners and the batter have reached home. In other cases, it is provided after all runners have reached their awarded bases.

> **Note: Player substitutions**
>
> The umpire-in-chief, after receiving notice from a team, is responsible for announcing any substitute players.

Tools of the Trade

Overview: The umpires have equipment to keep things running smoothly.

The plate umpire keeps home plate tidy — and clearly visible — with a hand brush like the one shown here.

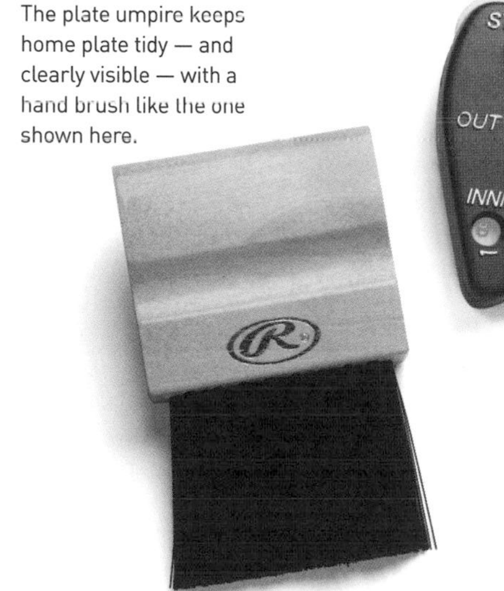

Plate umpires can use an indicator to keep track of strikes, balls, and outs. In the Major Leagues, umpires can also use the scoreboard to keep track.

Suspended and Called (Terminated) Games

Overview: A called game will either be replayed in its entirety, or ended prematurely with a final score. A suspended game will be completed either later that day or on another day.

Calling games due to weather or playing conditions

Before the start of the game, the home team's manager is responsible for determining if a game should be started or postponed because of bad weather or other unsuitable playing conditions (see page 198).

As soon as the game starts, the umpire-in-chief takes on this responsibility. He becomes the sole judge to determine:

- if and when a game should be suspended due to weather or other unfit playing conditions.
- if and when the game will be resumed.
- if and when the game shall be called (terminated) after the suspension.

The umpire's responsibility, according to the rules, is to try to complete the game if at all possible. His decision to eventually terminate the game is based on his judgment that weather or field conditions will not improve and there is no possibility of resuming play.

After calling a suspension, the umpire is required to wait at least thirty minutes before terminating a game. While thirty minutes is minimum, the suspension can last for any length of time, even several hours, as long as the umpire believes there is a chance to resume play.

Suspending a game

In the event of a game suspension, the umpire signals "time." He does this by raising both of his hands over his head. The ball is dead when the call is made.

On resumption of the game the umpire signals "play" and the next pitch can be made.

Suspended games and doubleheaders

Following the first game of a doubleheader, the umpire-in-chief of the first game determines if the second game should be started or postponed because of bad weather or other unsuitable playing conditions. The decision is not up to the home team's manager and not up to the umpire-in-chief of the second game.

Suspended games due to fitness of the field

The umpire-in-chief assumes command of the field's ground crew and ground crew assistants whenever a game is suspended because of the condition of the field. The umpire-in-chief's goal is to make the field suitable for play. An unfit field is considered a violation of the rules by the home team.

Penalty: If the cause of the violation is not corrected the umpire-in-chief will require the home team to forfeit the game to the visiting team.

See the Suspended and Terminated Games chapter for more information.

Ground rules

Each ballpark has a set of ground rules specific to that field's unique features — for instance, if the ball hits the roof in a domed stadium. The official rules state that the home team's manager may provide other special rules to the umpire and to the visiting team's manager. These rules will go into effect if both teams agree. If not, the umpire will impose his own rules regarding special conditions on the field, batted or thrown balls that hit spectators on the field, and other possible unforeseen events. None of these special rules, of course, will be allowed if they conflict with the official rules of the game.

Suspended and Called

When Umpires Don't Have Control

Suspension of late-season and postseason games

Under normal circumstances the umpire-in-chief has the authority to call or suspend a game, and to determine when or if it should be resumed. The most common reason for suspending a game is weather — but things like major equipment failure in the stadium can also cause a game to be suspended.

The umpire-in-chief also has the authority to call a game that has become a regulation game, and call a "no game" if the game in question has not been played far enough to have reached regulation status. A "no game" will be rescheduled for play at a later date.

However, there are exceptions, games in which decisions regarding suspension and resumption of play are too important to leave to the crew on the field. The games in which "higher authorities" will have the final word on suspensions include:

- a regular season game that has been added to the schedule to break a tie
- Wild Card games
- Division Series games
- League Championship Series games
- World Series games

One reason for this is that Major League Baseball officials, not confined to the field, may have better access to weather information than the umpires. But another significant reason is that there is a lot at stake in these games, including of course television broadcasts and contracts. Simply put, Major League Baseball officials may try harder to keep a game underway rather than have it rescheduled. This doesn't mean one of these games won't be rescheduled, but because doing so will have more severe repercussions than would be the case in a regular season game, MLB officials become involved in the decision.

Forfeits

Overview: A forfeit occurs when a game is prematurely ended by the umpire-in-chief due to a team's serious violation of the rules. He will declare the game ended with an automatic score of 9 to 0.

Forfeited games

For a serious rule violation, the umpire-in-chief may end a game before it is finished, or even before it starts, automatically imposing a score of 9 to 0.

When the umpire-in-chief calls a forfeit he is required within twenty-four hours to submit a written report to the League President. Failure to submit the report, however, does not affect the forfeit.

See the Official Scorer chapter, page 213, for rules regarding how a forfeited game is officially recorded.

Reasons an umpire-in-chief can call a forfeit

The umpire-in-chief is solely responsible for calling a forfeit. A forfeit can be called if:

1. the field is determined to be unsuitable for play. If the ground crew intentionally refuses to fix the problem, the umpire-in-chief may rule that the home team lost the game to the visiting team by forfeit.

2. one or more people enter the field during the game, preventing play, and the field cannot be cleared within a "reasonable time" by police or security personnel. The umpire-in-chief may rule that the home team forfeit the game to the visiting team. He must, however, allow a minimum of fifteen minutes for the field to be cleared before making this call.

3. a team refuses to take their position on the field or to play the game within five minutes from the time the umpire calls "play." A forfeit can be called, unless for some reason the umpire feels the delay could not be avoided.

4. a team attempts to either delay the game or shorten it.

5. a team refuses to continue playing, or following a suspension of play, delays the action by more that one minute after the call of "play."

6. following a warning, a team continues to violate the rules.

7. a team does not comply with a ruling to eject a player.

8. a team does not show up for the second game of a doubleheader within twenty minutes of the end of the first game (unless of course the interval time has been officially extended).

9. a team is unable, or refuses, to put nine players on the field.

Appeals and Protested Games

Overview: Umpires can be wrong. If a team manager disagrees with an umpire's ruling, he may appeal, requesting that a second umpire verify the decision. In extreme cases, if a wrongful decision affected the game's outcome, a manager can protest the entire game.

Appeals made on an umpire's decision (protesting a decision)

If a team manager believes an umpire made a decision that contradicts the official rules, he may appeal by asking that umpire to revise his decision. At this point the umpire who made the call may consult with another umpire on the field. However, this is the only means by which another umpire may become involved. Umpires are not permitted to involve themselves in other umpires' decisions unless the umpire who made the decision requests assistance.

If the issue is not resolved to the manager's satisfaction, and the manager believes the umpire did not adhere to the rules, the manager can protest the game.

Protested games

Either team can protest a game, charging that the umpire made a wrongful decision that was not in accordance with the official rules. A protest, however, cannot be made over the call of "ball" or "strike." This is a "judgment call," which is solely the decision of the umpire. (See the following page for a discussion on judgment calls and umpire decisions.)

The League President presides over protest decisions

To make a protest, the team making the complaint must speak up *immediately*. The protest must be made:

1. at the time of the play in question, and;

2. before a next pitch is thrown or a runner is put out.

If the call being protested occurs in the final play of the game, the team making the protest must file the complaint with the league office before noon the next day.

If the umpire's call, in the opinion of the League President, was incorrect and adversely affected the losing team's chances of winning the game, the League President may call for the game to be replayed. The game would be replayed starting at the point in the game when the incident occurred.

Appealing a call

A manager may make an appeal to an umpire who he believes made a wrong call. That umpire, at his option, may then ask other umpires for their thoughts on the play. (Other umpires can react only if asked by the umpire who made the call.)

If a call is reversed the umpires will "undo" any plays that took place following the call. For example, runners will go back to the bases that they would have occupied, interference or obstruction incidents will be ignored, etc. Beyond making the appeal no team member is allowed to argue that the umpires "should have exercised their discretion in a different manner." Arguments following an appeal's decision can result in ejection.

Calling Balls and Strikes

Overview: The game of baseball centers on the strike zone. While it is carefully defined in the rules, the strike zone is wide open to interpretation.

The landmarks used to define the actual strike area, in practice, are vague. Each plate umpire will therefore see it slightly differently. Unfair? Definitely. But this dependence on interpretation, and the inevitable arguments that ensue, are all part of the sport. Baseball wouldn't be the same without them.

The strike zone is defined and discussed in the chapters on pitching and batting. The important point, from the umpire's point of view, is that his call of "ball" or "strike" is the final word. (See pages 64 and 80-82 for more information.)

Balls and Strikes

Check Swings

Rulings on "check swings" (half-swings) by the batter

A check swing, also known as a "half-swing," is a partial swing by the batter that may or may not qualify as a swing. That means that if the pitcher delivers a pitch that is outside of the strike zone, and the batter only swings the bat halfway (without hitting the ball) his swing may or may not be considered a strike. It depends on the judgment of the plate umpire. In some cases, a team can appeal the umpire's call. The official rules state that:

- if on a half-swing the umpire calls a ball, an appeal *can* be made.
- if on a half-swing the umpire calls a strike, an appeal *cannot* be made.

The defensive team's manager, therefore, may elect to appeal the call of ball on a half-swing, believing that the batter swung the bat far enough to be counted as a swing-and-a-miss (i.e., a strike). However, the rules specifically state that the manager's appeal may only be based on the fact that the plate umpire did not ask for the opinion of another umpire before making the call, not that the plate umpire's call was incorrect. On the appeal, a field umpire must respond — the umpire positioned at first base for a right-handed batter, and the umpire positioned at third base for a left-handed batter. If the field umpire determines the swing went far enough to qualify for a strike, the "ball" will be changed to a "strike."

The appeal must be made before the next pitch, a play, or if the end of an inning, before the defense makes their exit from fair territory.

Implications if the appeal on a check swing is granted

If the "ball" is now a "strike" the status of runners may change. Forced runners who were freely advancing may suddenly be at risk. If they already reached their bases however, they may stay.

Therefore runners need to be on guard. If they are not touching a base they are liable to be thrown out. The catcher must also be on guard for runners stealing bases while the appeal is made, since the ball remains in play.

Example: With a runner on first and three balls in the count, the batter makes a check swing. The plate umpire calls a ball, walking the batter, and the runner from first starts walking to second on the awarded base. On appeal the call is changed to strike when the first base umpire says the swing went too far. The runner from first is now stealing second, and can be thrown out.

The Umpire and the Pitcher

Overview: While there are many rules a pitcher must follow, here are some unsportsmanlike acts that the umpire must look for.

Ball tampering

Umpires need to be on the watch for ball tampering. These rules are in place to prevent the pitcher from altering the performance of the ball, which could unfairly work to the pitcher's advantage.

Before the game starts the umpire is responsible for inspecting the baseballs to be used in the game, checking to see that they meet Major League Baseball standards. He is also responsible for making sure the balls continue to meet those standards during play.

As you can imagine when reading the list below, these are judgment calls. The umpire determines whether or not these rules have been violated. Additional details on ball tampering, including exceptions to specific rules, are covered on page 68 of the Pitching chapter.

The umpire must not allow the pitcher to:

1. apply any "foreign substance" to the ball.

2. spit on the ball, or on his hand or glove.

3. rub the ball using his glove, body, or clothing (although he can rub the ball using his bare hands).

4. deface or otherwise alter the ball.

5. scuff the ball, or use what the official rule book terms the "emery ball."

Penalty: The penalty for the above violations will be immediate ejection and a ten-day suspension.

6. touch his mouth or lips with his pitching hand while standing within the eighteen-foot-diameter pitching circle.

Penalty: The umpire will first remove the ball and warn the pitcher. If it happens again a "ball" may be called.

If the same pitcher repeats the violation the umpire may disqualify him, ejecting him from the game. The League President may also impose a fine for repeated violations.

Pitcher's behavior and possible ejection

The umpire is on special call to ensure fair play as well as the safety of the players. He therefore is required to take action against a pitcher who:

- **has a foreign substance in his possession.** The penalty for this violation is ejection from the game. The pitcher does not need to use the substance — just having possession of it is enough. For instance, an emery file in the pitcher's pocket can get him ejected.
- **deliberately delays the game** with the batter in position, by throwing the ball to fielders.

  Penalty: On the first offense the umpire shall deliver a warning. For a repeated offense the umpire shall eject the pitcher from the game.
- **deliberately attempts to hit the batter.** This is a judgment call by the umpire, who may:

  a. eject the pitcher, and possibly the manager as well, from the game, or

  b. warn the pitcher and the manager, with the intent that the next such violation will result in the ejection of both of them. This warning may be issued before the start of the game or at any point during the game.

The League President may follow up with other penalties, such as imposing a fine or suspending a player from participating in upcoming games.

Disputes about hitting the batter are prohibited

Team members are not allowed to leave the dugout or playing positions to argue a warning about hitting the batter. They will be given a warning to stop, and can be ejected.

Judgment Calls by an Umpire

Overview: The call of ball or strike is a judgment call that cannot be argued. Many other calls are up to an umpire's judgment as well, although these can (and will) be argued by a manager.

An umpire's call of "ball" or "strike" is final! Team members, according to the rules, anyway, are not permitted to object to the decision. The calls that fall into this category include:

1. Whether a pitch is a strike or a ball.

2. Whether a check swing qualifies as a full swing. A full swing would result in a strike.

Other decisions that are up to an umpire's judgment

In many instances, the official rule book uses the word "judgment" in reference to an umpire's call. Although these calls can sometimes amount to a tricky rule interpretation by the umpire, they can (and will) be argued.

3. The suitability of the baseballs being used in the game.

4. Weather. The umpire-in-chief determines if a game should continue due to poor weather or poor field conditions. Or, at the end of game one of a doubleheader, he determines if the second game should be started due to weather or field conditions. The umpire-in-chief also determines if and when a suspended game shall resume, or if it shall be terminated.

5. Forfeit. Whether or not a team should forfeit a game for failing to appear on the field or failing to start play within five minutes of the call of "play." (The umpire-in-chief will not declare a forfeit if he feels the delay was unavoidable.)

6. Helmet violation. If a team member does not correct a helmet violation "within a reasonable amount of time."

Concerning the pitcher

7. Injured substitute pitcher. Whether or not a substitute pitcher, who replaced a pitcher during a batter's time at bat, is injured before the at-bat is completed, preventing him from pitching and requiring another replacement pitcher for that batter.

8. Quick pitch. Whether the pitcher's quick movement to step on the pitcher's rubber and pitch qualifies as a quick pitch (an attempt to pitch before the batter is ready).

9. Ball tampering. Whether the pitcher spit on the ball or tampered with it in any manner.

10. When to issue a pitcher's first warning. If prior to the start of the game, or during the game, both teams received adequate official warning about pitches being thrown to hit a batter, pitchers can be ejected from the game on the first offense.

11. Hitting the batter. Whether the pitcher intentionally tried to hit the batter with a pitch.

12. Warm-up pitches. If a substitute pitcher will be allowed to take more than eight warm-up pitches.

Concerning the batter

13. Whether a batted ball is fair or foul.

14. Batter interferes with a fielder. Whether a batter who is running to first base, when more than halfway to first, stepped out of the baseline and interfered with a fielder or a throw to first base.

15. Which bases were reached when interference occurred. On a call of interference by the batter, the umpire will determine which bases were reached by the runners before the interference occurred.

16. Interference with the catcher. In a situation in which the batter swung the bat and hit the catcher, if the batter hit him intentionally.

17. Bat tampering. Whether or not a bat has been tampered with.

18. Thrown glove. In a situation where a fielder threw his glove, cap, or

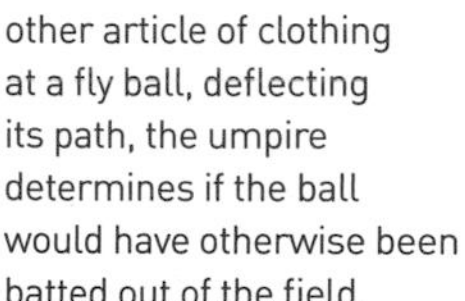

other article of clothing at a fly ball, deflecting its path, the umpire determines if the ball would have otherwise been batted out of the field.

19. **Whether a batter intentionally interfered with the hit to prevent a double play.** If a batter intentionally interfered with a batted ball or a ball that was being fielded, to thwart a double play, the umpire will call out both the batter and the runner closest to home.

20. **Fair or foul.** In cases where a batter hits a fly ball near the foul line, and a fielder touches (or catches) the ball before it hits the ground, whether that ball is considered fair or foul. This call depends on the ball's trajectory, not on whether the fielder himself is in fair or foul territory at the time he touched the ball. (If fair, the ball would remain in play. If foul, the ball would be dead.)

21. **Tagging up.** Whether or not a runner touched his base after a fly ball was caught. (A runner must be touching, or must retouch, his base after a fly ball is caught before attempting to reach the next base.)

22. **Batter's use of rosin.** If because of weather conditions a batter will be allowed to step out of the batter's box to use rosin or the pine tar rag to improve his grip on the bat.

23. **Whether or not the batter interfered with a batted ball** either by intentionally throwing his bat at it or dropping the bat in its path.

24. **Whether or not a batter or runner intentionally interfered with a ball in play** by throwing or dropping his helmet.

Concerning the runner

25. **If a runner is safe or out** on a force play or a tag.

26. **Whether the member of the offensive team tried to get out of the way of the fielder** in an interference situation.

27. **Whether a runner intentionally left the baseline and interfered with a fielder** making a play on the ball.

28. **The bases that were reached by runners,** including the batter-runner, at the instant a wild throw was made.

29. **The bases that would have been reached had an obstruction not occurred.** After a call of obstruction (an act in which a fielder impedes the advance of a batter or runner) the umpire will nullify the effect of the obstruction by awarding bases he believes the runners would have reached.

30. **Whether or not a runner has abandoned his base-running effort** by walking toward the dugout or his position on the field.

31. **If a runner not touching a base interfered with a fielder** who was making a play on the ball.

32. **If the runner on base intentionally interfered with a fielder** who was making a play on the ball.

33. **Whether a runner reached the spot that "would have been" occupied by the base** when a base has broken away from its designated location.

34. **Whether a runner intentionally interfered with either a batted ball, or a ball in play being thrown by a fielder, to thwart a double play.** If yes, the umpire will call out both the runner and the batter-runner on this violation.

35. **Whether the first base or third base coach physically touched a runner,** assisting him in running.

36. **Whether a runner intentionally kicked the ball** after a fielder missed a play on a batted ball.

Concerning the fielder

37. **On a call of obstruction, whether a fielder was "in the act of fielding the ball."**

38. **In cases of spectator interference, the bases that the batter and runners would have reached** had the interference not occurred. The umpire will award those bases.

(continued...)

Judgment Calls by an Umpire

continued

39. Whether the fielder held onto the ball long enough to be considered a catch in cases where a fielder drops a ball.

40. Whether or not a third out was made before a runner scored at home, meaning the run would not count. If the out was made after the runner scored, the run would count.

41. Whether the Infield Fly Rule applies — specifically, before a high fly ball that is hit into the infield lands, the umpire judges whether an infielder will be able to easily catch the ball.

Caught, then dropped

If a fielder securely catches the ball, but then drops it while making a throw, the umpire shall consider the ball to have been caught, then dropped. For instance, if the shortstop catches a thrown ball, tags second base to put out a runner, but then drops the ball while throwing to first base, the out at second base will count.

Concerning others

42. Whether or not interference by someone authorized to be on the field, but not a player, was avoidable — for example, if a bat boy or girl, police officer, base coach, etc., tried to get out of the way.

Judgment Calls

Judgment Calls *Not* Made by an Umpire

Some judgments are made by the official scorer, not the umpires

While umpires uphold the rules, the official scorer makes decisions that affect record keeping. The official scorer's judgment decisions include:

1. **Hit or error.** If a batter's advance is due to a hit or an error.

2. **Stolen base.** Whether a runner should be credited with a stolen base, or if he was safe only because of a fielding error.

3. **Sacrifice or a base hit.** Whether a bunt should be recorded as a sacrifice or a base hit.

4. **Sacrifice fly.** With runners on base and 0 or 1 out, when a fly ball or line drive into the outfield is dropped by a fielder, whether or not the hit will be recorded as a sacrifice fly.

5. **Error.** If, and to which fielder, an error will be attributed.

6. **Earned run.** Whether or not an earned run will be scored.

7. **The winning pitcher.** In cases in which the winning team's starting pitcher does not qualify to be named the winning pitcher, a substitute pitcher will receive that designation. If the team called in more than one substitute, under certain circumstances the substitute who would normally be recorded as the winning pitcher may be deemed unworthy by the scorer. In this situation the scorer will award the win to the substitute pitcher that, in his judgment, was more effective.

Note: To qualify as a winning pitcher the starting pitcher must have completed five or more innings, his team must have been in the lead when he was substituted, and his team must maintain the lead through the end of the game. See page 218 in the Official Scorer chapter for more on winning pitchers.

For more information on the official scorer's responsibilities in general, see the Official Scorer chapter beginning on page 206.

If an Umpire Gets in the Way

Overview: With four umpires on the field in a typical Major League game, they are bound to get in the way from time to time.

If the plate umpire interferes with the catcher's throw

If the catcher's throw is successful and the runner is put out, the umpire's interference will be ignored. If the throw cannot be completed or is not successful, the ball is dead and runners must return to their bases.

If an umpire interferes with a catcher returning the ball to the pitcher

The ball will be dead, no runners can advance.

Umpires on the field

If a ball batted into fair territory touches an umpire:

- before it touches the pitcher or other fielder, or
- before it goes past a fielder (other than the pitcher),

the ball becomes dead and the batter will be awarded first base.

If a batted ball touches an umpire in the infield after bouncing over or getting past the pitcher, untouched, the ball becomes dead and the batter will be awarded first base (see page 117).

If a fly ball batted into fair territory passes a fielder, or deflects off of a fielder, then hits an umpire or runner, and is then caught by a fielder before touching the ground, it will not be considered a catch (meaning the batter will not be out on the catch). The ball remains in play.

If a pitch hits the plate umpire

If a pitch gets past the catcher and hits the plate umpire, the ball remains in play.

If the ball bounces off of the umpire and is caught by the catcher or a fielder before touching the ground, the batter is not out on the catch. The ball remains in play.

If the batter barely hits the ball, and it bounces off of the umpire and is caught by the catcher before hitting the ground, the ball is dead and the batter is not out.

If a pitch hits an umpire or catcher and becomes stuck in his mask or equipment, runners are awarded one base. The ball is dead.

If the batter barely hits the ball and it becomes stuck in the umpire's mask or equipment, the ball is dead and the batter is not out.

If a thrown ball hits an umpire

If a thrown ball hits any umpire, the ball simply remains in play.

On the third strike

The third-strike rule applies when, under either of the two conditions below, a pitch is missed by the catcher on the third strike:

- there is no runner on first base, or
- there is a runner on first and two outs.

This rule applies even when the missed ball touches the umpire. Under the third-strike rule the batter becomes a runner and must attempt to advance to first base. This means the batter can be put out either by being tagged with the ball, or by a fielder with the ball in his possession tagging first base before the batter has reached it. If a batter in this situation makes no attempt to reach first he will automatically be called out. See page 83 for more on the third-strike rule.

If a pitch gets stuck on the third strike or fourth ball

The batter and all runners will be awarded one base when, on the third strike or fourth ball, a pitch gets stuck in the umpire's or catcher's mask or equipment (and therefore is out of play).

Umpire's Call of Obstruction

Overview: When a runner is obstructed, the umpire must assign awards or penalties that will nullify the act of obstruction.

Explanation: It is up to the umpire to determine the bases awarded for obstruction. The intent is to award all the runners, including the batter, the bases that they would have reached had the obstruction not occurred. The actual number of bases is a judgment call by the umpire. If a play was being made on the batter or runner who was obstructed, he will be awarded at least one base. Any runners forced to advance by the awarded base or bases would, of course, also advance. Other runners will be awarded bases if the umpire believes they would otherwise have reached those bases.

Calling "obstruction" and awarding bases

Umpires enforce the premise that runners have right-of-way to the base path. Obstruction is a violation committed when a fielder, without the ball in his possession and not in the act of fielding the ball, gets in the way of a runner within the baseline. This includes the catcher, who has no right to block a runner trying to score at home, unless he is in the act of fielding the ball or has the ball in his possession.

The umpire signals obstruction by pointing to the source of the infraction and yelling "That's obstruction!" The ball is dead on the call.

Whether or not a fielder is "in the act of fielding the ball" becomes a judgment call by the umpire. A fielder placing himself in position to catch a thrown ball can be considered to be in the act of fielding even if the ball is still in flight. If the fielder misses the catch, his "act of fielding" has ended and obstruction can be called if he gets in the way of a runner after missing the catch.

Example: A fielder who dives for a ball but misses, and ends up on the ground, blocking the baseline, must immediately attempt to get out of the way of any oncoming runners.

If there *is* a play being made on the runner when he is obstructed, or if the batter-runner is obstructed before he reaches first base the umpire will make the call immediately. At the very least, the obstructed runner will be awarded one base beyond the base he last reached before he was obstructed.

Note: When a wild throw is made during a play in which a runner or batter is obstructed, and an umpire calls "obstruction" while the throw is in flight, the wild-throw rules will take precedence. This is to the advantage of the offensive team, since on a wild throw all runners will be awarded two bases beyond the last base they reached.

If there *is not* a play being made on the batter or runner at the time he is obstructed the umpire will let the play proceed. Although he will call and signal "obstruction" when it occurs, it will only be enforced at the completion of the play. A putout will be ignored if it was made on the obstructed player before he reached the base he would have otherwise attained.

Penalty: As penalty for obstruction the umpire will award bases to the batter and runners as he deems appropriate — the bases he believes the batter and runners would have reached had the obstruction not occurred. If a batter or runner was put out before reaching the base he otherwise would have attained, the out will be ignored.

If the play is allowed to proceed to completion after the obstruction, if the obstructed runner continues to advance beyond the base that in the umpire's opinion he should be awarded, and he is put out, that out will stand.

Example 1: Obstruction, immediate dead ball

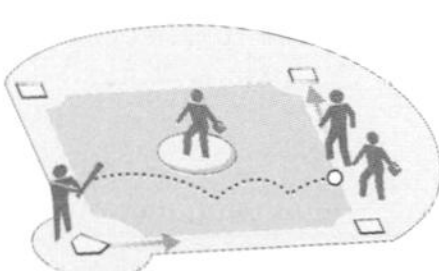

A runner on first is stealing second base when the batter hits a ground ball toward the first baseman.

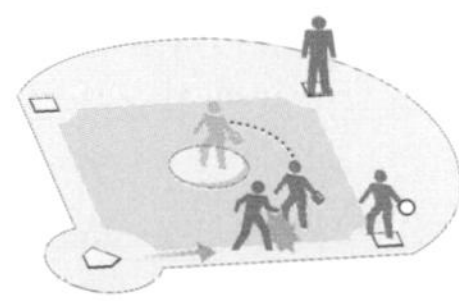

The pitcher runs to the first base line to cover the base, but his assistance is not needed. Just before the first baseman tags first, the pitcher obstructs the batter-runner.

The umpire immediately calls "obstruction" and the ball is dead. The batter-runner is awarded first base. The runner from first is awarded second base.

Example 2: Wild throw

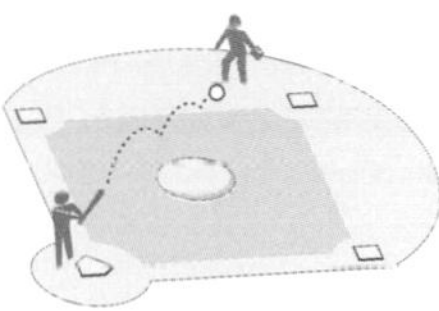

The batter hits a ground ball to the shortstop, who has trouble fielding it. The shortstop picks up the ball and makes the throw.

As soon as the ball leaves the shortstop's hand the first baseman gets in the batter's way. The umpire signals obstruction, but the shortstop's throw goes wild into the dugout.

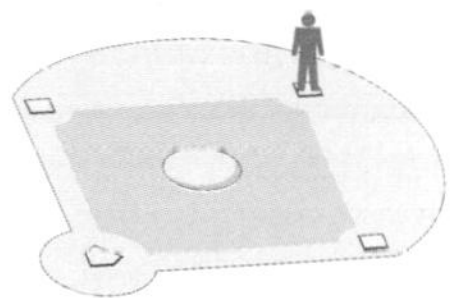

The batter will be awarded two bases on the wild throw, so he will advance to second base. The call of obstruction will be ignored.

Example 3: Delayed dead ball

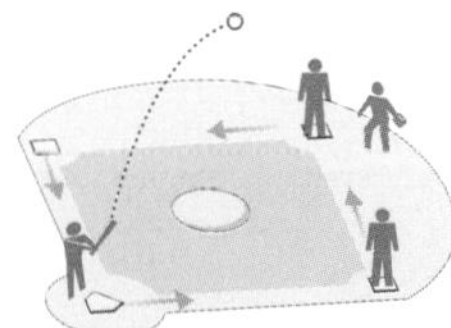

With runners on first and second, the batter gets a hit to deep left field.

The runner coming from second is thrown out at home plate. At the same time, the runner coming from first is obstructed after passing second.

The umpire waits before making a call, because he wants to see if the obstruction affects the play.

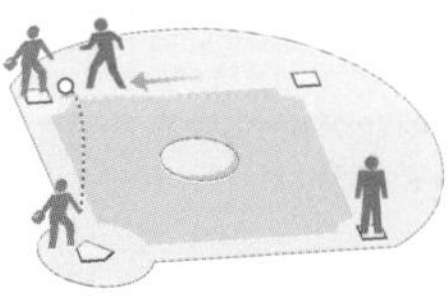

The runner who was obstructed is tagged out while trying to reach third base, and the play ends.

After the play, the umpire calls obstruction and awards the runner third base on the assumption that he would have made it there safely if the obstruction had not occurred.

Ejections and Removals

Overview: For really bad behavior, a player or other team member may be ejected from the game — banished to the clubhouse.

Ejecting players, managers, and others from the game

Any umpire is authorized to disqualify a player, manager, coach, or other team member from further play in the game, and to eject the disqualified player from the field.

The umpire also has authority to eject other people, non-team members who may have permission to be on the field. This includes members of the ground crew, seating attendants, photographers, news crew, spectators, and others.

Eject vs. Remove

"Ejecting" and "removing" a team member are two options for the umpire specified in the official rule book. Technically, ejecting a player will ban him from the field, sending him to the locker room. Removing a player may simply send him to the dugout. Decades ago, removals were common, but in recent years, removals by umpires have come to mean the same as ejection.

Our discussion of ejections and removals in this section stays true to the official rules, differentiating between the terms. However, this is simply for nostalgic reasons. In practice, consider a removal to be the same as an ejection.

See the Misbehavior chapter, pages 188 and 189, for more on ejections and removals.

A thankless job

Umpires put up with a lot of grief during the normal course of their job. The scene below shows a typical day at the office for umpire Emmett Ashford, who is being verbally assaulted by Earl Weaver and Boog Powell during the 1970 World Series. As much as an angry player may resent it, the umpire has the final word. If things get really out of hand, umpires have every right to eject a team member.

Ejections

Reasons for Ejections or Removals

Ejecting (or removing) a player

An umpire cannot eject or remove a player or other team member while a play is in progress. He must wait for the play's completion, then call "time."

The team member who is ejected must immediately leave the field and may no longer participate in the game. An ejected player must either confine himself to the clubhouse, or he may change out of his uniform and leave the ballpark. He may also sit in the stands, but far from the dugout or bullpen.

If a team fails to comply with an ejection (i.e., if the ejected team member does not leave the field) the umpire may call a forfeit of the game, giving the win to the other team.

Reasons an umpire may eject or remove someone include, but are not limited to, the following:

1. **Helmet violations.** This includes batters, catchers, and bat boys and girls.

2. **A batter uses a tampered bat,** an illegal attempt to improve his hitting. (The League President may impose additional penalties for this violation.)

3. **A pitcher has a "foreign substance" in his possession,** even if he did not use it to affect the ball.

4. **Non-team members.** An umpire may, if he feels it is warranted, eject anyone who has permission to be on the field. This includes members of the ground crew, seating attendants, photographers, news crew, spectators, and others.

5. **Unauthorized persons.** An umpire may eject anyone not authorized to be on the field.

6. **Fights and brawls.** An umpire may eject a player for assaulting someone or for being involved in any sort of physical altercation.

7. **Players, managers, or coaches leave their position to argue a call of ball or strike.** Leaving a fielding position, the coach's box, or the dugout to argue a call of ball or strike is prohibited. If the team member continues toward home plate after receiving a warning, the umpire may eject him.

8. **Unauthorized persons in the dugout.** During a game, only players (including substitutes), managers, coaches, trainers, and bat boys and girls may be in the dugout.

9. **First or third base coaches** who are either not in uniform, or who leave their coach's box position. See page 187.

10. **A team member tries to incite a demonstration,** attempting to rouse the spectators.

11. **A team member uses foul language** against a player, umpire, or spectator.

12. **A team member tries to cause the pitcher to balk** by calling "time" or employing other unsportsmanlike tactics.

13. **Physical contact with an umpire,** applying to any team member who intentionally makes contact.

14. **A fielder positions himself to block the batter's line of vision** or who otherwise attempts to distract the batter.

15. **A pitcher spits on the ball** after being warned for a first offense.

16. **A pitcher tampers with the ball** (see page 68).

17. **A pitcher delays the game** by throwing the ball to fielders other than the catcher.

18. **The manager makes a second visit to the pitcher's mound.** The pitcher will be removed when the manager visits him at the pitcher's mound twice in the same inning.

(continued...)

Ejections

Reasons for Ejections or Removals continued

19. A second visit to the pitcher during the same at-bat. If a manager visits the pitcher a second time while the same batter is at bat, both the manager and the pitcher will be removed — the manager immediately, and the pitcher upon completion of that current batter's turn at bat.

Note: The umpire must have warned the manager on his way to the mound.

20. A pitcher throws the ball with the intention of hitting the batter. The umpire may also eject the manager when this offense occurs.

21. Intentionally damaging or discoloring the ball. The player who tampered with the ball, or, if he cannot be identified, the pitcher, will be removed (see page 68).

22. A player previously removed reenters the game. If the umpire believes the manager knowingly reentered a player that had been removed, he faces ejection.

Note: MLB's Official Baseball Rules can be daunting. They often use different terms to mean the same thing. For ejection, they state a player should be "ejected" for the reasons numbered here as 1 through 7, "removed from the game and leave the playing field" for 8 through 14, "disqualified" for 15 and 16, "removed" for 17, 18, 19, 21, and 22, and "expelled" for 20.

Ejections

Reporting Ejections

Umpires must report ejections to the League President

The umpire has specific responsibilities to the League President for reporting ejections from the game. At the conclusion of a game the umpire must report ejections:

- **within four hours**

  If the ejection concerned obscene or indecent language, or an assault on an umpire or any team member, the umpire must convey details of the circumstances surrounding the incident within four hours of the conclusion of the game.

- **within twelve hours**

  If the ejection occurred for reasons not mentioned above, or if the umpire feels that a rule violation or other incident that occurred during the game is "worthy of comment," the umpire must convey details of the incident within twelve hours of the conclusion of the game. This includes, but is not limited to, any other ejections of team members from the game (other than those that needed to be reported within four hours).

The League President may penalize the parties involved

The League President, after receiving the umpire's report describing ejections or other incidents, will:

- **penalize the team member(s).** The League President determines the appropriate penalty, which may include a fine, a suspension, or both.
- **notify the affected parties.** This means he will notify both the team member who is being penalized and the manager of that team about the penalty.

If a fine is involved, upon being notified, the team member has five days to pay. If he does not pay within five days he will not be allowed to play in any game, and not even be allowed to sit on the bench with the other players on his team during a game, until the fine is paid.

Video Replay Reviews

Overview: Video replays have been part of Major League Baseball since 2008 — but their use has been expanded.

Since August 2008 umpires could elect to view video replays to verify whether certain hits qualified to be home runs. In the 2014 season video replays, to the joy or dismay of many, were put to more extensive use, to confirm or deny a call made on the field. These replay reviews are not made at the stadium — a high-tech facility in New York City is staffed with MLB umpires and technicians ready to review challenged calls for every game.

The Crew Chief

The crew chief is the umpire on the field with the most experience. This may be, but is often not, the umpire-in-chief. Among his other responsibilities the crew chief communicates with league officials concerning replays.

At the start of a game each team is granted one "manager challenge," to be used to request a replay review to verify one or more calls made during a single play. If a call on that play is overturned by MLB's replay official, a second manager challenge will be allowed — but that's all, two maximum. Beyond that a manager can ask that a call be reviewed by replay, but it's up to the discretion of the crew chief.

Managers can request a replay review to verify...

- on a home run call, whether the ball hit the top of a fence or railing, it was fair or foul, or a spectator interfered
- whether a live ball bounced out of play, it hit the top of a fence or railing, a spectator interfered, or a catch was made by a fielder who fell into the stands
- whether a hit landing at or beyond first or third base was fair or foul
- whether a fielder successfully tagged a runner or a base to put him out
- whether a fly ball or line drive to the outfield was successfully caught
- whether a runner passed a runner in front of him
- whether a runner scored before the third out
- whether a runner touched his base
- whether a pitch touched the batter
- collision calls at home plate

Calls that are *not* eligible for review include...

- umpires' judgment calls
- whether a fly ball or line drive to the infield was successfully caught
- whether a fielder tagged the base on a call of out in a force play at second
- whether a runner tagging his base left early
- whether a batter rounded first base and started toward second
- whether a runner abandoned his effort to reach the next base
- whether a pitch touched the bat
- whether a batter tried to avoid being hit by a pitch

The crew chief can request a review on:

- certain home run calls — e.g., whether the ball was fair or foul, it made it over the wall, or if a spectator interfered
- collision calls
- beginning in the seventh inning, any reviewable call, on his own or at the request of a manager who has no remaining challenges

On a manager challenge or a crew chief's request...

1. The crew chief points and walks toward the communication headset on the field. **2.** The crew chief speaks with the replay official in New York City. **3.** The replay is reviewed and the decision to uphold or overturn the call is conveyed by the replay official. **4.** The crew chief announces the decision. **5.** If the call is overturned, the "definitive video" that was used in the decision is shown on the scoreboard and released to broadcasters.

12 The Manager and Coaches

A team includes one manager and many coaches. The manager directs the team and represents them when dealing with umpires. First and third base coaches are required to be on the field during the game.

As with the players, the rules of baseball provide guidelines for the responsibilities and behavior of the team's managers and coaches.

The Manager and Coaches: contents

Basics for Managers and Coaches

Overview: A team will have one manager and many coaches. The manager is responsible for directing the team's actions. He also represents the team in ruling disputes, and often acts as spokesman to the press. In addition to a manager, two coaches are required by the rules — a first base coach and a third base coach. Other coaches may also be employed. The manager's and coaches' responsibilities, as they pertain to the rules, are discussed in this chapter.

Basics

Managing and Coaching

Manager

Before every game each team must identify one person to act as its manager. In addition to directing the team and interacting with the umpires, the manager may also play in the game — although in practice this is the exception to the norm.

A manager may delegate some of his managing responsibilities to members of his coaching staff.

Required coaches

The rules require teams to position two coaches on the field:

- first base coach
- third base coach

Other coaches on the team's roster

In addition to the first and third base coaches, the coaching jobs listed below are typical. The actual coaching staff varies with each team — as do the coaches' specific titles:

- bench coach
- pitching coach
- hitting coach
- bullpen coach

First and third base coaches' boxes

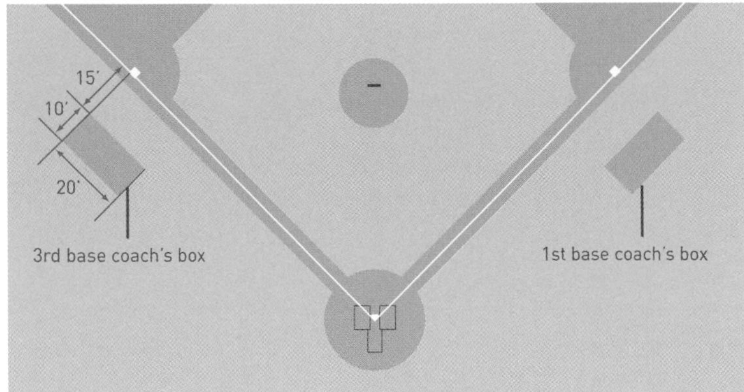

Manager's and Coaches' Job Descriptions

Overview: The rules of baseball delegate specific responsibilities to the manager and the first and third base coaches.

Job Descriptions

The Manager's Job

The manager's job is to direct the team's actions and to speak for his team in communications with the umpire and with the opposing team. The manager must be identified to the umpire-in-chief or the League President by the team at least thirty minutes prior to the game's scheduled start time.

The manager is also accountable for his team's behavior and adherence to the rules. He is ultimately responsible for his team's recognition of the umpires' authority in the game — a point that is often tested when disagreements arise.

In addition to the responsibilities inferred from a coach's title, the manager may delegate portions of his specific managing responsibilities to a coach, making that coach accountable for certain aspects of his team's performance pertinent to the rules. The umpire will be notified of this beforehand, and from that point forward the actions of that coach relevant to his assigned responsibilities will be considered official — as if those actions were taken by the manager himself.

Substitute managers

In the event a manager must leave the field, he must name a coach or a player to act in his place. If he fails or refuses to designate a substitute manager, the umpire has the right to assign the responsibilities to a team member.

When a manager/player substitutes another player for himself

When another player enters the game as a substitute, taking over a manager's position on the field, the manager will continue to serve in his role as manager. His "new" position on the field will be on the bench or in a coach's box, not a player.

Job Descriptions

The Coaches' Jobs

Teams typically have five to seven coaches on their roster. Most teams will include the following six coaches, although their actual titles are not limited to the titles shown:

The first base coach directs runners at first.

The third base coach directs runners at third.

The bench coach assists the manager in the dugout.

The pitching coach works with pitchers to improve their performance.

The hitting coach works with players to improve their batting.

The bullpen coach works with the relief pitchers warming up in the bullpen.

Base coaches

A base coach's job is to direct the runners — instructing them to advance, continue advancing, hold up at the base, or take other actions in their quest to score.

The rule book calls for two base coaches to be appointed per game. When their team is at bat the base coaches take their positions in the coach's boxes at first base and third base. Each base coach is required to wear the team's uniform and, with exceptions, must restrict himself to the coach's box during play.

Job Descriptions

Base Coaches' Positions

Definition of "within the coach's box"

The official rule book provides guidelines for a first or third base coach's position within the coach's box — although in practice umpires are very lenient on these rules. According to the rule book, base coaches may be permitted to do the following:

- **Position one foot outside the coach's box.**
- **Position both feet outside, but near, the coach's box lines,** provided the opposing team's manager does not object. If there is an objection, the umpire will require base coaches on both teams to strictly stay within the lines.
- **Leave the coach's box.** If there is a play being made on a runner at the base coach's base, the base coach may be permitted to leave the coach's box to advise the runner — signaling him to continue on to the next base, slide, or return to a previous base. In doing so the base coach cannot, of course, touch the runner or physically interfere with the actual play. This is considered interference, and as a penalty the runner will be called out.

Touching a runner

A base coach is allowed physical contact with a runner if it's simply to exchange equipment.

Before the Game

Overview: Before the game begins the home team's manager is in charge of the field.

Before the game begins, the home team's manager, not the umpire-in-chief, is in charge of the field. He is the sole judge determining if weather or other field conditions warrant postponement of the game.

Exception: In the final weeks of the season, the League President may assume this responsibility — for concern that the manager's decision could potentially be influenced by factors other than the weather. The visiting team may appeal to have this shift in responsibility enacted.

Once the game begins, and between games of a doubleheader, the umpire-in-chief takes charge, determining if weather or field conditions will permit a game to begin on time. Between games of a doubleheader, the umpire-in-chief of the first game remains in charge of this decision for the second game.

Before the start of the game, the home team's manager may propose to the umpire-in-chief any special ground rules concerning spectators on the field, covering, for instance, cases where a batted or thrown ball may go into a crowd that has overflowed onto the field. If accepted by the opposing team's manager, these rules will be in effect. If not, the umpire-in-chief becomes responsible for creating and enforcing any special rules he deems necessary. None of these rules can contradict the official rules of baseball.

The batting order

Five minutes prior to the start of the game, the umpires and the managers of both teams meet at home base to do the following:

- the home team's manager hands two identical copies of the home team's batting order to the umpire-in-chief.
- the visiting team's manager hands two identical copies of the visiting team's batting order to the umpire-in-chief.
- after the umpire-in-chief confirms that each team's copies are, in fact, identical and contain no mistakes, he hands to each manager the opposing team's duplicate copy of the batting order. The umpire-in-chief retains the other copy for himself.

Note: A manager may opt to have a team member handle batting order duties for him. See page 28 of the chapter Before the Game Starts for more details.

The Team Captain: The position of team captain is primarily an honorary title given to a player. Although he may have other responsibilities designated to him by his team, the team captain may simply lead his team onto the field. The position of captain is only mentioned once in the official rules of baseball: if the umpire-in-chief discovers an error in the batting order, he may inform either the team manager or the team captain.

Teams are under no obligation to appoint a captain.

Requesting a Time Out, and Substitutes

Overview: A manager may request a time out to replace a player with a substitute, or to speak with a player.

Manager's request for a time out

The manager can ask the umpire to call "time" when:

- the manager wishes to make a substitution.
- the manager wants to have a discussion with a player.

The umpire may also call "time" if he wants to speak with one or both managers.

Upon calling "time" the ball is dead and no runners may advance.

Substituting a player, and the batting order

The manager must inform the umpire-in-chief when he substitutes a player, providing the player's name, field position, and position in the batting order. The new player will replace that player on the field and will come to bat in that player's position in the batting order.

The double-switch

A double-switch can occur when two substitutes come into a game at the same time — the manager will specify which vacated position each substitute will take in the batting order. A double-switch often involves a pitcher.

Example: The incoming pitcher will take the pitcher's place on the field, but the outgoing fielder's place in the batting order. The incoming fielder will take the outgoing fielder's place on the field, but the outgoing pitcher's place in the batting order.

The umpire-in-chief, in turn, will notify the game's official scorer.

If the manager does not provide the double-switch information, the umpire-in-chief can decide which player fills each vacated spot in the batting order.

Double-switch notice

The manager must inform the umpire-in-chief before signaling to the bullpen for a new pitcher.

Attempting to Reenter the Game

Overview: Once substituted, a player cannot reenter the game. Rules are in place in the event he, or his manager, tries.

Once a player has been substituted he is not allowed to return to the game "in any capacity." The umpire-in-chief will order the manager to remove the player immediately, having noticed it himself, or having been informed by another umpire or by the manager of either team.

Actions taken depend on when the umpire-in-chief notices the improper player on the field:

Before any play with the improper player takes place

If the umpire-in-chief orders the improper player off the field before a play takes place, then the player he is supposed to be substituting can continue in the game. In other words, nothing really changes.

After a play with the improper player takes place

If the umpire-in-chief orders the improper player off the field after a play has taken place, the play will count — however, the improper player must leave the game. The player for which he was substituting, since he is now also considered to have been removed, cannot reenter the game either. A new player must come in.

If the substituted player is also the team's manager

If the player that was ordered off the field is a player-manager, he will be allowed to continue as manager in the game.

Grounds for ejection

If, in the opinion of the umpire, the manager knew that the player had been removed and put him back in the game anyway, the umpire can eject the manager as penalty.

When a pitcher crosses the line

At the start of a half-inning, if a pitcher that is already in the game walks from the dugout toward the pitcher's mound, once he crosses the foul line he is committed to pitch to the first batter. He must pitch to the batter until he is out or until he reaches first base (unless a substitute batter takes that batter's place, or the pitcher becomes injured).

If the pitcher is on base or at bat when the inning ends, and he walks directly to the pitcher's mound without crossing a foul line, he is not obligated to pitch until he engages the pitcher's rubber and begins warming up.

The Manager and the Pitcher

Overview: Among other things, the rules limit the number of times a manager can visit the pitcher during an inning.

Pitchers may take another position on the field.

A manager may move a pitcher to a different playing position and later that inning move him back to pitch again. If he does, he cannot move him again during that same inning.

The umpire may eject a manager when the pitcher throws to hit a batter.

Pitching to hit a batter is strictly prohibited. The umpire will eject the pitcher, and at his discretion may eject both the manager and the pitcher when a pitcher deliberately throws a pitch to hit a batter.

On the first occurrence, the umpire may warn the managers and the pitchers of both teams. When warranted, the umpire may choose to issue this first warning prior to the start of the game, or at any point thereafter. This means the pitcher, and possibly the manager, may be ejected on the first pitch that, in the umpire's opinion, is intentionally aimed at the batter.

Managers' and coaches' visits to the pitcher's mound

Visits to the pitcher's mound are discussed in detail on page 71 in the Pitching chapter. Here's a quick synopsis:

The number of times a manager or coach can visit a pitcher is limited to just once per inning. On a second visit the pitcher must be removed and a substitute must take his place. A "first visit" to the new pitcher is allowed in that same inning.

There are some exceptions:

- Visits during the pitcher's warm-up time are not included in the count of visits.
- Managers are free to visit the pitcher when an umpire calls "time" at the request of the opposing team.

If a manager ignores the umpire's warning about making a second visit:

- the manager will be immediately ejected from the game, and
- the pitcher, following that batter's turn at bat, will be ejected from the game.

Therefore, as a last move the umpire may remind the manager that on his way to the locker room he should have a substitute pitcher start warming up in the bull pen — they'll be needing him soon.

The eighteen-foot circle

While a manager's visit to the mound starts when he crosses the foul line, it ends when he leaves the eighteen-foot circle surrounding the pitcher's rubber. There is a minor quirk in the wording of this rule: while the mound is eighteen feet in diameter, the rubber is not exactly in the center — it's located eighteen inches behind the center, toward second base. This is almost, but not quite, the area defined by the mound.

Protested Games

A protest is an official complaint filed with a League President charging that an umpire made a decision that does not comply with the official rules of baseball — or that an umpire failed to make a crucial call.

Any call other than those considered "judgment calls" can be protested.

A manager from either team can protest a game, speaking for his team when the protest is made. He must make the protest *immediately*. This means:

1. **at the time the play is made,** or

2. **before the next play,** meaning before the next pitch is thrown or before a next play is attempted.

If the call being protested occurs in the final play of the game, the manager making the protest must file the complaint with the league office before noon the next day.

Each league has the ability to establish its own procedures for handling protested games. If the League President determines the rule violation affected the outcome of the game, he may require that the game be replayed. On the rescheduled date the game may be restarted from the point the protested play took place, rather than replaying the entire game.

Rescheduling a game is, of course, a major decision and a rare event. The League President will have the final word on this decision.

Note: Judgment calls cannot be protested. A judgment decision is completely up to the umpire and, although a team can appeal to that umpire by asking him to seek a second opinion from another umpire, a judgment call cannot be argued or officially contested — no matter how incorrect that call may seem.

Of course, in reality, players express their displeasure over umpires' calls, including judgment calls, all the time. But the umpires are protected by the rules.

For more information on protests and on judgment calls, see the Umpires chapter starting on page 140. For more on appeals see page 151.

Rulings on check swings cannot be protested

An umpire's call of "ball" or "strike" is a judgment call. If a batter's check swing (a half-swing) is called a ball, the defense may appeal to obtain a second umpire's opinion, hoping the swing actually went far enough to be called a strike. The umpire's subsequent decision, however, cannot be protested. As a judgment call, the umpire's word is final. Also see pages 83 and 152.

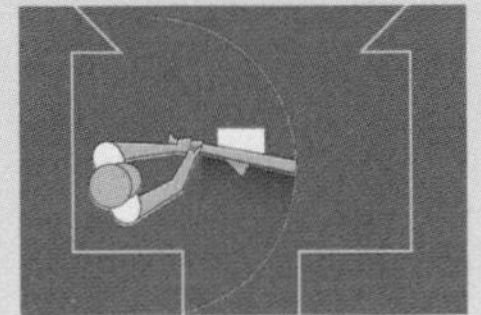

Example of a protest

In a 1983 game between the Kansas City Royals and the New York Yankees, Yankee manager Billy Martin charged that George Brett's ninth-inning two-run home run for the Royals was made with an illegal bat. Pine tar was applied to the handle beyond the eighteen-inch limit. Brett was called out, and then ejected after expressing his feelings to the umpire. The Yankees won 4-3. Despite the fact that the rules at the time supported the umpire's decision, the Royals protested the call.

The League President upheld the protest because he felt the results of the umpire's decision was not in the "spirit and intent" of the rule. The game was replayed several weeks later, picking up after the completed home run play. The rule was later changed to state that when a pine tar infraction is discovered the bat should simply be removed from the game while play continues unaffected.

13 | Misbehavior

Clearing the dugout to brawl with members of the opposing team is against the rules. So is arguing with an umpire. Umpires are responsible for maintaining proper discipline and sportsmanlike conduct. The way this is handled in practice depends on the situation — and on the umpire.

The following pages explain what the rules say about various types of misconduct. In practice, each umpire will interpret these rules differently and will determine, individually, when someone has made the transition from sportsmanlike to unsportsmanlike behavior.

Misbehavior: contents

Misbehavior

Overview: Team members must conduct themselves in a proper manner before and during a game. According to the rules, this means they can't be friendly.

Umpires are in charge of maintaining proper conduct during the game.

Umpires are responsible for maintaining proper conduct and discipline on the field during the game. They can impose penalties for what can be termed "unsportsmanlike conduct." Violations by team members can range from those that are almost indiscernible, such as ball tampering, to out-and-out brawls that can empty the dugouts. The pages in this chapter discuss rules that pertain to various aspects of behavior, or misbehavior, by a player or other team member. Rules regarding the behavior of spectators will be discussed in the next chapter.

In addition to enforcing rules specifically laid out in the official rules of baseball, umpires have the authority to make a ruling on any actions not covered by the rule book. An umpire may eject from the game any team member who acts in an unsportsmanlike manner through actions or language.

Team members may not interact with spectators or the opposing team.

Managers, coaches, or players dressed in a team uniform are not permitted to interact with spectators either before, during, or after the game. This rule includes both friendly and unfriendly exchanges.

The official rules also prohibit team members in uniform from interacting with members of the opposing team — although in reality this commonly takes place. The rule specifically states that players of opposing teams shall not "fraternize" while in uniform. The dictionary defines "fraternize" as socializing with people with whom you "should not be friendly." Apparently, according to the official rules of baseball, this includes any member of the opposing team ranging from the manager to the bat boys and girls.

Team members cannot discuss decisions with the official scorer.

Managers, coaches, and players are not permitted to communicate in any way with the official scorer regarding his decisions.

Players must carry their equipment off of the field.

At the end of each half-inning the defensive team's players are responsible for carrying all gloves and other equipment with them as they leave their field positions. They may not leave equipment lying in either fair or foul territory.

Misbehavior | Bad Behavior That Can Lead to a Forfeit

A team loses a game by forfeit when they:

- refuse to enter the field, or refuse to begin playing within five minutes of the call of "play" by the umpire.
- delay the game, or attempt to shorten the game.
- refuse at any point in the game to continue playing.
- following a suspension of the game (due to weather, field conditions, etc.) do not resume playing within one minute of the umpire's call of "play."
- after being warned by the umpire, continue to deliberately violate the rules of the game.
- do not comply with an umpire's order to remove a player.
- do not show up on the field for the second game of a doubleheader within twenty minutes of the conclusion of the first game (unless the interval between the two games has been officially extended).
- refuse or are not able to put nine players on the field.

Steroids and Other Drugs

Overview: Major League Baseball's policies covering steroid and other drug use are not covered in the official rule book. Drug policies are covered in the Major League Constitution, an agreement between Major League Baseball and the leagues.

The use of steroids and other illegal drugs is strictly prohibited in baseball. The Major League Constitution goes into great detail about drug testing procedures, and all players are subject to drug testing as outlined in that contract.

Players who test positive for drug use are placed on a "clinical track" to receive treatment. In addition, players face fines and suspensions that increase if subsequent tests also prove positive.

Refusal to take a drug test, or failure to show up for a drug test without good cause, is considered the same as a positive result.

In addition to steroids, other drugs specifically mentioned in the agreement include cocaine, LSD, marijuana, heroin, codeine, morphine, ecstasy, and PCP.

Drug use is a serious issue in baseball and the Major League Constitution will continually be updated to reflect an increasing focus on this problem.

Misbehavior and Interference

Overview: The term *interference* typically refers to an act by a member of the offensive team that hampers a fielder's attempt to make a play on a ball. The interference can be through physical contact with the ball or the fielder, or through acts meant to distract or otherwise hinder the fielder's attempt at making the play.

There are five types of interference:

The official rules of baseball discuss five different types of interference:

1. **Offensive interference** occurs when a member of the team at bat interferes in any way with a fielder making a play.

2. **Umpire interference** can occur in several ways:

- when an umpire hinders a catcher's return throw to the pitcher,
- when an umpire hinders a catcher's throw to pick off a runner,
- when an umpire hinders a catcher's throw to prevent a runner from stealing a base,
- when a ball batted into fair territory comes in contact with an umpire before going past a fielder.

3. **Spectator interference** occurs when a spectator enters the field or reaches from the stands into the field, touching a live ball or otherwise affecting a fielder's play on the ball.

4. **Defensive interference,** commonly called "catcher interference," occurs when any fielder, not just the catcher, interferes with a batter, hindering or preventing him from hitting a pitched ball.

5. **Interference by others** occurs when any other person, authorized or not to be on the field, hinders a fielder's play on the ball. This list includes photographers permitted by the home team, police and security personnel, spectators, and others. By being within the field boundaries they are all in a position to possibly interfere with a play.

Note: *Interference by others* is not an official baseball term. We are using it here to identify occurrences of interference identified in the rule book, but which do not fall into the other categories.

Interference vs. obstruction

"Interference" should not be confused with the call of "obstruction." Interference is an act that hinders a fielder's efforts to make a play. Obstruction refers to an act that hinders a runner's advance — a fielder blocking a runner on his way to the next base, for instance.

However, to confuse things somewhat, "defensive interference" can occur. The word *interference* in this case describes a fielder's act that hinders a batter.

Intentional vs. unintentional interference

The actions taken following a call of interference for an act committed by a member of the offensive team can depend on whether their interference was, in the umpire's opinion, intentional or unintentional. Upon making this judgment call the umpire will take the appropriate steps.

Intentional interference

Interference is considered intentional when a person deliberately performed the act. For instance, if a person other than a player catches a ball in play, it's intentional.

Touching a live ball can be intentional and innocent at the same time.

Example: A bat boy picks up a ball, unaware that the ball is still in play. Although it was an innocent act, the interference is still, for purposes of the rules, considered intentional.

When the umpire judges interference to be intentional, the ball is dead and the umpire may impose any penalties or actions that he feels will make up for the interference.

Unintentional interference

The interference is unintentional if the person involved made an honest attempt to avoid the interference. If he or she did, the interference is ignored and the ball remains in play.

Example: If a ball hits a person who tried to duck to avoid it, it's considered unintentional.

The penalty for interference is an out.

On a call of offensive interference, the batter or the runner will be called out.

Making room in the dugout

According to 2007 rule revisions, a fielder is not allowed to step into the dugout to make a catch. He can, however, reach into the dugout. When completing the catch at least one foot must be on or over the playing surface, and no foot may be on the ground inside the dugout.

Members of the offensive team are required to clear away from any area needed by a fielder to field the ball, including a reach into the dugout. If a fly ball is headed for the offensive team's dugout and a catch is possible, everyone in the dugout is required to get out of the way. Failure to do so will result in a call of interference, and the batter or runner on whom the fielder was making the play will be called out.

Rules are not in place requiring the defensive team to clear their dugout for a fielder — because they will be helping their own teammate, their willingness to make way for the fielder is not an issue.

Misbehaving in the Dugout and Sidelines

The dugout

Only players, managers, coaches, trainers, and bat boys and girls are permitted in the dugout. When not participating in the play at hand, they are all required to remain in the dugout. Failure to to do so will result in a warning by the umpire.

Penalty: On the second offense, the team member will be ejected from the game.

Players on the disabled list

The dugout is open to players on the disabled list. While the injured players may take part in pregame activities, during the game they must stay in the dugout. They are not permitted on any part of the field during the game.

Causing trouble from the sidelines

No member of a team — managers, coaches, players, substitute players, trainers, bat boys, or bat girls — may act in an unsportsmanlike manner, either from the bench or from any other part of the field.

Team members may not, or instance:

- attempt to stir up or provoke the spectators.
- use foul or obscene language against an opposing player, an umpire, or a spectator.
- try to cause the pitcher to commit a balk (for instance, by calling aloud "time" to trick the pitcher).
- physically make contact with an umpire.
- obstruct the batter's view, or otherwise try to distract the batter.

Penalty: As penalty, that team member will be removed from the field.

If team members in the dugout show "violent disapproval" of an umpire's decision, then after issuing a warning, the umpire has the right to order the team member or members to the clubhouse.

If the umpire cannot identify the specific team member or members responsible, the umpire may order all substitute players to the clubhouse. In this case a substitute will only reappear when he is called into the game by the manager.

If the Pitcher Misbehaves

Pitching to intentionally hit the batter

In addition to an immediate ejection, the pitcher could be fined and/or suspeneded.

Pitchers must pitch within twelve seconds

Pitchers are responsible for keeping the game moving. When there are no runners on base and with the batter in position, the pitcher must deliver the pitch within twelve seconds of receiving the ball, or the umpire can call a "ball."

Ball tampering

Tampering can affect the way the flight of the ball.

Tape, a Band-Aid, Super Glue, bracelets, and licorice are a few of the illegal foriegn substances mentioned in the rules.

See page 68 for more on ball tampering.

Ball tampering by other players

If the ball has been tampered with by another player and that player cannot be identified, the pitcher may receive the punishment.

Ball tampering carries severe penalties

Ball tampering is considered a serious offense. The penalty for ball tampering will be immediate ejection from the game and an automatic suspension.

If a Batter Misbehaves

A batter must take his turn at bat.

A batter is penalized if he refuses to take his place in the batter's box. The umpire will call "strike," the ball will be dead, and runners cannot advance. The batter will be called out after the third strike is called, even if the batter has not come to the batter's box at all. Before the third strike, however, the batter may take his proper position in the batter's box. The strikes will remain in the count and the umpire will proceed to call balls and strikes on new pitches, as usual.

Batters must remain in the batter's box.

Once a batter has taken his position in the batter's box he may leave only if:

- the umpire grants the batter's request for a call of "time," or
- there is a delay in the game for any reason. This includes a delay by the pitcher.

When either of these occur the umpire will allow the batter to step outside of the box.

The batter may also briefly step outside of the batter's box between pitches, before the pitcher is in position.

Time may be granted to the batter when the pitcher is in the first stages of the pitching sequence. However, time will not be granted once a pitcher has left the set position or has started his windup. If a batter steps out of the batter's box at this point the umpire will call an automatic strike, and the ball will be dead. See page 85.

If the batter hits the ball with one or both of his feet touching the ground but outside of the batter's box, the batter will be called out. The batter will also be called out if he steps outside the batter's box to swing at the ball when being intentionally walked by the pitcher. See page 87.

If the batter delays the game by leaving the box, the umpire will issue a warning. If he does it again he'll receive "appropriate discipline" from the League President.

A batter must accept being "walked."

Rather than risk a base hit by a strong batter, a pitcher may intentionally walk a batter by pitching four balls far outside the strike zone, allowing the batter to freely advance to first base. A batter who refuses to advance to first base after being walked (possibly angry about being intentionally walked) will be called out.

If the batter interrupts the pitcher

With a runner on base, if the batter unintentionally interrupts the pitcher after he started his windup, the pitcher can stop his pitch.

If the batter interferes with the catcher

Interference by the batter against the catcher depends on the batter's intent — or more specifically, the umpire's opinion as to whether the batter's act of interference was intentional.

For instance, if a batter steps outside the batter's box to interfere with a catcher who is fielding the ball or throwing to a base, or if a batter interferes with a play at home base, interference will be called.

- the batter will be out
- the ball will be dead
- runners will return to the last base legally touched before the interference occurred.

Interference must have an effect.

Even if the batter's interference was intentional, if the catcher's fielding attempt or throw is successful and a runner is called out on the play (including a runner attempting to score at home plate), interference will not be called. The batter will not be out.

(continued...)

If a Batter Misbehaves continued

If the batter hits the catcher with his bat

If the batter's backswing unintentionally interferes with the catcher (meaning, as long as the umpire believes the contact was unintentional) the swing is simply a strike.

For example:

- the batter's swing may come fully around and unintentionally hit the catcher.
- the bat may swing fully around and contact the ball on the backswing.

In either of these two cases interference will not be called. If the catcher makes a throw despite the contact and the throw puts the runner out, the play stands. Otherwise, the ball is dead and runners cannot advance.

If the batter throws the entire bat into fair territory

Intentionally or unintentionally, if the batter throws the entire bat into fair territory and it interferes with a fielder making a play, interference will be called.

The batter is not allowed to intentionally hit the ball with his bat a second time.

The rules regarding a hit ball being hit by the bat a second time depend on whether or not the batter's second hit was intentional.

Intentional: Batters are not allowed to hit a ball a second time. If for instance, the batter swings, partially hitting the ball and sending it straight up into the air, the batter may not hit that ball again.

Likewise, a batter cannot deliberately throw his bat or his helmet at a batted ball. If he does and the bat or the helmet makes contact with the ball in fair territory, and if in the eyes of the umpire this was the batter's intent, the batter will be out, the ball will be dead, and runners may not advance.

Unintentional: If, following a hit, a ball in fair territory comes in contact with the bat a second time, or contacts a helmet or another object, and if this second contact is judged by the umpire to be unintentional, the ball remains in play and no penalty is called.

For instance, interference will not be called, and the ball will remain in play, if:

- the batter drops the bat after hitting the ball and the bat inadvertently contacts the ball in fair territory,
- the bat breaks and the broken part of the bat comes in contact with the ball, a fielder, or a runner, in fair territory.
- a batted or thrown ball accidentally hits a helmet or other object lying in fair territory.

Switch hitters cannot quickly change sides.

Some batters are switch hitters, able to bat right-handed or left-handed. If a batter switches sides when the pitcher is in position, he will be called out. Between pitches a batter is allowed to step between the two batter's boxes.

Pine tar

A batter may apply pine tar to his bat to improve his grip — but it may not be applied more than eighteen inches past the end of the handle. If the eighteen-inch limit is exceeded, however, it is not considered tampering. The bat will simply be removed from the game, and no other penalties against the batter will be imposed.

If the batter uses or attempts to use a tampered bat

Altering (tampering with) the bat can improve its performance — and is illegal. Bat tampering is a serious offense that will result in the batter being ejected from the game. Additionally the League President will fine and suspend the batter.

If a tampered bat is detected, before or after the ball is hit:

- the batter will be out,
- no runners will advance on the hit, and
- any runners who were put out on the play made with a tampered bat will remain out.

Exception: Any advances that were not due to the use of the illegal bat will be allowed, including stolen bases, advances due to a balk, a wild pitch, or a passed ball.

Batter Misbehaves

Misbehavior on the Winning Run

It's not over till it's over

Players can sometimes get overexuberant on winning a game. They can sometimes even forget to complete the win. In an awarded base situation, for a run to score a runner must touch home plate and the batter must reach first — even though home is an awarded base.

Exception: If, on the winning run, spectators mob the field before the batter has reached first base, or before the runner at third base has reached home, blocking their advance, the run will score as if both the batter and the runner had successfully reached their bases.

Example: The batter doesn't touch first, or the runner doesn't touch home plate.

With the bases loaded, the batter gets a walk. This forces in the winning run from third base.

In the excitement, the batter neglects to advance to first base, and/or the runner on third neglects to advance to home plate.

The umpire will call the offending players out and continue with the game.

Note: This rule deals specifically with a game-winning situation and does not appear in reference to a normal inning. Presumably, the level of celebration necessary to forget to score would only occur during a game-winning play.

If, on the winning run, the batter refuses to advance to first

If in the example above, the batter refuses to advance to first base, the following will apply. In both cases, the official scorekeeper will attribute an out to the batter.

With 0 or 1 out:

- the runner at third base will score, winning the game, but
- the batter will be called out.

With 2 outs:

- the batter will be called out,
- the runner at third base will not score, and
- the half-inning will be over. The game will continue into the next half-inning.

If a Runner Misbehaves

A runner will be called out if:

- to avoid being tagged out, he runs more than three feet away from the baseline.
- after successfully reaching first base, he later gives up his attempt to advance to subsequent bases.
- after successfully reaching a base, he tries to confuse the fielders by running the bases in reverse order.
- when attempting to score at home base, he misses the base, does not attempt to touch it, and enters the dugout (either because he believes he touched the base, or he is bluffing). In this case, the defense can appeal for an out.

See page 105 in the Running chapter for more ways a runner can be put out.

A runner may not interfere with a batted ball.

If a runner drops or throws a helmet at a batted ball, making contact with the ball in fair territory, and the umpire judges the act to be intentional:

- the runner will be out
- the ball will be dead
- all other runners will return to the last base they legally reached before the interference occurred.

Runner Misbehaves

Running the Bases in Reverse

Why this is a rule

Like many rules in baseball, this was put in place when some clever player tried a legal but underhanded trick. In 1911 Germany Schaefer, second baseman for the Washington Senators, was a runner on first base with a teammate on third. He stole second base with the thought that the catcher would try to throw him out, allowing the runner on third to score. When that didn't work, he tried it again — but to do so he had to run back to first base, essentially "stealing first." He tried, but that didn't work either. A protest ensued. In the confusion, teammate Clyde Milan, the runner on third base, attempted to steal home but was thrown out.

In 1920, nine years later, the rule was implemented. To this day, it is prohibited to run the bases "in reverse order for the purpose of confusing the defense or making a travesty of the game." "Time" will be called, the ball will be dead, and the runner will be called out.

If a Fielder Misbehaves

Throwing things

A fielder at times may be tempted to throw things at the ball — his glove or other piece of equipment or clothing.

Throwing things at batted balls

A fielder is not allowed to throw his glove or other things at a batted ball, or to use an item "detached from its proper place on his person." For example, he may not use his cap to catch a ball. Penalties are imposed (bases are awarded) if these items make contact with the ball in fair territory — but not if the thrown item misses the ball.

Example: A batted ball is on its way over the center field fence for a home run. The fielder, unable to reach the ball and in a desperate attempt to prevent the home run, throws his glove at the ball. The glove hits the ball, and the ball falls in center field. The home run will be awarded and the batter and all runners will score at home.

If the fielder throws something at a batted ball that landed, or is about to land, in fair territory (a hit not destined to be a home run), and the item contacts the ball, the batter will be awarded three bases. This means the batter will advance to third base and all other runners will freely advance to home to score. Because the ball will still be in play, after reaching third base the batter may elect to run from third to home — but if he does he risks being put out.

The rules regarding thrown gloves and other items do not apply if the gloves or other items come loose accidentally, or become detached in the act of making a play.

Example: A fielder reaches to make a catch and his glove flies off his hand from the momentum, contacting the ball. The umpire believes the contact was unintentional, therefore the ball remains in play and no penalties will be imposed.

Touching a pitched ball

If a fielder uses any detached part of his uniform to touch a pitched ball the batter and all runners will be awarded one base. The ball remains in play.

Throwing things at thrown balls

A fielder is likewise not allowed to throw his glove or other items at balls thrown by fielders. The penalties in this case call for two bases to be awarded to the runners and to the batter who made the hit on the play. As with items thrown at batted balls, no penalties will be imposed if the thrown item does not actually touch the ball.

Defensive interference: if the catcher or another fielder interferes with the batter

The batter may freely advance to first base when the catcher or another fielder interferes with his attempt to bat. Runners who are forced will advance, as will runners who were stealing a base at the time of interference. However, if the batter gets the hit and reaches first base, and all other runners advance at least one base, the interference will be ignored.

Note: If the catcher interferes with the batter before the pitch is delivered, the umpire will call "time." Interference will not be called.

(continued...)

Fielder Misbehaves

If a Fielder Misbehaves continued

The offensive team's manager can accept or decline the penalty.

The offensive team's manager can decide whether to accept a call of defensive interference or not. He may or may not consider the call to be to his team's advantage.

Example: The catcher interferes with the batter, the batter is put out, but a runner on second base advances to third base on the play. The manager has two options:

1. he may elect to accept the call of defensive interference, leaving him with runners on first and second, or

2. he may reject the call of defensive interference, letting the out stand but putting a runner on third base, where he may have a better chance of scoring.

Fielders may not obstruct a runner.

Runners have right-of-way when running within the baselines. A fielder who gets in his way will be charged with obstruction, unless he is actively fielding the ball, or he is in possession of the ball and is attempting to tag the runner out.

The rules differ depending on whether or not a play is being made on the obstructed runner.

If a play *is* being made on the obstructed runner:

When obstruction occurs the umpire will call "That's obstruction" and point to the scene of the crime. On the call of obstruction the ball is dead immediately.

If a play *is not* being made on the obstructed runner:

If fielders were directing their attention to a play elsewhere on the field and there was no play being made on the obstructed runner, the play will continue to completion, even after obstruction is called. If the obstruction had no ultimate effect (meaning, if the runner reached his base in spite of the obstruction) the call will be ignored.

In both cases, as a result of the call the umpire will award the batter-runner and all runners the bases that, in his opinion, they would have reached if the obstruction had not occurred.

See page 130 for more on obstruction.

Actions by a catcher or a fielder can result in the pitcher being charged with a balk.

The pitcher will be charged with a balk (awarding runners a base), the batter will be allowed to advance to first base, and the ball will be dead if:

- the catcher or a fielder comes in contact with the batter or his bat.
- the catcher or a fielder not in possession of the ball blocks a runner from third base who is attempting to score through a squeeze play or by stealing home.

Squeeze play: a play in which, with a runner on third, the batter bunts in hopes that runner will score.

Misbehavior by Managers and Coaches

Overview: Several rules pertain to the behavior of the managers and the first and third base coaches.

Managers' and coaches' behavior

A manager or coach (or any other team member in uniform) is not allowed to speak to or communicate with any of the spectators.

Managers, coaches, and other team members, while in uniform, are also not permitted to socialize with members of the opposing team at any time. The umpires are rather lax about the enforcement of this rule, however.

During their team's time at bat, base coaches are required to be in uniform and to remain in their coaches' boxes.

Managers and coaches can be ejected from a game.

A manager or coach can be ejected from the game and ordered to leave the playing field for the following reasons:

1. If he tries to incite a demonstration by the spectators.

2. If he uses foul language against a player, umpire, or spectator.

3. If he tries to cause the pitcher to commit a balk — by calling "time" or through other tactics.

4. If he intentionally makes physical contact with an umpire.

5. If a first or third base coach is not in uniform or if he leaves his coach's box position.

Note: Reasons 1 through 4 apply to all team members, not just managers and coaches.

A manager, coach, trainer, or other team member who is ejected from a game must vacate the field. He is no longer allowed to participate in the game. Failure to comply can result in his team forfeiting the game.

Upon exiting the field he must either confine himself to the clubhouse or change out of his uniform. If he chooses the latter, he must either leave the ballpark or he may sit in the stands far from the dugout or bullpen.

An ejection subjects the team member, at the discretion of the League President, to a suspension, a fine, or both. A suspended manager, coach, or other team member is prohibited from entering the dugout or a press box during a game.

See page 160 in the Umpires chapter for more on ejections and removals.

If a base coach is touched by a thrown ball or interferes with a thrown ball

- If a base coach is touched by a thrown ball, by accident, the ball remains in play.
- If a base coach deliberately interferes with a thrown ball while a play is being made, the ball will be dead and the batter or runner will be called out.

Interference by a base coach

There are two circumstances under which interference will be called on a base coach:

- If either the first or third base coach physically contacts a runner, helping him to advance, remain on, or return to a base.
- If, with a runner on third base, a base coach leaves his position in the coach's box or performs movements that attract a throw by a fielder.

Remaining in the coach's box

Umpires typically do not strictly enforce the rules requiring the first and third base coaches to remain in their boxes — although getting too close to the foul line is not allowed. For one thing, if too near the foul line coaches may be able to see the signals being given by the catcher to the pitcher.

Ejections

Overview: The most severe penalty for misbehavior by a team member during a game is ejection.

An ejected team member must leave the field, and may face additional penalties — a fine as well as a suspension from participating in future games for a specified number of days. Following are a few of the ways team members can get themselves ejected. (Also see page 160.)

Reasons a pitcher may be ejected include:

- **ball tampering**
- **having any foreign substance in his possession** on the suspicion that he would be using it to his advantage to affect his throw or the ability of the batter to hit his pitch.
- **delaying the game by throwing the ball to other fielders** unless, of course, he is making a play on a runner. When the batter is in position, the pitcher is required to pitch. The first time he delays the game, the pitcher will receive a warning from the umpire. If it happens again, the umpire will remove the pitcher from the game.
- **pitching with the intention of hitting the batter.** This is a serious (and dangerous) violation of the rules that can result in the pitcher's immediate ejection, and possibly an ejection of the manager as well.

Note: Team members who leave the dugout or their field positions to argue a warning from the umpire to the pitcher will also face ejection. (Also see pages 67, 153, and 171.)

Reasons other team members may be ejected include arguing balls, strikes, and other judgment calls.

The rules of baseball specify certain calls made by the umpire to be judgment calls. These decisions are solely up to the umpire. No team member is permitted to argue a judgment call.

The calls classified as judgment calls are listed on page 154.

The umpire's call of ball or strike is a judgment call. Therefore the batter, runners, fielders, manager, coaches, and other members of the team are strictly prohibited from leaving their positions on the field or the bench to argue a call of ball or strike. On first violation the umpire may issue a warning. The second time, the umpire may eject that player from the game.

The same is true when a manager attempts to argue a ruling on a batter's check swing (half-swing), since arguing the call of a check swing is essentially arguing the call of ball or strike.

While a manager cannot argue a judgment call, he may, on any call by the umpire, make an appeal. This means he can ask the umpire who made the call to ask for assistance from another umpire.

Of course, during a game, team members disagree with the umpires' calls often. It is up to the umpire to determine when the disagreement has gone too far.

Umpires shouldn't argue

An umpire is not permitted to criticize or argue a call made by another umpire. He may only advise that umpire if asked by that umpire for his opinion.

Brawls and outbursts

Serious violations of the rules of conduct may include anything from the use of obscene language to an out-and-out brawl. When violations of this magnitude occur the umpire is required to submit details of the incident (or incidents) to the League President.

In some cases, one short outburst may be enough for an umpire to immediately eject the player or team member.

Reporting violations after the game ends

Violations concerning rules of conduct that occurred during a game, including ejections of team members, must be reported by the umpire to the League President within twelve hours of the game's completion. The time limit for reporting bad behavior is reduced to four hours for blatant violations.

The League President may impose a fine on the team member and may also suspend that player or team member from participating in upcoming games. If a fine is imposed by the League President the team member must pay that fine within five days of receiving notice.

See page 162 for more information on umpires' responsibilities after the game.

Eject, remove, disqualify, and expel

The Official Baseball Rules use four different terms regarding actions an umpire can take against a misbehaving team member: *eject, remove, disqualify,* and *expel*. All four terms essentially refer to the same thing — ejecting the player or other team member from the game, and banning him from the field. That team member may also face a suspension and a fine.

In past years a "removal" by a umpire meant sending him to the dugout, no further penalties involved. However, few people can remember the last time this took place. Players and team members today are simply ejected.

(Don't confuse this, however, with a manager's removal of a pitcher to put in a substitute. This is a different use of the word *removal*, and happens often.)

14 | Spectators

Of the handful of rules that pertain to spectators, two have caused significant confusion in the past and will continue to do so in the future: 1) fielders are allowed to reach into the stands to make a catch, and 2) spectators are under no obligation to get out of a fielder's way.

These and other rules pertaining to spectators are discussed on the following pages.

Spectators: contents

Basics for Spectators

Overview: Baseball would be nothing without its fans. Spectators are an integral part of the sport. They can influence a team's performance, affecting a player's psyche through cheers or through uninhibited criticism. They sometimes can become a bit too involved in the game. This chapter covers the rules of baseball that pertain to the fans.

The rules of baseball provide specifications for the infield, the outfield, and the foul areas. There are no limits, however, on seating areas. In some stadiums fans may surround the players from every direction. Inevitably, they may on occasion get too close. Intentionally or unintentionally, mischievously or innocently, they may contact the ball or somehow hamper a fielder's attempt to field the ball.

Spectator Interference

Overview: Spectator interference occurs when a fan gets too close to the action, touching a ball in play or a fielder making a play on the ball anywhere on the field.

The issue of spectator interference can be extremely controversial. A spectator interferes with the play when he or she reaches into the playing field, or enters the playing field, touching a ball in play or otherwise interfering with the action. In some cases the umpire's call, laying blame on a spectator, will be obvious to all — but in cases where a fielder is reaching near or into the stands to catch the ball, and at the same time a fan sees that ball as a souvenir in flight, controversy can arise. The question as to whether the fielder reached into the stands, or the spectator reached into the field to interfere with the play, can be a point of contention.

Spectators are under no obligation to vacate their position in the stands to make room for a fielder making a play. That, matched with the prospect of returning home with a souvenir and a story, can lead to chaos. Therefore, while the rules are clearly written, actual circumstances can make things fuzzy.

Spectator interference is treated like interference by a member of the offensive team.

When spectator interference occurs:

- the ball is immediately dead,
- no runners may advance,
- the umpire imposes awards or penalties based on his opinion of what would have happened in the play had the interference not occurred.

The umpire may call an out (or outs), or may allow the batter and runners to freely advance to the bases that the umpire feels they would have reached had the interference not occurred. Or, he may call for a combination of outs and base awards.

Example: A spectator reaches into the playing field to try to catch a ball, and his action prevents a fielder from successfully catching the ball. The umpire will call the ball dead and the batter out. On the same play, however, if there was a runner on third base and the umpire believes that he would have reached home, tagging up on third after the fielder's catch then running to home, then in addition to the out the umpire will allow that runner to freely advance to home base to score.

If a fielder catches the ball in the stands

A ball is considered legally caught even if a fielder made the catch in the stands. Before or after catching the ball a fielder may reach, leap, or fall into the stands. As long as he hangs on to the ball the catch is still good. (See page 123.)

If the interference occurred in the stands

In cases where a ball is hit into the stands and hits or is touched by a spectator, even when the fielder is reaching into the stands to catch the ball, there will be no call of interference. The ball is already out of bounds. The hit is simply a foul, a home run, or a ground rule double, depending on the circumstances.

If the fielder reaches, leaps, or falls into the stands and misses or drops the ball, for whatever reason, the ball is simply considered not caught. Interference does not apply.

If the ball bounces back onto the playing field

If a ball is hit into the stands, bounces off the seats or off of a spectator, and lands back onto the playing field, the hit is simply a foul, a home run, or a ground rule double, depending on where it first landed. When the ball bounces back it is no longer in play — the ball became dead when it crossed into foul territory.

Spectator Interference

Spectator Interference with a Thrown Ball

If a thrown ball goes into the stands

If a thrown ball goes near or into the stands, the same situation can occur as if a hit ball goes near or into the stands — there is potential for spectator interference. The same spectator interference rules apply to thrown balls as hit balls.

If spectator interference is called, the ball is dead and bases or outs will be awarded.

If a thrown ball goes into the stands, the ball is already out of bounds and interference is not called, even if a spectator prevents a fielder from making a catch. Wild-throw rules will apply: the batter and runners will be awarded two bases from the last base legally touched at the time the throw was made (the time the ball left the thrower's hand).

Team Members and Spectators

Players cannot socialize with spectators.

While in uniform, before, during, or after a game, players, managers, and coaches are not permitted to interact with spectators. The rules specifically prohibit team members in uniform from sitting in the stands. (Team members in uniform are also not allowed to interact with members of the opposing team.)

Team members cannot incite spectators.

The rules prohibit any member of a team — from manager to bat boy — from communicating with spectators, vocally or through actions, to incite the crowd. This means a team member cannot act as a cheerleader, rousing his team's fans.

Likewise, a team member cannot argue or use foul or abusive language against a spectator, and any physical contact is forbidden.

The penalty for violating any part of this rule will be ejection from the game.

Spectator interference — when to call security. Fans erupted at Wrigley Field during game six of the 2003 National League Championship Series between the Chicago Cubs and the Florida Marlins, when Cubs fan Steve Bartman grabbed for a foul ball being fielded by the Cubs' Moises Alou. Even though Alou would probably have made the catch had it not been for Bartman, no rule was broken. From many angles of view, the ball had crossed into the spectator area before Bartman touched it.

Angry Cubs fans expressed their feelings and Bartman needed to be escorted from the field by security for his own protection.

The following season, Cubs fans ceremoniously exploded the ball, blowing it to smithereens in hopes of breaking the curse that has kept them out of the World Series since 1945.

Spectators on the Field

Spectators are not permitted on the playing field.

The following people are allowed on the playing field during a game. They are not considered spectators. The people allowed on the field include:

- players and coaches in uniform
- managers
- umpires
- authorized photographers
- police and security personnel
- ground crew and other home-team employees

By special permission, spectators may be permitted to view the game from the field.

The official rules of baseball allow for special ground rules to be established covering an overflow of spectators onto the field. Before the start of the game the home team's manager will propose special rules concerning balls that are batted or thrown into the spectators on the field. The visiting team's manager must agree to these rules. If not, the umpire-in-chief will determine any ground rules he believes are required, provided they are in accordance with the official rules.

If a spectator or a group of spectators enters the playing field

The home team is responsible for providing security and police protection during a game. If a single spectator or a group of spectators enters the field, the visiting team may suspend play. The home team will be given time — a minimum of fifteen minutes — to eject the spectators from the field.

The umpire will determine what is a "reasonable length of time" for clearing the spectators from the field. If the field cannot be cleared within this time, the home team will forfeit the game to the visiting team. Under the rules of forfeit the visiting team will automatically win the game.

If spectators rush onto the field at the end of a game

Runs are not scored until the runner or runners have touched all bases, including home base. This is true even if a pitch results in a home run or a base on balls that will allow the team at bat to "automatically" win the game. Runs are not scored until home plate is touched.

An exception is made, however, if exuberant fans rush onto the field, blocking the batter's or the runner's advance. The umpire in this case will award the run or runs — a runner's inability to advance to home will be blamed on the spectators.

Interference rules differ for authorized individuals on the field and spectators.

The rules involving interference with people authorized to be on the field are different than the rules governing interference by spectators. The umpire's call in the first case depends on whether he believes the interference caused by the authorized person was intentional or unintentional. If ruled intentional, the ball is dead. If ruled unintentional, the ball remains alive and in play.

Interference with a spectator is never treated as "unintentional," regardless of the spectator's actual actions or intent at the time the incident took place. Interference will be called even if there was no malicious intent on the part of the spectator.

15 | Suspended and Terminated Games

The umpire's goal is to see that a game is completed. Sometimes this is not possible. This chapter discusses the effect of weather delays and the rules in place for suspending play, resuming play, and terminating a game. In the process, it defines what exactly constitutes a "regulation game."

Suspended and Terminated Games: contents

Weather: Who's in Charge?

Overview: Factors such as rain or poor field conditions can affect a decision to begin the game, to delay play of a game in progress, or to end the game prematurely.

Before the game, the home team's manager is in charge.

Before the start of a game the home team's manager is in charge of the field. He decides if the game will start or be delayed due to weather or field conditions.

Once the game starts, the umpire-in-chief is in charge.

During the game the umpire-in-chief takes command from the home team's manager. More specifically, the authority is transferred to the umpire-in-chief as soon as the home team hands him the batting order a few minutes before the start of the game.

The umpire-in-chief remains in charge throughout the game. From that point, among other responsibilities, he becomes the sole authority concerning decisions about:

- if and when weather, poor field conditions, or other factors warrant that a game be suspended.
- if and when a suspended game is to be resumed.
- if and when a suspended game should be terminated (or "called") because resumption of play is not possible.

Certain rules exist to guide exactly when and where these decisions can be implemented. They are described in this chapter.

In games that may affect a team's standing in the league

Near the end of a season a game may significantly affect a team's standing in the championships. The League President may be asked to stand in for the home team's manager to decide, before the game begins and the umpire-in-chief takes control, if a game should be postponed due to weather or other factors. This prevents the home team manager's decision from being biased — having his decision influenced by his team's chances of winning the game that day.

For example, if the home team has a star player on the injured list, it may be to the home team's advantage to postpone the game.

The visiting team can appeal directly to the League President (because at this point before the game the umpire-in-chief is not yet in charge). If the appeal is granted, the League President takes charge of the decision concerning whether or not to reschedule the game.

The number of rain delays is not limited

The umpire's goal is to see that a game is completed if at all possible. This means calling multiple rain delays if necessary. As long as there is a chance that a game can be completed, the umpire-in-chief should extend the delay. His authority to order teams to suspend play or resume play due to weather or other factors is, according to the official rules, "absolute."

Weather: Who's in Charge?

Doubleheaders

In a doubleheader, the umpire-in-chief of the first game decides whether to start the second game.

If there is a doubleheader scheduled the umpire-in-chief of the first game, not the home team manager, will be in charge between the games, deciding if weather, field conditions, or other factors will affect the start of the second game.

Delayed or rescheduled doubleheaders

If the first game of a doubleheader is delayed due to weather or other conditions, the first game played will be the first game originally scheduled for that day — even if that game would begin during a time that the second game would have been played.

If a doubleheader is taking place because an entire game needed to be rescheduled, the rescheduled game will be the second game played that day.

Minor League rules

While baseball games are typically nine innings long, the Minor Leagues (also called the National Association) will allow their teams to play seven-inning games on days when a doubleheader is scheduled. One or both games of a doubleheader may be seven innings long. In these games, rules that typically apply to the ninth inning will apply to the seventh inning.

Weather: Who's in Charge?

Suspended vs. Terminated: Definitions

Once a game has started the umpire-in-chief becomes the sole judge for making the decision to suspend or terminate a game.

Suspend: A suspended game will be resumed after a delay, or if poor weather or other conditions seem unlikely to change, on another day.

The umpire-in-chief is the sole judge determining when play should be halted.

Resume play: The umpire-in-chief also decides when to continue play. A suspended game will resume from the point it was suspended. Runners, fielders, and the batter will all take the positions they held at the time of the suspension.

Terminate: A terminated game describes a game that has been prematurely ended by the umpire-in-chief. The game has been officially completed and play will not be resumed.

Terminating a game (a.k.a. "calling" a game) is a very last resort. The umpire-in-chief will only make this call when there is no chance of continuing play.

Understanding the fate of a game halted because of weather or other factors first requires an understanding of the concept of "regulation games." The definition of a regulation game, suspended and terminated games, and a "no game" are discussed in detail on the following pages.

Regulation Games

Overview: A game must reach "regulation" status to be counted as a game in the eyes of the official scorer. Simply stated, to qualify as a regulation game at least half of a standard nine-inning game must be completed. The actual "halfway point," however, may be anywhere between the end of the first half and the end of the second half of the fifth inning. The rules ensure that, when needed, both teams have equal chances to bat.

Regulation games

When a game must be halted due to rain or other conditions, the decision to suspend the game, declare it to be a *no game*, or end the game with one team a winner depends on whether enough of the game has been played to qualify as a regulation game.

A game becomes a regulation game when:

- the fifth inning has been completed.
- the game is in the fifth inning, the visiting team has just completed their turn at bat, and the home team is ahead in the score.
- the game is in the second half of the fifth inning and the home team has just scored one or more runs to tie the game. It becomes a regulation game as soon as the home team's tying run scores.

A game becomes a "regulation game" in the fifth inning in one of three ways

To be considered a regulation game the visiting team must have completed their turn at bat in the fifth inning. Sometime between that point and the moment the home team completes their turn at bat in the fifth inning, the game will have become a regulation game.

	1	2	3	4	5	6	7	8	9
VISITING TEAM	0	1	0	1	0				
HOME TEAM	0	0	1	2	-				

The game becomes a regulation game sometime during the fifth inning.

1. If the home team is ahead the game becomes a regulation game as soon as the first half of the fifth inning ends (seen in the scoreboard above, where the home team is ahead 3 – 2).

However, if the score is tied when the first half of the fifth inning ends, it is not yet a regulation game.

2. If the visiting team is ahead and if the home team scores one or more runs in the bottom half of the fifth inning, to either tie the game or to take the lead, the game becomes a regulation game the instant the home team's runner crosses home plate to tie the score.

3. Any score: Regardless of the score, as soon as the second half of the fifth inning has been completed the game has become a regulation game.

Suspended and Terminated Games

Overview: When a game is called due to weather or other factors, that game will either be suspended or terminated. A suspended game will be resumed, either after a rain (or other) delay, or it may be rescheduled to continue play on another day. A terminated game will be ended — either declaring one team the winner or calling a "no game."

A terminated game will conclude in one of two ways:

One team will win: If a game has become a regulation game when it is terminated, the team with the most runs will be declared the winner.

No Game: A *no game* is a game that has been started but has not yet advanced to be considered a regulation game. A *no game* will be rescheduled for another day, and will be replayed in its entirety.

Note: A *tie game* was eliminated with rule changes in 2007. If a tied game must be terminated before it has become a regulation game, it is a *no game*. If a tied game is terminated after becoming a regulation game, it is suspended.

Suspended and Terminated | Major vs. Minor League Rules

Major League rules:

No game: If a game must be terminated before it has become a regulation game, the umpire-in-chief will declare it a *no game*, unless it qualifies to be suspended. A *no game* will be replayed in its entirety on a later date. Statistics from a *no game* will not be counted.

Suspended game: With any score, if a game is stopped *before* it has become a regulation game, the game will be suspended, not terminated — but only if it was stopped for any of the six reasons discussed on the next page. In a suspended game play will resume on another day, picking up where it left off.

Minor League exception

If the last game of the season between two Minor League teams has not yet become a regulation game, and is called because of weather, a time limit, a curfew, or with a tied score, a *no game* will be called.

Minor League rules:

The Minor Leagues may adopt rules that circumvent a *no game*, allowing a game to be suspended even if it has not yet become a regulation game. This means that innings already played will not need to be replayed.

If a Minor League game has not become a regulation game: If the suspended game has not progressed enough to qualify as a regulation game, and it is scheduled to resume prior to another regularly scheduled game, the regularly scheduled game will be a seven-inning game.

If a Minor League game has become a regulation game: If the suspended game has progressed enough to qualify as a regulation game, and it is scheduled to resume prior to another regularly scheduled game, the regularly scheduled game will be a nine-inning game.

Suspended Games: Causes and Next Steps

Overview: Although weather is typically the cause, a game may be suspended for several reasons. The umpire's job is to see that a game is completed on its scheduled day, if at all possible. In any case, a suspended game must be completed.

A game can be suspended for the following reasons:

1. If weather conditions, in a regulation game with an inning underway and the visiting team in the lead, make further play impossible.

2. A time limit has been set for the game (which can be permissible under league rules).

3. A legal curfew is in effect.

4. Vital equipment has stopped working and is preventing play. (Equipment may be related to water removal, a retractable roof, tarpaulin placement, or other equipment necessary for keeping the field in playable condition.)

5. "Darkness" prevents further play. Since all Major League stadiums are lit electrically, this rule is rather antiquated — unless of course there is a light failure.

6. A regulation game needs to be stopped and the score is tied.

A game will be suspended whenever light failure or other equipment failure makes further play impossible.

A game that must be stopped because of light failure or other major equipment failure (or an operator error) in the stadium will be considered suspended regardless of how many innings of the game have been played. The game will eventually be completed.

Suspended games must be completed.

If a suspended game needs to be resumed on another day, the remaining innings will be played:

1. Immediately before the next scheduled game in the same stadium between the two teams.

2. If no single game between the two teams remains on the schedule, the suspended game will be completed immediately before the next scheduled doubleheader in the same stadium.

3. If the suspended game was the last game to be played between the two teams at that stadium, the above rules will apply to the visiting team's stadium.

4. If following the suspension of a game there are no more games in the season scheduled between the two teams, the game will be considered complete (terminated), not suspended. The score will be final.

When a suspended game is resumed:

A suspended game resumes with the game picking up exactly where it was suspended, either later the same day or on another day. It is simply a continuation of the game.

The batting order and the team's lineup will be unchanged. However, any of the players may be replaced with new players, provided that the replacement player did not play in the game before the suspension occurred.

Team members who have just signed up with a team may play in the game when it resumes. This is the case even if, when they joined the team, they replaced a player who played in the game but was replaced before it was suspended.

Pitchers. If just before the game was suspended a substitute pitcher came to the mound, and he did not complete the half-inning or did not pitch to a batter who reached first base, that pitcher is not required to pitch when the game resumes. However, he will be considered to have been substituted, and he will not be permitted to pitch for the remainder of that game.

Suspended Games

Suspended and Regulation Games

A game can be suspended if it has become a regulation game and the score is tied.

The game becomes a suspended game if the game has reached or passed a halfway point (to become a regulation game) and the score is tied.

If a suspension is declared on a game that is being played near the end of the season — either a regular season game or during the playoffs — and the suspended game is the second-to-last game scheduled between those two teams, the game will be completed prior to the next day's (or date's) game between them.

Exception: If a final game between the two teams is suspended and all possible dates to complete the game have been exhausted, the game will be "called." A winner will be declared, if possible, according to the rules.

A game ending in a tie is possible

A game ending in a tie is possible, but only under certain circumstances. Late in the season, if a score is tied and the game is suspended, the League President may determine that replaying the game is unnecessary if it wouldn't affect the championship standings.

If a regulation game is suspended before an inning has been completed:

If a game has reached regulation status and the umpire-in-chief needs to stop play while an inning is still underway — because of, for instance, sudden, severe weather conditions, light failure, or other factors make completion of the inning impossible — under the following circumstances the umpire-in-chief can only suspend the game, not terminate it.

The regulation game will be suspended when:

- The score is tied.
- The visiting team has scored one or more runs during the inning in progress to take the lead.

These rules simply ensure that the home team cannot lose the game unfairly — before they have had a chance to bat the same number of innings as the visiting team.

New players

When a suspended game resumes, players who have just joined the team may enter the game. This means, theoretically, if a player is traded between the two teams before the rescheduled date, he could conceivably play on both sides in the same game.

If a final game between two teams is suspended before an inning has been completed:

If a game has reached regulation status, the visiting team is ahead in the score, and it is the last scheduled game in the regular season between the two teams, the final score will be the score at the end of the previous inning. (As mentioned above, this could possibly result in a tie game.)

The same is true if the visiting team tied the score during the inning. Because the home team has not had a chance to complete their half-inning, the score will revert to the score at the end of the previous inning.

Rain Checks

A rain check is a "new" ticket issued to a spectator when a game is canceled or suspended due to weather or other factors. It allows the spectator entrance to the rescheduled game, or to a future game.

In cases in which the game reached the fifth inning and has become a regulation game, the League President may decide if rain checks are to be honored (see "Regulation Games" on page 200). Aside from the regulation game stipulation, specific rain check policies are up to the individual stadiums.

Typically if a game needs to be rescheduled, the original ticket becomes the ticket for the new game. If the game is suspended, the ticket stub can be used.

Darkness

Still in the official rule book is a regulation stating that a game can be suspended on account of "darkness." A game will be called for darkness "when a law prevents the lights from being turned on." Otherwise, the umpire-in-chief has the authority to order the lights on when he feels they are needed. Assuming there has been no major electrical malfunction, darkness is no longer a factor in Major League games.

Electric lights

With much hoopla, lights were installed in Wrigley Field in Chicago in 1988, making it the last Major League stadium to go electric. Night games could finally be scheduled, and darkness ceased being a concern in Chicago.

Field Conditions

Field conditions can also be responsible for suspended games. A wet or flooded field, for instance, can make it unsuitable for play. The umpire-in-chief will direct the ground crew to rectify the situation. However, if it is not possible to solve the problem within a reasonable time, the game will be rescheduled.

Game delays are not included when reporting a game's time duration.

One of the many statistics recorded by the official scorer at the end of the game is the time it took to play the game. If the game was delayed due to weather, light failure, or other reasons, the delay time is not included. The official scorer's responsibility is to report the time spent actually playing the game.

Weather — Batting and Pitching

Weather conditions and batting

If weather conditions are affecting the batter's grip on the bat, the umpire may grant the batter permission to step out of the batter's box to apply rosin or pine tar to the bat's handle. Otherwise, unless "time" has been called or unless there is a pause in the action, once the batter steps into position in the batter's box he is not permitted to step out.

A batter's request for "time" will not be granted for any reason, even for weather-related complaints, once a pitcher has started his windup or has come to the set position. This includes a batter's complaints about dust in his eyes, steamed glasses, or other problems.

Weather conditions and pitching

At the beginning of the game the home team will place a rosin bag at the far side of the pitcher's rubber. If it is raining or if the field is wet, the umpire may direct the pitcher to keep the rosin bag in his pocket instead of on the ground. The pitcher may apply the rosin to one or both of his bare hands, but not to his glove or anywhere else.

In cold weather, a pitcher may be allowed to bring his hands up to his mouth to blow on them in order to warm them. Under normal conditions, however, the pitcher is forbidden from bringing a hand in contact with his mouth — a rule imposed to prevent spitballs (see page 68 for rules regarding ball tampering).

Pine tar, rosin, and resin

Pine tar is a sticky, dark brown substance derived from pinewood. It is used by batters to improve grip. Pine tar is typically applied to a rag, and then rubbed onto the handle of the bat. Pine tar may not be applied more than eighteen inches from the bottom of the bat's handle.

In addition to pine tar, both "rosin" and "resin" are mentioned in the official rules of baseball. They refer to the same material. A resin is a sticky substance derived from any number of plants or trees. Rosin is a specific type of resin derived specifically from the sap or from the stumps of pine trees. Sports equipment manufacturers use the more specific term "rosin" when describing their products.

Rosin is used by the pitcher or batter to improve his grip on the ball or bat. It is lighter in color than pine tar, ranging from amber to brown, and is contained in a rosin bag. The pitcher or batter applies the rosin by rubbing the bag between his bare hands.

16 | The Official Scorer

An official scorer is required at every game, responsible for recording virtually everything that happens. The scorer's report is entered into the permanent record books of Major League Baseball. Each game will generate long lists of numbers and names.

The umpires are not the only officials making judgment calls. Once a call is made, the official scorer in many cases may need to interpret the call, determining which player or players will receive the credit, or the blame, for the action on the field. The scorer, however, has no authority over the game's action.

The Official Scorer: contents

Basics for the Scorer

Overview: Major League Baseball appoints an official scorer to every game — the Office of the Commissioner appoints the scorer for Major League games, and the Minor League President for Minor League games. The scorer operates behind the scenes — or more accurately, in the press box. After a play occurs or an umpire makes a call it is up to the official scorer to determine which players were officially responsible for the actions that took place. His report will be entered into MLB's permanent record.

The official scorer

The official scorer records many aspects of the game for Major League Baseball's official records. When an umpire makes a call, the scorer will determine which player will receive the credit, or the blame. This means that the umpires are not the only officials in a game making judgment decisions.

The official scorer is positioned in the press box because part of his or her responsibility is to communicate these judgment decisions to the press.

The official scorer is employed by Major League Baseball, and like an umpire, he or she is an official representative of the sport. The rules require team members to treat the scorer with respect and dignity. Any disrespect or violation of the scorer's rights will be reported directly to the Executive Vice President for Baseball Operations.

Note: The official rules still state that the scorer can communicate decisions through a speaker system, or through the old-fashioned method of hand signals.

Example: Box scores and abbreviations

Hitters	AB	R	H	RBI	BB	SO	#P	AVG	OBP	SLG
Ellsbury CF	4	1	1	0	1	0	18	.262	.322	.349
Gardner LF	4	0	1	0	0	1	13	.260	.346	.405
Rodriquez DH	3	0	1	1	0	1	14	.252	.356	.490
Beltrán RF	4	0	1	0	0	0	13	.275	.334	.466
Headley 3B	4	0	1	0	0	1	16	.263	.326	.377
Bird 1B	4	0	1	0	0	2	18	.250	.329	.521
Murphy C	4	0	2	0	0	1	17	.286	.325	.422
Gregorius SS	3	0	0	0	1	0	14	.266	.316	.368
Refsnyder 2B	4	0	1	0	0	0	23	.259	.286	.407
Totals	**34**	**1**	**9**	**1**	**2**	**6**	**146**			

AB = At-bat
R = Runs
H = Hits
RBI = Runs Batted In
BB = Bases on Balls
SO = Sacrifice Outs
#P = Number of Pitches
AVG = Batting Average
OBP = On-base Percentage
SLG = Slugging Percentage

The Official Scorer's Report

Overview: The official scorer includes many records in his report. The next few pages provide quick lists of the statistics recorded for each player. The rest of the chapter goes into detail about these records. In addition to recording the game's final score and the winning and losing teams, the official scorer's report contains performance records for each player.

Scorer's Report

Pitching Records

Number of occurrences: The pitcher's records will include the number of:

1. **innings that he pitched,** counted in fractions of one-third according to how many batters he put out (see the examples below).
2. **batters to whom he pitched.**
3. **batters to whom he pitched who qualified for an at-bat.** An "at-bat" will *not* be charged if the batter:
   - hits a sacrifice fly or a bunt (although the batter is out, he advanced the runner)
   - is walked by the pitcher
   - is hit by a pitch
   - is awarded first base as the result of a call of interference or obstruction.
4. **hits made by the batters.**
5. **runs that the pitcher allowed.**
6. **earned runs that the pitcher allowed.**
7. **pitches that were hit for a home run.**
8. **sacrifice hits allowed.**
9. **sacrifice flies allowed.**
10. **total walks** (bases on balls) that he pitched.
11. **walks that were intentional.**
12. **batters hit by a pitch.**
13. **strikeouts.**
14. **wild pitches thrown.**
15. **balks charged to the pitcher.**

Name of the pitcher: The names of the pitchers will be recorded for:

16. **the winning pitcher.**
17. **the losing pitcher.**
18. **the starting pitcher** and the pitcher in place at the end of the game.
19. **the pitcher deserving credit for the save** (see page 219 regarding saves by a relief pitcher).

Example: Innings pitched

Example 1: If a starting pitcher is replaced in the fourth inning after putting one batter out, he will be credited with pitching three and one-third innings. If the substitute pitcher completes that inning, but a third pitcher starts the fifth inning, the first substitute pitcher will be credited with two-thirds of an inning. If the third pitcher completes the nine-inning game, he will be credited with having pitched five innings (innings five through nine).

Example 2: If the starting pitcher is substituted in the fourth inning, but before any batters were put out (even if one or more batters reached a base or if runs were scored in the fourth inning), that pitcher will be credited with having pitched three innings. The increments of one-third of an inning are counted only after an out is recorded.

Example 3: If a substitute pitcher enters the game and a runner is called out on an appeal play, the substitute pitcher will have pitched one-third of an inning.

Scorer's Report

Batting and Running Records

Number of occurrences. The batter's and runner's records will include the number of:

1. **at-bats:** the number of times he came to bat and got a hit or made an out. (Not every plate appearance counts as an at-bat, as noted below.)

2. **sacrifice flies.**

3. **sacrifice bunts.**

4. **walks:** the number of times he received a base on balls.

5. **walks that were intentional:** when the pitcher deliberately pitched four balls for a base on balls, rather than risk a hit by that batter.

6. **times he was hit by a pitch.**

7. **times he was awarded first base as a result of a call of interference or obstruction.**

8. **hits resulting in the batter safely reaching base.**

9. **runs batted in (RBI).**

10. **hits by which he reached second base.**

11. **hits by which he reached third base.**

12. **home runs.**

13. **grand slams:** hitting a home run with runners on first, second, and third.

14. **total bases reached on hits:** one if he singled, two if he doubled, three if he tripled, and four if he hit a home run.

Example: If in the batter's first two at-bats in a game, he reaches second base on a hit during his first at-bat and third base during his second at-bat, the total bases he reached so far during that game will be five.

15. **times he struck out.**

16. **runners who remained on base when an inning ended.** The number of runners does not include runners who were put out or runners who scored.

This number will include the batter himself, whose hit put out another runner for a third out, on the basis that the batter reached, or would have reached, first base.

17. **times he reached home to score.**

18. **bases he stole during the game.**

19. **times he was caught stealing.**

20. **times he hit ground balls resulting in:**

- **force double plays.** A force double play is a play in which two runners are forced to run and are put out.
- **reverse force double plays.** A reverse force double play is a play in which the possibility of a force out exists for two runners, but the trailing runner is put out first, removing the force on the runner ahead of him. With the force removed, this requires the defense to tag the runner who was ahead of him for the second out, not just tag the base.

An "at-bat" will *not* be charged when:

- the batter hits a sacrifice fly or a bunt (putting himself out to advance another runner).
- the batter is walked by the pitcher.
- the batter is hit by a pitch.
- the batter is awarded first base as the result of a call of interference or obstruction.

Because the number of "at-bats" are factored into a batter's batting average, the exclusion of sacrifice flies or bunts, walks, and awarded bases provides a more accurate reflection of his performance as a batter.

Scorer's Report

Catching and Fielding Records

Number of occurrences. The catcher's and fielder's records will include the number of:

1. pitches missed by the catcher. Known as "passed balls," these are pitches that he should have caught but because he missed, a runner or runners advanced or scored.

2. putouts: times he put out a batter or runner.

3. assists: plays in which he fielded or contacted the ball prior to a putout made by another fielder.

4. errors: fielding mistakes that benefited the offense.

5. double plays in which he was involved.

6. triple plays in which he was involved.

Scorer's Report

At the End of the Game

Numbers. At the end of the inning or game, the scorer will record:

1. the number of outs in the inning when the game was won. If a game is won by the home team in the second half of the last inning their number of outs can be fewer than three.

2. the score at the end of each inning.

Names. The official records will also include:

3. the names of the umpires officiating at the game, listed in this order:

- the plate umpire
- the first base umpire
- the second base umpire
- the third base umpire
- the left field umpire (if there was one)
- the right field umpire (if there was one)

The time duration of the game

The official scorer's report includes the time it took to play the game. This number is the actual playing time. Suspensions for weather, light failure, or other reasons are not included in the playing time. Time spent due to an injury to a player, however, *is* included.

Note: Team members are prohibited from communicating with the official scorer about his decisions.

Starting Players, Substitutions, and Improper Batters

Overview: The official scorer's report will contain the names of the players on both teams, their field positions, and their positions in the batting order.

Players' batting order positions and their fielding positions

In the official scorer's report, players' fielding positions will be their nominal positions. If, for instance, a second baseman positions himself far behind second base, putting four fielders in the outfield, for purposes of record-keeping his position will still be considered second base.

If a substitute batter or substitute runner enters the game, the official scorer will use a special symbol that will refer to a separate part of his records, describing what the substitute did in the game. To keep the written records consistent, the rules instruct the scorer to refer to substitute players by using lower case letters for substitute batters and numbers for substitute runners.

Example: The scorer may write something like "player [a] hit a double for Williams in the fourth inning," or "player [2] ran for Anderson in the fifth inning."

In cases where a substitute is announced, but before actually entering the game he himself is substituted, then the official record will consider the second substitute to be a substitute for the first substitute, not a substitute for the original player.

Example: Player [a] is announced as a substitute batter for Williams, but before player [a] even has a chance to enter the game, player [b] is announced as a substitute, taking the position held by [a] in the batting order. Player [b] is considered to be a substitute for player [a], not for Williams.

Notations for substitute batters and runners

The rules specify that in his written records the scorer should use lowercase letters (a, b, c, etc.) when referring to substitute batters, and numbers (1, 2, 3, etc.) when referring to substitute runners. See the examples above.

Attributing outs when a batter bats out of turn

Situation 1: If a batter bats out of turn, is put out, and the proper batter who missed his turn is called out for missing it:

- the proper batter is charged with an at-bat and an out.
- the fielder (or fielders) receive credit for the putout and any assists, the same as if the proper batter had batted.

Situation 2: If an improper batter becomes a runner and the proper batter who missed his turn is called out for missing it:

- the proper batter is charged with an at-bat.
- the catcher receives credit for a putout (even though he didn't play an active role).
- the improper batter's advance to a base doesn't count, and the records ignore everything that occurred during his time at bat.

Situation 3: If multiple batters bat out of turn:

- the batters continue batting, skipping the batter who missed his turn at bat.
- the records for the batter's missed turn at bat remain empty.

Box Scores

A box score is a table of numbers and letters that displays each player's accomplishments during a game. The table lists the names of the players of each team down the left-side column. Across from his name are shown his number of at-bats, bases on balls received, sacrifice flies and bunts that he hit, and other statistics from the game (see page 208 for an example).

The box score records will be accurate when the sum of:

at-bats
bases on balls
hit batters
sacrifice flies
sacrifice bunts
bases awarded by interference
bases awarded by obstruction

equals

runs
putouts by the opposing team
runners left on base

Called (Terminated) Games

If the game is called after it has become a regulation game (i.e., if more than half the game was played), all of the game's records up to that point will be entered into the official scorer's report.

Forfeits

The Official Baseball Rules state that the umpire-in-chief will declare a forfeited game ended with an automatic score of 9 to 0. The official scorer, however, will report the actual events of the game up to that point (not the 9 to 0 score), along with the fact that the game was ended by forfeit.

If a game that has been played more than halfway through to become a regulation game ends with the umpire-in-chief calling a forfeit, the records up to the point the forfeit is called will be entered in the official scorer's report.

If the team that is declared the winner by forfeit is:

- ahead in the score at the time the forfeit is called, the winning and losing pitchers will be named as if the game had been called at that point.
- behind in the score or tied at the time the forfeit is called, winning and losing pitchers are not named.

If not a regulation game:

If the forfeit is called before the game starts, or before it has become a regulation game, no records will be included in the official scorer's report. The report will only declare that the game was forfeited.

Wild Pitches and Passed Balls

Wild pitches and passed balls are only recorded when they allow a runner or runners to advance.

A pitcher will be charged with a wild pitch when the pitch is so high, so low, or so wide that the catcher, with "ordinary effort," cannot catch or control the ball. However, if the official scorer believes the pitch was controllable, the catcher will be charged with a passed ball (a missed catch). In either case a runner or runners must advance for the charge to be recorded. (Also see page 231.)

Note: A pitch that hits the ground before reaching home plate is not automatically charged as a wild pitch unless it bounces in a way that makes it impossible for the catcher to handle, and one or more runners advance as a result.

Bases on Balls (Walks)

A base on balls is commonly known as a "walk." It is an award of first base to the batter when a pitcher pitches four balls (a pitch outside of the strike zone on which the batter does not swing). The official scorer charges a base on balls to the pitcher.

If, when pitching the fourth ball, the pitch touches the batter, the official scorer will record a "hit batter."

Intentionally pitching a base on balls

As part of his strategy, a pitcher may intentionally walk a batter rather than risk a base hit that could advance other runners or send them home. An intentional base on balls is indicated by the pitcher's last pitch. Regardless of what he threw previously, if the fourth ball is pitched way outside the strike zone, requiring the catcher to leave his catcher's box to make the catch, the official scorer will record an intentional base on balls.

Note: If the batter refuses to advance to first base after receiving four balls and being awarded the base, the umpire will call him out. In this case, a base on balls is not recorded. Rather, it qualifies as an at-bat. The catcher receives credit for the automatic putout.

Strikeouts

A strikeout can take place in four ways:

1. When a batter receives his third strike and the pitch is caught by the catcher.

2. When, with 0 or 1 out and a runner on first base, a batter receives his third strike (even if the pitch is not caught).

3. When the "third-strike rule" is in effect. This occurs when, with no runner on first base, or a runner on first and two outs, the pitch is not caught by the catcher. The batter in this situation becomes a runner.
Even though the batter becomes a runner the official scorer still records a strikeout.

4. When, with two strikes in the count, a pitch is bunted foul (unless the bunt is hit into the air and the catcher or another fielder catches the ball before it touches the ground for an out).

Note: If a batter has two strikes against him when a substitute takes his place, and the strikeout is completed by the substitute, the first batter will be charged with the strikeout. Any other outcome of that time at bat, a base on balls for instance, will be attributed to the substitute batter.

Earned Runs

Earned runs

An earned run is a run attributable to a pitcher's performance, or lack thereof. It means that the offense "earned" the run off the pitcher (as opposed to, for instance, getting the run on a fielding error). For the pitcher, fewer earned runs is better.

To determine the number of earned runs, reconstruct the inning without fielding errors, catcher interference, or passed balls (pitches missed by the catcher). Do not count any runs scored after a fielding error that would otherwise have resulted in a third out — the pitcher isn't responsible for them.

An earned run *will* be counted when the offense earned it, due to:

- a hit
- a sacrifice bunt
- a sacrifice fly
- stolen bases

An earned run will also be counted if the run was the result of fielder's choice or pitching performance:

- fielder's choice or putouts being made on another runner or runners
- a base on balls (a walk)
- a batter hit by a pitch
- a balk
- a wild pitch, including a wild pitch on a third strike that allows a batter to run

If catcher interference (defensive interference) is called, an earned run will be charged if a runner scored at home before the catcher interference call was made.

A run will not be counted as an earned run if the runner reached first base or advanced to a base at any time due to a fielding error.

A run *will not* count as an earned run when made by a runner who reached first base due to:

- a fielding error.
- a fielder who missed catching a fly ball in foul territory. (This is because without that fielding error, the batter would have been out.)
- a call of interference or obstruction.

A run *will not* count as an earned run when made by:

- a runner who could have been put out while running the bases, except for a fielding error.
- a runner who advanced one or more bases as the result of a fielding error, a passed ball, defensive interference, or obstruction (provided the official scorer believes that the runner would not have otherwise advanced during the play).

The official scorer must make judgments about fielding errors.

Before counting an earned run, the official scorer must evaluate the effect that a fielding error had on a current or previous play. On plays in which fielders committed errors he must determine whether a runner would have advanced had the play been error-free. If he would have advanced, his eventual crossing of home plate will count as an earned run. If he was only able to advance because of the fielding error, his run will not be included in the count of earned runs.

Give the pitcher the benefit of the doubt

In determining the effect of a fielding error, the official scorer is instructed to give the pitcher the "benefit of the doubt." If there is any doubt, blame for the runner's advance should be attributed to the fielding error, not to the pitcher. If that runner eventually reaches home plate to score, his run should not be included in the count of earned runs.

Earned Runs

Earned Runs and Substitute Pitchers

When a substitute pitcher enters the inning with runners on base, the number of earned runs already scored and the number of runners who are on base will determine the maximum number of earned runs that can be attributed to the first pitcher.

For instance, if the first pitcher puts runners on first and second bases, and is then substituted, the next two runs to score in that inning will be included in the first pitcher's earned run count.

His number of earned runs will be reduced if one or both of the runners he put on base are put out for reasons not associated with batting, for instance, if they were caught stealing a base, or if they were thrown out at a base (picked off) because they were not touching the base.

His number of earned runs *will not* be reduced if their outs are associated with a batter's performance, for example, if they were forced out at a base or tagged out while running the bases after a hit. In this case subsequent runs scored will be attributed to the first pitcher, up to his maximum number, even if the runners who actually scored were put on base by the substitute pitcher.

Examples: **Earned runs applied to substitute pitchers**

Example 1: Pitcher 1 puts Adams on second base and Brown on first base. He is then substituted. Pitcher 2's pitch to Clark results in a home run, scoring three runs.

Pitcher 1: two earned runs
Pitcher 2: one earned run

Example 2: Pitcher 1 puts out Adams, then Brown. He is then substituted. Clark hits a ground ball to second base, but reaches first due to a fielding error. Davis hits a home run, scoring two runs.

Pitcher 1: no earned runs
Pitcher 2: one earned run

Note: Pitcher 1 is not charged with an earned run because if the inning were reconstructed without the fielding error Clark's hit would have resulted in the third out, ending the inning with no runs scored. Pitcher 2 is charged with one earned run (the home run).

Example 3: Pitcher 1 puts Adams on first base. He is then substituted. Pitcher 2 puts Brown on first base, but Adams is forced out at second (an out associated with batting). Clark hits a ground ball that puts him out at first, but advances Brown to second. Davis gets a hit and Brown scores.

Pitcher 1: one earned run

Example 4: Pitcher 1 puts Adams on second base and Brown on first base. He is then substituted. Adams is put out when he is caught stealing (an out *not* associated with batting). Pitcher 2 walks Clark. The next pitch to Davis results in a home run. Three runs score.

Pitcher 1: one earned run
Pitcher 2: two earned runs

Example 5: Pitcher 1 puts Adams on second base and Brown on first base. He is then substituted. Pitcher 2 pitches to Clark, who reaches first base, but Adams is forced out at third base (an out associated with batting). The next pitch to Davis results in a home run. Three runs score.

Pitcher 1: two earned runs
Pitcher 2: one earned run

Example 6: Pitcher 1 puts Adams on second base and Brown on first base. He is then substituted. Pitcher 2 pitches to Clark, who reaches first base, but Adams is forced out at third (an out associated with batting). Pitcher 2 is substituted. Pitcher 3's pitch to Davis results in a home run. Three runs score.

Pitcher 1: two earned runs
Pitcher 2: no earned runs
Pitcher 3: one earned run

Earned Runs

Bases on Balls (Walks) and Substitute Pitchers

Substitute pitchers are not accountable for the first pitcher's count.

If a substitute pitcher relieves a pitcher while a batter is still at bat, the substitute pitcher will not be responsible for a walk (a base on balls) if the balance of balls and strikes in the count is in the batter's favor.

The first pitcher will be responsible for a walk if the count is:

- 2 balls and 0 strike
- 2 balls and 1 strike
- 3 balls and 0 strike
- 3 balls and 1 strike
- 3 balls and 2 strikes

In the case that the batter is eventually walked, that batter and the base on balls will be attributed to the first pitcher.

If the balance of balls to strikes in the count are in the pitcher's favor when the substitute pitcher comes in, that batter and his actions will be charged to the substitute pitcher.

The substitute pitcher will be responsible for a walk if the count is:

- 0 ball and 1 strike
- 0 ball and 2 strikes
- 1 ball and 0 strike
- 1 ball and 1 strike
- 1 ball and 2 strikes
- 2 balls and 2 strikes

The substitute pitcher will be held responsible if the batter is walked. The substitute will be charged with the base on balls.

If that batter reaches first base for any other reason, for example, if he gets a hit or he is touched by a pitch, that batter's advance will be charged to the substitute pitcher.

Shutouts

A shutout is a game in which one team does not score any runs.

The opposing pitcher will be credited with a shutout when:

- he pitches the entire game,

or when both of the following conditions are met:

- he enters the game in the first inning, with no runs by the opposing team and no outs, and
- he pitches for the remainder of the game without allowing any runs.

If two or more pitchers took part in a game that ended in a shutout, the league statistician must note that fact.

The Winning and Losing Pitchers

Overview: A winning and losing pitcher will be named for each game. In some cases the official scorer must make a judgment call to determine which pitchers qualify.

Determining the winning and losing pitchers

By the end of each game a winning and a losing pitcher will be selected. The following rules guide the official scorer in determining which pitchers qualify for each title.

A pitcher will be named the winning pitcher if his team takes the lead while he is in the game as pitcher (even if he is removed during that inning), provided his team maintains that lead.

Starting pitcher

In order for the starting pitcher to receive credit for winning the game, he must pitch five complete innings or more.

Note: The "five innings" requirement pertains to games that lasted at least six innings. (A game may be terminated before the normal nine innings are complete when, for instance, the umpire-in-chief needs to end play because of bad weather.) If the game was terminated after only five innings, the pitcher must have pitched at least four innings to qualify to be the winning pitcher (the other requirements listed above will still apply).

If the score becomes tied:

If the score becomes tied the selection of winning and losing pitchers starts anew. If the opposing team takes the lead, no pitchers prior to that point will qualify for the title of winning pitcher. However, if the pitcher who was pitching when the opposing team took the lead continues to pitch, retakes the lead, and his team retains that lead for the remainder of the game, he will be declared the winning pitcher.

When the starting pitcher doesn't qualify to be the winning pitcher

If the starting pitcher doesn't meet the five-inning requirement, a substitute pitcher will be declared the winning pitcher. That substitute will be the pitcher in place at the time his team took the lead, provided they retained that lead and won the game. To qualify, a substitute must pitch for at least one inning, or pitch at the time an important out is made.

Exception: If a substitute pitcher is ineffective in his role as pitcher, and a new substitute comes in who is instrumental in helping his team retain the lead, the new substitute may be credited with winning the game.

The official scorer can judge the first substitute to be ineffective if he pitches for less than an inning and allows the opposing team to score two or more earned runs — including runs that, in the scorer's report, are charged to a previous pitcher (runs will be charged to a pitcher if the scoring runners were on base at the time the pitcher was replaced).

In determining which substitute was more effective, the number of runs, earned runs, and runners put on base need to be considered. If two or more substitute pitchers were equally effective, preference goes to the first substitute.

Note: Even when a substitute batter or substitute runner stands in for a pitcher, that pitcher is still considered the current pitcher. Runs scored by his team will still be credited to his turn as pitcher, and if his team takes the lead he will receive the credit.

Losing pitcher

The losing pitcher will be the pitcher who gave up the run that put the opposing team ahead (provided the opposing team maintained that lead).

Saves for Relief Pitchers

The official scorer can credit a substitute pitcher (a relief pitcher) with a "save." To qualify, all four of the following conditions must be met:

1. His team won and he was the last pitcher for his team, and

2. he is not named as the winning pitcher, and

3. he pitched for at least one-third of an inning (meaning, he put at least one batter out), and

4. one of these three conditions apply:

- he pitched for three or more innings, or
- his team was ahead by one, two, or three runs when he entered the game, and he pitched at least one inning, or
- when he entered the game, the opposing team's potential tying runner was already on base, at bat, or on deck (scheduled to be the next batter up).

Note: On the last condition, since the "tying run" can be the batter on deck, the pitcher's team could be ahead by up to five runs when he enters the game. For instance, the pitcher's team could have been ahead by four runs if he entered the game with two runners on base, or ahead by five runs if the bases were loaded.

The Winning Pitcher in the All-Star Game

In a non-championship game, the All-Star Game for example, pitchers may be scheduled to take the mound for a predetermined number of innings. In this case the winning pitcher will be the pitcher in place when his team takes the lead and they retain the lead throughout the remainder of the game.

The official scorer may credit the win to a subsequent pitcher, however, if he believes that the subsequent pitcher is more deserving.

Base Hits

Overview: A base hit is scored when the batter safely reaches first base — even if he is put out after that. There are exceptions.

A base hit *will* be scored when:

1. **The batter successfully reaches first base, or any other base,** when he hits a fair ball that touches the ground or a fence before being touched by a fielder, or hits a ball over the fence in fair territory.

2. **A batter successfully reaches first base, or any other base, after hitting a ball on which the fielders cannot make a play.** The base hit will be scored even if the fielder misjudges the play or if one fielder interferes with another fielder in an attempt to make a play.

3. **A batter reaches first base, or any other base, on a hit that takes an unexpected bounce.** For example, a ball may hit a rock and the fielder is unable to catch it in time. The ball may also take a wild bounce after hitting the pitcher's rubber, home plate, or one of the other bases.

4. **The batter hits a ball that rolls or flies into the outfield before being touched by a fielder,** allowing the batter to reach first base or any other base.

Exception: It will not be a base hit if the scorer believes the fielder could have fielded the ball with "ordinary effort."

5. **When the batter hits a fair ball that touches a runner or an umpire** before being touched by a fielder.

Exception: If an infield fly touches a runner who is not touching his base, the runner will be called out. No base hit.

6. **When on a hit a fielder tries, without error, to put out a runner in front of the batter (fielder's choice),** fails to put out that runner, and the official scorer believes the batter would have been safe at first even if the fielder had tried to put the batter out.

Note: The official scorer is instructed to **favor the batter,** scoring a base hit when the batter reaches a base and "exceptionally good fielding" does not result in a putout.

Even if a batter successfully reaches a base, he may not be credited with a base hit. In some cases this is because a runner in front of him was forced out. Here are the reasons a batter may reach first base but will *not* be credited with a base hit.

A base hit will *not* be scored when:

1. **A hit forces a runner out** — or, if not for a fielding error, the runner would have been forced out.

2. **A batter safely reaches first, but a runner who is forced to advance fails to touch the next base** to which he advances, and is called out on appeal by the defense. The scorer will attribute an at-bat to the batter, but not a base hit.

3. **The pitcher, catcher, or infielders (without the aid of outfielders) put out a runner in front of the batter** as that runner is trying to advance or trying to return to a base. A base hit will also not be scored if the fielders could have put out a runner, but made a fielding error.

4. **Fielder's choice** applies in a play in which a fielder, in the official scorer's judgment, could have put out the batter at first base but attempts instead to put out another runner and fails. No base hit.

Note: The fielder must actually make an attempt to throw out the other runner, not simply turn his head toward that runner, or fake a throw in that direction.

5. **An umpire calls interference on a runner ahead of the batter,** declaring that runner out.

Exception: The scorer will credit a base hit to the batter in this situation if he feels that the batter would have reached first base even if the interference had not occurred.

Base Hits | Singles, Doubles, Triples, and Home Runs

The rule for singles, doubles, triples, and home runs is simple. On a hit, the official scorer credits a batter with a one-base hit if the batter reaches first base, a two-base hit if he reaches second, a three-base hit if he reaches third, and a home run if he reaches home.

Base Hits | If a Runner Ahead of the Batter Is Put Out

Doubles: If the batter reaches second base, he is credited with only a one-base hit, not a two-base hit, if the runner ahead of him is put out at third (or if the runner would have been put out at third if it weren't for a fielding error).

Triples: If the batter reaches third base, he is credited with only a two-base hit, not a three-base hit, if the runner ahead of him is put out at home plate (or if the runner would have been put out at home if it weren't for a fielding error).

Note: Except for these two cases, the number of bases credited to a batter does not depend on the number of bases reached by the runner ahead of him.

Example: Batter hits a double

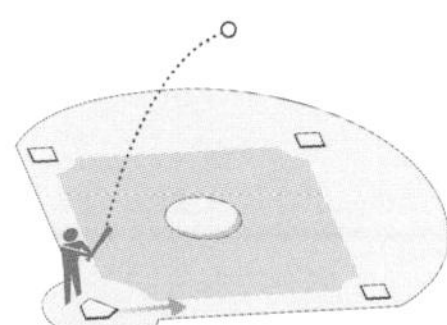

1. With no runners on base the batter hits a ball to left field that gets past the outfielder.

2. The batter safely reaches second base. **He will be credited with a two-base hit.**

Example: Batter hits a double, but the runner ahead is, or could have been, put out

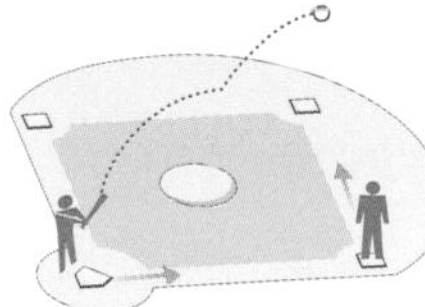

1. With a runner on first the batter hits a ground ball into the outfield.

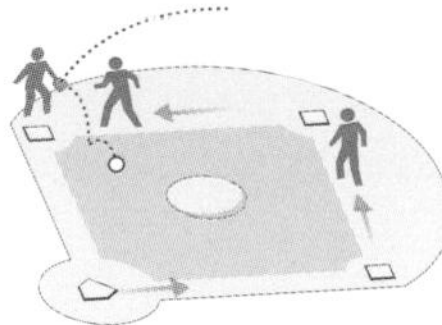

2. The runner who was on first reaches third base safely, but only because an outfielder made a bad throw to third base. The batter reaches second.

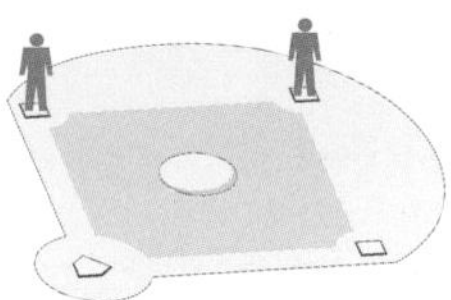

3. Even though the batter reached second, in this situation **he will only be credited with a one-base hit**.

Base Hits

Counting Base Hits

Running beyond a base, then being tagged out, counts.

If a batter touches a base, continues running beyond it to the next base, and is then tagged out, he will be credited for the last base he touched.

Example: The batter hits a ground ball into the outfield. He successfully reaches first base, continues his run to second but is put out. He will be credited with a one-base hit. If he was put out after running beyond second base he would be credited with a two-base hit, or if he was put out after running beyond third base, he would be credited with a three-base hit.

Awarded bases count as base hits.

If a batter gets a home run, or if he is awarded: two or three bases because a fielder used his cap, mask, or thrown glove to touch a ball; two bases because a ball bounced over the wall and went out of play; or two bases because a thrown ball went out of play — those bases will be counted.

Fielder's choice doesn't count.

Fielder's choice occurs when a fielder opts to put out a runner ahead of the batter rather than the batter. When a batter gets a hit with one or more runners already on base, and he successfully reaches second base or beyond on the hit, the official scorer must use his judgment in recording the play. He must decide whether the batter's hit qualifies as a two-base hit, a three-base hit, or whether the batter only advanced to those bases because the fielder was more concerned with putting a lead runner out.

Oversliding a base doesn't count as reaching a base.

If a batter overslides a base and is tagged out, he will *not* be credited with safely reaching that base.

Example: If a batter reaches first base, continues running toward second, and slides into second but his slide takes him past the base and he is tagged out, he will only receive credit for a one-base hit.

Missing a base doesn't count as reaching a base.

If a batter hits the ball but while running misses touching a base, and is called out, he will only be credited with having reached the last base he actually touched.

Example: If a batter gets a hit that allows him to run to third, but misses second base in the process, and is called out on appeal by the defense, he will be credited only with a one-base hit. If he missed touching first base, he will not be credited with a hit at all, only an at-bat.

If a batter's hit wins the game

If the batter makes a game-winning hit he will receive credit for the number of bases advanced by the runner who scored the winning run at home — but not more than that. To receive this credit, the batter himself must have safely reached at least as many bases as were advanced by the winning runner.

Example: With a score of 5 to 4 in the last half of the last inning, with runners on second and third, a batter hits the ball deep into the outfield. The runners from third and second score, winning the game. If the batter only touches first base, he will be credited with a one-base hit. He must touch second base to be credited with a two-base hit. Even if the batter makes it all the way to third base, he will still be credited with only a two-base hit — the number of bases the winning runner advanced to win the game.

If a home run wins the game

If the batter hits a home run out of the ballpark to win the game, the batter and all runners who were on base at the time will score. The home run will be credited.

Example: Game-winning home run. With a tie score of 5 to 5 in the last half of the last inning, with runners on second and third bases, a batter hits the ball over the outfield wall for a home run. The two runners and the batter will score. The batter will receive credit for the home run. The final score of the game will be 8 to 5.

Runs Batted In (RBI)

Overview: Runs batted in is a measure of a batter's performance, crediting the batter with every run that scores as a result of his time at bat.

Runs batted in (RBI)

An RBI will be credited to the batter for every run scored as the result of that batter's:

- hit (in which he safely reaches a base)
- sacrifice fly
- sacrifice out
- batted ball that results in an out made in the infield, or an out made by "fielder's choice" (where a fielder opted to throw out a runner ahead of the batter)
- award of a base that forces another runner to score because the bases were loaded (there were runners on first, second, and third bases). The awarded bases may be due to:
  - being walked (i.e., the batter received a base on balls)
  - a pitch touching the batter
  - a call of interference or obstruction

RBI and home runs

A home run will result in an RBI for every run that scores as the result of that home run. A home run with bases loaded, for example, will result in four RBIs for the batter.

RBI and errors

An RBI will be credited to the batter if, with 0 or 1 out:

- a runner from third scores, and
- an error is made on the play, and
- the runner from third would have scored even without the error.

An RBI will *not* be credited for runs scored when:

- a batter hits a ground ball resulting in a force double play or a reverse force double play
- a fielder makes an error on a play at first base that otherwise would have resulted in a force double play

See page 210 for a description of force double plays and reverse force double plays.

The scorer determines if an RBI counts when fielders make errors.

The scorer must determine if an RBI should be credited when a fielder hesitates or makes an error — for instance, if a fielder holds on to the ball, or does not throw to the correct base.

The official rules instruct the scorer to:

Credit the RBI if the runner runs continuously, without pausing.

Do not credit the RBI if the runner pauses, then runs after noticing the fielder's hesitation or mistake.

In the second case, the run will be attributed to fielder's choice, not to the batter.

Sacrifices

Overview: A sacrifice occurs when a batter hits or bunts the ball in a way that is likely to put him out, for the purpose of advancing another runner. This is a deliberate, strategic move by the offensive team. Therefore, the batter is not penalized with an at-bat that results in an out.

Sacrifice flies

The official scorer will record a sacrifice fly when all of these conditions are met:

- there is 0 or 1 out
- a ball is hit into the outfield (in fair or foul territory)
- any fielder catches the ball in flight, in the outfield, to put the batter out
- a runner already on third base tags up and scores a run on the play.

Note: If the fielder misses the catch, and a runner scores, the sacrifice fly will still be recorded as long as the official scorer believes the runner would have scored even if the catch was made. In this case the sacrifice fly will be scored even if another runner is forced out by the batter's action.

Sacrifice bunts

The official scorer will record a sacrifice bunt when either of these conditions are met:

- With 0 or 1 out, the batter bunts, putting him out at first base, but advancing at least one other runner. (A sacrifice bunt will also be recorded if the batter is safe at first because of a fielding error, but would have been put out had the error not occurred.)
- With 0 or 1 out, the batter bunts, and the fielders, in an errorless play, try but fail to put out a runner in front of the batter. The batter may be safe on first.

Exception: The batter will be credited with a base hit, not a sacrifice, if after the bunt:

- the fielders try but fail to put out a runner in front of the batter, and
- had the fielders instead attempted to put out the batter at first base, the official scorer believes the batter would still have been safe at first.

A sacrifice bunt will *not* be scored when:

- any runner is put out trying to advance on the bunt, or, if there was a fielding error on the play, would have been put out. The batter will instead be charged with an at-bat.
- in the official scorer's judgment, the batter is bunting to reach a base, not to sacrifice himself for the purpose of advancing a runner.

  Note: In making this judgment, when the batter's motive may be questionable, the scorer is instructed to allow the batter the "benefit of the doubt" and record a sacrifice bunt.

Sacrifice flies and bunts

One difference between a sacrifice fly and a sacrifice bunt is that a runner must score in order for a sacrifice fly to be recorded, but a runner only needs to advance for a sacrifice bunt.

Stolen Bases

Overview: In some cases a runner can advance simply by running.

A stolen base is defined as a successful advance by a runner that is not enabled by:

- a hit
- a putout
- a fielder's error
- a force out
- fielder's choice (a fielder's decision not to throw the runner out while stealing the base, even though he could have)
- a catch that was missed
- a wild pitch
- a balk

If the runner is stealing a base and the pitcher pitches wild or the catcher throws wild

The following rules are in place for these situations:

- If the attempt to steal a base begins before the pitcher throws his pitch, and the pitch results in a wild pitch or the catcher misses the catch, the runner will still be credited with a stolen base.
- If the runner is able to advance beyond that stolen base as a result of a wild pitch or a missed catch, the scorer will record the stolen base as well as the wild pitch or missed catch.
- If the runner steals a base and the catcher makes a wild throw in his attempt to put out the runner, the runner will be credited with a stolen base.
- If the runner is able to advance beyond that stolen base as a result of the catcher's wild throw, or any other runner is able to advance as a result of the wild throw, the scorer will record an error for the catcher in addition to the stolen base.

Stolen bases and run-down plays

The following applies if a runner begins to steal a base, or takes a lead off of a base, and becomes caught in the run-down play (in which fielders on either side of him attempt to put him out). If the runner is not put out and manages to advance to the base (not as the result of a fielder's error), he will be credited with a stolen base. If another runner takes this opportunity to also steal a base, both runners will be credited with stolen bases. If one runner steals a base but the other safely returns to his original base, the runner who advances will be credited with the stolen base.

Stolen Bases | Caught Stealing

A runner will be charged with "caught stealing" when:

If in attempting to steal a base a runner is put out, or if in the official scorer's opinion he would have been put out except for a fielder's error, the runner will be charged with "caught stealing." This will be the case when the runner:

- attempts to steal a base and is tagged out
- overslides a base during a steal and is tagged out
- is thrown out when he takes a lead off of a base and is "picked off" (tagged for an out as he attempts to move toward the next base)

A runner will *not* be charged with "caught stealing" when:

- he attempts to steal after the catcher misses a pitch, but is put out, or
- he is obstructed and a base is awarded

Stolen Bases

Situations in Which Runners Will Not Receive Credit for a Stolen Base

Runners will *not* be credited with a stolen base:

1. If two (or three) runners attempt to steal a base at the same time and any one of them is put out before reaching the base, then none of the runners will be credited with a stolen base.

2. If a runner in the act of stealing a base overslides that base, either when advancing to the base or returning to the base, and he is tagged out, he will not be credited with having stolen that base.

3. When a runner stealing a base is only safe because a fielder missed or mishandled a throw:

- the runner will not receive credit for a stolen base, but instead will be charged with "caught stealing" — even though he is safe on the base.
- an assist will be credited to the fielder who made the throw.
- an error will be charged to the fielder who missed or mishandled the throw.

4. If in stealing a base a runner reaches it only because the fielder opted to allow the steal and not to make the play, then the runner will not be credited with a stolen base. The scorer will record the advance as "fielder's choice."

The official scorer considers the totality of circumstances.

In determining whether a runner should be credited with a stolen base the scorer must judge whether he actually earned the stolen base, or if the fielders simply allowed him to advance. It's a tough decision, based on factors that include:

- the inning and the score
- whether the fielders were holding the runner on base
- the pitcher's previous pickoff attempts on that runner prior to his advance
- whether a fielder made any attempt to cover the base being stolen by the runner
- whether the defense had a legitimate, strategic reason to allow the runner to steal
- whether the defense purposely allowed the runner to freely advance to prevent him from being credited with a stolen base

Example 1: A runner is nearing a record for his number of stolen bases (for instance, a career or a league record). The defense doesn't want to see him succeed, because one of their players is also nearing that record. To prevent another stolen base credit they allow the runner to advance freely. The official scorer may decide to credit the stolen base in spite of the fact that the fielders allowed the advance. By doing so, it discourages this sort of behavior on the field and gets the teams back to playing baseball as they should.

Example 2: In the last inning of the game the defensive team is ahead in the score by many runs. A runner attempts to steal. Is a fielder's sluggish performance a true effort, or is he indifferent because he assumes his team will win the game despite the advance? The scorer must decide.

Stolen bases may be the scorer's most difficult call.

A scorer needs to weigh many factors when judging whether a stolen base should be credited or not. It's probably a scorer's toughest call. The issue is "fielders' indifference" — a factor that can be impossible to clearly determine. The game's score, team strategy, or simply a reluctance to see an opposing team's runner advance his stolen base record can all be at play.

Putouts and Assists

Overview: Putouts and assists are measures of a fielder's performance.

A fielder will receive credit for a putout when:

- he catches a hit ball before it touches the ground, either in fair or foul territory.
- he catches a thrown ball to put out a batter or a runner running to a base.
- he tags a runner who is not touching his base.
- he tags a base to put a runner out on an appeal play (for instance, if a runner missed a base).

Putouts and Assists

Automatic Putouts

The catcher will receive credit for an automatic putout when:

- the batter strikes out.
- the batter is out on the call of an illegally batted ball (for example, when the batter hits the ball with one or both of his feet outside of the batter's box).
- a batter refuses to advance to first base after being walked, hit by a pitch, or interfered with by the catcher.
- a runner is called out because he refuses to advance from third base to home.
- the batter is called out because he interfered with the catcher.
- the batter is out because he was touched by the ball he just hit.
- a batter is called out for missing his turn at bat.
- the batter bunts a ball on the third strike, and the ball goes foul.

  Exception: If the bunt is hit into foul territory, and is caught before hitting the ground, the fielder who caught the ball will be credited with the putout.

Other types of automatic putouts

Other automatic putout situations occur when:

- a batter is called out on an infield fly that is not caught. Credit for the putout goes to the fielder who, in the official scorer's judgment, would have caught it (see page 124).
- a runner is called out because he was touched by a ball hit into fair territory, including an infield fly. The putout will be credited to the fielder closest to the ball when it touched the runner.
- a runner is called out because he ran more than three feet away from his baseline to avoid being tagged. The fielder who was trying to tag him will receive credit for the putout.
- a runner is called out because he passed a runner in front of him. The fielder who was closest to the runner as he passed the other runner will receive credit for the putout.
- a runner is called out because he runs the bases in reverse order (in an attempt to confuse the other team). The fielder who was covering the base from which he began his reverse run will receive credit for the putout.

(continued...)

Putouts and Assists

Automatic Putouts continued

- a runner is called out because he interfered with a fielder. The fielder will receive credit for the putout. However, if the runner interfered with a fielder who was throwing the ball to another fielder, the fielder who was receiving the throw will get credit for the putout, and the fielder who was throwing will be credited with an assist.
- interference is called against a runner who was already on base, and a batter-runner is called out as a result. The first baseman will receive credit for the putout. If the fielder with whom the runner interfered was in the process of throwing the ball, that fielder will be credited with an assist.

Note: On these last two points, only one assist will be credited on the play.

Putouts and Assists

Assists

Credits for assists

An assist is a credit given to each fielder who assisted the fielder who received credit for the putout. An assist is awarded if he fields a batted or a thrown ball, throwing or deflecting it toward another fielder whose play results in an out. An assist will be awarded even if the other fielder mishandles the ball and fails to put out the runner.

In a run-down play, only one assist will be credited to each fielder who threw or deflected the ball to help put out the runner. Credit will be given even if the runner was not put out due to a subsequent error on the play.

Even though a fielder can receive credit for an assist if he deflects the ball, it only counts if the deflection has an effect — for instance, if the ball's trajectory was affected, or the ball's movement was slowed, enabling another fielder to make the out.

An assist *will* be credited to:

- a fielder who throws or deflects a batted or thrown ball, and that action leads to, or could have led to, an out.
- a fielder who throws or deflects a thrown or batted ball, and that action leads to a runner being called out for interference or called out for running outside of the base path.
- a pitcher who, if a catcher misses a catch on a third strike, fields the ball and throws it to another fielder for an out. (This could occur, for instance, if the catcher misses the catch and the pitcher is able to get to the ball before the catcher.)

An assist *will not* be credited to:

- a pitcher who simply strikes out the batter.
- a pitcher in a play in which the catcher, after catching a pitch, puts out a runner — for instance, if the catcher tags a runner coming into home, or makes a throw to put out a runner attempting to steal a base.
- a fielder who throws wild — even if, in spite of the wild throw, a runner is eventually thrown out on the play.

Assists can be awarded on an appeal play

When a runner is called out after an appeal by the defense, an assist will be credited to each fielder who fielded, threw, or deflected the ball, helping to make the out. However, if the appeal is made by the pitcher who, after the play ended, made the appeal by throwing the ball to a fielder, only the pitcher will be credited with an assist.

Fielding Errors

Overview: An error is charged whenever a fielder mishandles the ball, and as a result extends a runner's time on a base, allows a runner to advance, or extends a batter's time at bat when the batter otherwise would have been retired by "ordinary effort."

Exception: An error must be a *physical* mishandling of the ball. If a fielder handles the ball slowly but is in control of the ball, an error will not be charged. Similarly, if a fielder misjudges a play without touching the ball, an error will not apply. With a runner on third base and 0 or 1 out, a fielder may decide not to catch a foul fly ball, holding the runner on third to prevent him from possibly scoring. That fielder will not be charged with an error.

Fielding Errors

Nine Ways an Error Can Be Charged

An error will be charged when:

1. a fielder mishandles the ball, extending a runner's stay on bases, allowing a runner's advance, or extending a batter's time at bat.

2. a fielder mishandles a foul fly ball, extending a batter's time at bat.

3. a fielder fields a batted or thrown ball at first base but fails to tag the batter or the base (if in the scorer's judgment he could have put him out).

4. similarly, a fielder fields a batted or thrown ball in a force play but fails to tag the runner or the base (if in the scorer's judgment he could have put him out).

5. a fielder makes a wild throw, missing an opportunity to put out a runner or the batter.

Exception: A wild throw made during an attempt to put out a runner stealing a base will not be counted as an error.

6. a fielder makes a wild throw during an attempt to put out a runner, and that throw enables that runner, or another runner, to advance.

Note 1: Although this may seem unfair, an error will also be charged against a fielder if runners are able to advance because his throw hit the ground and bounced unpredictably, or bounced off the pitcher's rubber or a base, or touched an umpire or a runner — even if the throw itself was accurate. Every advance must be accounted for. Advances in these situations will be attributed to a fielder's error.

Note 2: On any wild throw, regardless of how many runners advanced or how many bases they reached, only one error will be charged.

7. a fielder fails to catch or stop an accurately thrown ball, and a runner advances. If this occurs on a throw to second base the official scorer will decide whether that throw should have been fielded by the second baseman or by the shortstop. If the official scorer believes the fielder threw the ball without good reason, then the fielder who made the throw will be charged with the error.

8. a fielder is charged with obstruction, or with defensive interference, causing the umpire to award one or more bases. An error will be charged against the fielder.

Note: Similar to the wild-throw situation, only one error will be charged on a call of obstruction or defensive interference, regardless of how many runners advanced or how many bases they attained as a result. An error will *not* be charged if, in the official scorer's opinion, the infraction did not have an effect on the outcome of the play.

9. a fielder causes another fielder to mishandle the ball — for example, by running into him and causing him to drop the ball. The fielder who ran into him, not the fielder who dropped the ball, will be charged with the error.

Fielding Errors

Assists and Fielding Errors

Additional plays made after a fielder's misplay will be treated like a new play.

If a fielder makes a mistake (making an error or otherwise mishandling the ball) any subsequent action will be treated as if it were a new play. This means that a fielder who handled the ball before or during the misplay will not receive credit for an assist (assuming a runner was eventually put out on the play). That is, unless that fielder handles the ball again after the misplay occurred.

If a ball goes through a fielder's legs

A fielder does not need to touch the ball to be charged with an error. Balls that "could have been" handled by a fielder, but weren't, will be considered errors. For instance, if a ball goes between a fielder's legs, or passes by an infielder's side, or an outfielder misses a pop fly, the official scorer will charge that fielder with an error — as long as he believes that the fielder, with "ordinary effort," could have fielded the ball and secured an out on the play.

Fielding Errors

Errors Will Not Be Charged

An error will *not* be charged when:

1. a fielder throws to the wrong base.

2. a fielder's wild throw is not to blame — meaning, if the official scorer believes the runner or runners would have reached their bases safely even if the throw was accurate, then no error will be charged.

3. a fielder makes a wild throw in an effort to complete a double play or triple play.

Note 1: In situations 2 and 3 above, when as a result of the wild throw a runner advances to a base beyond the base he was attempting to reach, or if the wild throw enables any other runners to advance, an error *will* be charged.

Note 2: If the fielder on the receiving end of a throw mishandles the catch, allowing a runner or runners to safely reach a base, then that fielder will be charged with an error. The fielder who threw the ball, assuming he threw it accurately, will be credited with an assist, as if the receiving fielder's error had not occurred.

4. a fielder mishandles the ball but the batter-runner, or any runner who is forced to advance, is put out at that base in spite of the misplay.

5. with 0 or 1 out and a runner on third base, a fielder intentionally allows a fly foul ball to hit the ground, rather than catch it for an out.

Note: This instance describes a strategic decision for which the fielder should not be penalized with an error. If he had caught the ball, it would remain in play and the runner from third may be likely to score at home. By letting it drop, the ball is dead and runners stay put.

Note: Ordinary effort is defined by the average skill of all fielders — not an individual's past performance. It takes into account field and weather conditions.

"Mental mistakes"

An error *will not* be charged for a "mental mistake" (Major League Baseball's terminology). This includes throwing to the wrong base and other misjudgments. An error *will* be charged if the mental mistake leads to a physical misplay — for example, when a fielder mistakenly believes there are three outs and throws the ball into the stands.

An error against a pitcher or a catcher will *not* be charged in certain cases.

The pitcher and catcher handle the ball much more frequently than the other fielders. Special rules are in place to protect them while making plays that otherwise would have been called errors.

An error will *not* be charged when:

- a pitcher:
  - pitches four balls, or
  - hits the batter with a pitch, or
  - throws a wild pitch, or
  - pitches but his pitch is missed by the catcher.

  Even though the batter may be awarded or otherwise advance to first base as a result, an error is not charged.
- a runner or runners advance because of a wild pitch, a balk, or a missed catch.
- a wild pitch results in a fourth ball, and because it goes wild:
  - it allows the batter to advance to second base or beyond.
  - it allows a runner or runners who are forced to advance to reach a base beyond their forced base.
  - it allows any other runner, not forced, to advance one or more bases.
- a wild pitch on the third strike enables the batter to reach first base. Although no error will be charged, both a strikeout and a wild pitch with be recorded for the pitcher.
- the catcher, after catching a pitch, throws to a base to catch a runner stealing, and his throw goes wild (unless that runner continues to successfully advance).
- the catcher misses a pitch (not wild) on the third strike, enabling the batter to reach first base. Although no error will be charged, a strikeout and a passed ball will be recorded for the pitcher and the catcher, respectively.
- on a wild pitch or a missed catch that occurs on the third strike, the catcher is still able to make a play, putting the batter out by tagging him or by throwing to first, but other runners advance. The official scorer will record:
  - a strikeout for the pitcher.
  - the putout to the catcher, or to the appropriate fielder and an assist to the catcher.
  - the base advances of the runners, recorded as fielder's choice.

Fielding Errors

Credits for Double and Triple Plays

Credit is given for participation in a double play or a triple play

In plays in which the defense puts out two or three players, credit for the double play or triple play is given to every fielder who made a putout or an assist (unless an error or misplay also took place). The putouts must take place between the time the pitch is made and the time the play is over (when the ball becomes dead, or the pitcher is again in his pitching position and in possession of the ball).

However, if one or more of the putouts was the result of an appeal by the defense, then even if the appeal is granted after the pitcher has taken possession of the ball, credit(s) for the double play or triple play will be awarded.

Wild pitches and passed balls

No fielder will be charged with an error on plays in which a wild pitch or passed ball is recorded. See page 214 for more on wild pitches and passed balls.

Consecutive Streaks

There are three types of consecutive records (also known as cumulative performance records) that concern the official scorer:

Consecutive hitting streaks

A batter's consecutive hitting streak refers to the number of consecutive times he came to bat and made a hit that put him safely on base.

A hitting streak will continue if a batter's appearance at the plate results in a base on balls, he is hit by a pitch, the umpire calls defensive interference or obstruction, or he hits a sacrifice bunt. His streak will end if he hits a sacrifice fly.

Consecutive-game hitting streaks

A batter's consecutive-game hitting streak refers to the number of consecutive *games* in which, at some point in the game, he made a hit that put him safely on base.

His consecutive-game hitting streak continues if one or more at-bats in a game results in a base on balls, he is hit by a pitch, the umpire calls defensive interference or obstruction, or he hits a sacrifice bunt. The streak will end if his only hit during a game is a sacrifice fly.

Consecutive-game playing streaks

A player's consecutive playing streak refers to the number of consecutive games he played.

His streak will continue if:

- the player plays at least one half-inning on defense, or
- an at-bat results in his reaching a base or being put out, or
- he is ejected from the game, even if he is ejected before he can fulfill the requirements above.

If the player simply pinch-runs for another player, his appearance is not enough to extend his streak.

Cumulative performance records and suspended games

In calculating consecutive streaks, a player's performance in a suspended game that needs to be rescheduled and resumed on another day will be treated as if the game were completed on the day it was originally scheduled.

Reporting the Scoring Results

Decisions must be made within 24 hours of the game's conclusion

The official scorer is required to finalize all decisions within 24 hours of the game's conclusion or suspension. After that, changes to any decisions in his report can only be made with approval of the Executive Vice President for Baseball Operations. He must also submit a reason for the change or the erroneous entry.

Challenging the scorer

A player or team can challenge a scorer's decision by submitting a request, in writing or by approved electronic means, to the Executive Vice President for Baseball Operations. The request must be submitted within 72 hours of the scorer's call or revision of a call.

Upon review of videos or other evidence the Executive Vice President for Baseball Operations may order that the scorer's decision be changed.

For repeated or frivolous appeals regarding the scorer's decisions, a warning may be issued to the team or team member, followed by penalties if it continues.

Scorer's mistakes

The Office of the Commissioner will order changed any decisions not in keeping with the rules.

Reporting

Results

Called, forfeited, and suspended games

The reporting times will also apply to called, forfeited, and suspended games. In the case of a suspended game, where a game had to be rescheduled due to weather or other reasons, the official scorer must submit his report as soon as possible after the game's completion. If a game is called, as soon as possible after termination.

Reconstructing suspended and protested games

Suspended games must be resumed using the same playing situation as when the game was suspended. This means the game will pick up using the same batting order, fielders, pitcher, etc., as if a time delay had not occurred. The same is true if a protest is upheld (a rare event where an umpire's decision is found to be in error, and it affects the game's outcome). A protested game, when rescheduled, will pick up from the exact play that caused the protest. Runners, if any, will be placed in the same position and the same batter will come to bat with the same count of balls and strikes. The official scorer's information will serve as the official record on which to base reconstruction of the game.

Consistency

The official scorer's responsibilities are spelled out in the official rule book to ensure consistency in record keeping from game to game. If any scoring situations arise that are not covered in the rule book, the official scorer has the authority to impose rules (just like an umpire can impose decisions for situations not covered in the rules).

The official scorer and the umpire

The official scorer:

- must abide by the official rules of baseball.
- does not have the authority to override an umpire's decision.
- if he notices that a batter has come to bat out of turn, must refrain from informing the umpire or the teams. (Similarly, if an umpire notices that a batter is batting out of turn, he also must refrain from reporting this fact. They must wait until one of the teams takes action.)

Changing sides too soon

The official scorer will notify the umpire-in-chief if the teams start to change sides before a third out is made.

Included in the scorer's report:

The official scorer's final report will include:

- the date the game was played
- where it was played
- the names of the two teams involved
- names of the umpires officiating at the game
- the score
- records of each player's performance during the game (as discussed in this chapter)

Submitting the report

The official scorer must submit his report as soon as practical (but within 24 hours) to the Office of the Commissioner, and to the league office — or if requested by the league, directly to the statistician.

Games must reach "regulation game" status

Games must reach "regulation game" status before they can become official and be counted in the official record. In general, this means that at least half the game must have been completed (see page 200 for details about when a game becomes a regulation game).

Individual Championships

Overview: Several awards are given to individual players for their performance over the course of the season. This section describes how they are selected.

The individual batting, slugging, or on-base percentage champion will be the player with the highest batting average, slugging, or on-base percentage. However, during the season he must have made, as a minimum, this number of appearances at the plate:

number of games scheduled in the regular season x 3.1 = minimum number of plate appearances required

Example: Since a team is scheduled to play 162 Major League games in the regular season (not including playoff games) then each batter must have come to the plate at least 502 times to qualify for an individual batting championship.

162 x 3.1 = 502.2

For the Minor Leagues the multiple is 2.7, not 3.1. If a Minor League team plays 140 regular games, then:

140 x 2.7 = 378.0

Note: When the result is a fraction the number is rounded up or down to the nearest whole number.

The number of times he came to the plate equals the total of:

- his official at-bats
- bases on balls (walks) that he was awarded
- times he was hit by a pitch
- sacrifice bunts
- sacrifice flies
- times he was awarded first base on a call of interference or obstruction

Note: If a batter did not meet the minimum requirement for number of plate appearances — for instance, if he only came to bat 499 times rather than 502 times — an alternate calculation can be used. If the minimum required number of appearances, 502, is used in place of 499 when calculating his batting average, slugging percentage, or on-base percentage, and the result is still the highest, he will be awarded that championship title.

See pages 236 and 237 for more information.

The individual pitching champion will be the pitcher with the lowest ERA (earned run average). As a minimum requirement he must have pitched a number of innings equal to the number of regular games scheduled in that season. The rules for the Major Leagues differ from the Minor Leagues, whose minimum requirement is eighty percent of the number of regular scheduled games. See page 238 for calculating ERAs.

Major Leagues:

minimum number of innings = number of scheduled games in the regular season

With 162 games scheduled in a season, a pitcher must have pitched at least 162 innings to qualify.

Minor Leagues:

minimum number of innings x 80% = number of scheduled games in the regular season

If 142 games are scheduled in a season, for example, a Minor League pitcher must have pitched at least 114 innings to qualify: 142 x 80% = 113.6 (round up to 114). Note that the number of games in a regular season among Minor League teams will vary.

Individual Championships

Fielding Championships

The individual fielding champion will be the player with the highest fielding average. If the player's position is:

- **catcher,** he must have played in at least one-half of the games scheduled for each team during the season.
- **infielder or outfielder,** he must have played in at least two-thirds of the games scheduled for each team during the season.
- **pitcher,** he must have pitched at least as many innings as the number of games scheduled for each team during the season.

Exception: If a pitcher does not meet the minimum requirements for pitching champion, but in his fielding role:

- he has a fielding average that is equal or higher than other fielders, and
- he had more opportunities to field the ball during the season (even though he played in a fewer number of innings),

that pitcher will be selected to be the fielding champion.

The Official Statistician

Another position appointed by each League President is the official statistician. For every player and every game the statistician will generate tables displaying all individual and team records. Regular season games, postseason games, and games scheduled at the end of the season to break a tie within a division will all be included in the statistician's records.

The rules state that, in his report, the statistician must:

- identify each player by his first and last name,
- indicate whether each player bats right-handed, left-handed, or switches between the two,
- for each fielder, including the pitcher, indicate if he throws with his right or left hand.

All players in a team's starting lineup will appear in the batting statistics as being in the game. If, however, a starting player bats in the first inning but is replaced before he becomes a fielder, his appearance will be recorded in the batting statistic but not in the fielding statistics, since fielding statistics require that a fielder be on defense for at least one pitch or play.

Similarly, if a substitute pitcher is named but the game is called (due to rain, for instance) before he can throw a pitch or before a play is made, he will receive credit in the batting statistics for a game played, but will not appear in the defensive statistics.

Calculations

Calculated statistics include:

- Batting average (AVG)
- Slugging percentage (SLG)
- On-base percentage (OBP)
- Pitcher's earned run average (ERA)
- Percentage of games won (W-L)
- Fielding percentage (FP)

Discrepancies between the scorer's and the statistician's records

In cases where there may be a discrepancy between the scorer's and the statistician's records, the scorer's records will prevail.

Statistics

Overview: The following pages explain the meaning, and the math, for some common measures of performance.

Statistics |

Batting

Statistics: Batting

Batting performance can be measured by three different statistics:

- Batting Average (AVG)
- Slugging Percentage (SLG)
- On-Base Percentage (OBP)

Batting average (AVG):

Batting average measures a player's frequency of getting a safe hit. It is calculated by dividing the number of times he safely got on base with a single, double, triple, or home run by his total number of at-bats.

$$AVG = \frac{\text{Number of base hits}}{\text{Number of at-bats}}$$

For example, if after 200 at-bats a player had 66 hits, his batting average would be:

$$AVG = \frac{\text{66 base hits}}{\text{200 at-bats}} = .330$$

A higher AVG indicates better batting performance.

Slugging percentage (SLG):

Slugging percentage, unlike batting average, takes into account the number of bases the batter reached with each base hit.

$$SLG = \frac{\text{Number of bases reached}}{\text{Number of at-bats}}$$

The calculation counts one base for each single, two bases for each double, three bases for each triple, and four bases for each home run. Let's say a player had 200 at-bats times and 66 hits. Those hits consisted of 50 singles, 10 doubles, 2 triples, and 4 home runs. He therefore reached a total of 92 bases on those hits.

50 singles x 1	=	50	bases
10 doubles x 2	=	20	bases
2 triples x 3	=	6	bases
4 home runs x 4	=	16	bases
66 hits	=	92	total bases reached

Divided by his total number of at-bats, his slugging percentage is .460:

$$SLG = \frac{\text{92 bases reached}}{\text{200 at-bats}} = .460 \text{ bases per at-bat}$$

Note: A base hit is a hit that gets a batter safely to first base.

On-base percentage (OBP)

On-base percentage measures the frequency the batter gets on base. This includes base hits, walks, and getting to first by being hit by a pitch.

To calculate on-base percentage, divide the number of times a batter got on base by the sum of:

- his number of at-bats,
- the number of times he was walked,
- the number of times he got to first by being hit by a pitch, and
- the number of sacrifice flies he hit.

When calculating OBP, ignore awards of first base due to interference or obstruction.

$$\text{OBP} = \frac{\text{base hits} + \text{walks} + \text{times hit by a pitch}}{\text{at-bats} + \text{walks} + \text{times hit by a pitch} + \text{sacrifice flies}}$$

For example, after 490 appearances at home plate, a player made 131 base hits, was walked 42 times, was hit by a pitch 8 times, and hit 6 sacrifice flies. Of those plate appearances, 434 qualified as at-bats:

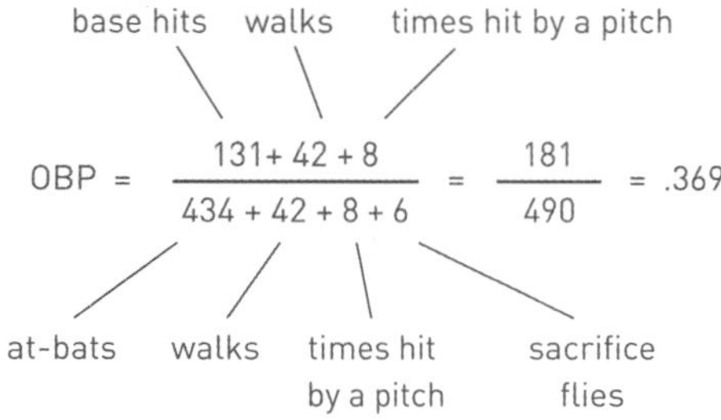

His OBP equals .369. Higher OBP numbers indicate better batting performance.

Not every plate appearance counts as an "at-bat."

Plate appearance: occurs every time a player comes to bat, regardless of the results of that appearance (an out, hit, walk, sacrifice fly, etc.)

At-bat: is counted only when a batter gets a hit , makes an out, or reaches base due to a fielding error.

Plate appearances that result in a sacrifice fly, sacrifice bunt, walk, hit by a pitch, or an award of first base as a result of interference or obstruction do not count as an at-bat.

Statistics

Pitching

Pitching performance can be measured by:
- Earned run average (ERA)
- Win-loss percentage (W-L)

Earned run average (ERA)

The earned run average measures a pitcher's ability to prevent runs from scoring. The number represents the average number of runs a pitcher gives up in nine innings. The other team must "earn" the run for it to be counted in the ERA. Runs scored as the result of a fielding error or passed ball do not count as earned runs because they are not considered to be the pitcher's fault.

ERA is calculated by:

$$\text{ERA} = \frac{\text{number of runs earned by the other team}}{\text{number of innings pitched}} \times 9$$

For example, if a pitcher gives up 18 earned runs and pitched 60 complete innings:

runs earned by the other team — innings in a typical game

$$\text{ERA} = \frac{18}{60} \times 9 = 2.70 \text{ runs every 9 innings}$$

innings he pitched

If the pitcher pitched part of an inning, that fraction of an inning (1/3 or 2/3) should be included in the calculation (i.e. 60.333 if he pitched 60 and 1/3 innings).

Less is more!

ERA measures how many runs the pitcher is likely to give up in nine innings. Fewer is better — a lower number indicates better pitching performance.

W-L percentage (win-loss percentage) for a pitcher

This calculation measures a team's performance in games where the pitcher had significant involvement. It simply takes the number of games won and divides it by the total games he pitched.

$$\text{W-L percentage} = \frac{\text{games won by a pitcher}}{\text{total games he pitched}}$$

If a pitcher pitched 19 games, winning 12 of them and losing 7, his W-L percentage would be:

$$\text{W-L percentage} = \frac{\text{12 games won}}{\text{19 total games played}} = .632$$

The pitcher wins 63.2% of the time.

Statistics

Fielding

A fielder's performance is measured by his fielding percentage (also referred to as "fielding average").

Fielding percentage

The fielding percentage is determined by dividing a fielder's successful fielding attempts by his total number of fielding attempts. This is a measure of his "chances" of successfully fielding the ball in future plays. Fielding percentage is calculated by:

$$\text{Fielding percentage} = \frac{\text{putouts + assists}}{\text{putouts + assists + errors}} = \text{percentage of success}$$

For example, if a fielder has 198 putouts and 214 assists, but made 5 errors, his fielding percentage would be:

$$\text{Fielding percentage} = \frac{\text{198 putouts + 214 assists}}{\text{198 putouts + 214 assists + 5 errors}}$$

$$= \frac{\text{412 successful attempts}}{\text{417 total attempts}} = .988$$

Statistics

Team Standings

Toward the end of the season, in addition to knowing which team is ahead in the standings, it is helpful to know how many wins are needed to clinch the title.

Magic number

The magic number in baseball indicates the minimum number of future games a team needs to win in order to clinch the season title.

The number is calculated by adding 1 to the number of games remaining to be played, then subtracting the number of games by which that team is ahead:

$$\text{Magic number} = \text{number of games remaining} + 1 - \text{number of games ahead of the second place team}$$

For example, the first-place team has 90 wins, putting them 3 games ahead of the second-place team, which has 87 wins. The first-place team has 14 games remaining in the season. To calculate their magic number:

$$\text{Magic number} = \text{14 games remaining} + 1 - \text{3 games ahead} = \text{12 games}$$

For each game a team wins, or each game the nearest competitive team in the same division loses, the magic number is reduced by 1. A magic number of 0 means a team has clinched the title.

W-L percentage (win-loss percentage) for a team

A win-loss percentage for a team is similar to the win-loss percentage for a pitcher:

$$\text{W-L percentage} = \frac{\text{games won by a team}}{\text{games they played}}$$

The team, on average, wins this percentage of the time.

Glossary

Appeal is a claim by a player or manager, to the umpire, that a rule has been broken.

Assist is a credit by the official scorer to a fielder who fielded or contacted the ball, intentionally or unintentionally, prior to a putout.

At-bat describes a player's turn in the batter's box that results in a hit or an out (not including hit by a pitch, a walk, or a sacrifice fly).

Automatic out is an out attributed to a violation of the rules — i.e., interference.

Awarded base is a base "given" to a batter or runner, allowing him to advance without risk of being put out.

Balk is a penalty charged against the pitcher, when a runner or runners are on base, typically for attempting to deceive a runner. A balk results in an award of one base to all runners (i.e., a runner on third would score.)

Ball is a pitch that does not pass within the strike zone, or that hits the ground before passing through the strike zone.

Base coaches are members of the coaching staff positioned in the boxes outside first base and third base to advise the batter and runners.

Base on balls (walk) is an award of first base given to the batter after the pitcher has pitched four balls.

Base hit is a hit that gets a batter safely to first base, without a fielding error or fielder's choice.

Base path is a six-foot-wide lane, three feet to either side of the baseline.

Baseline is a straight line between the runner's position at the instant a tag is first attempted, and the base.

Batter's box is an area to either side of home plate, where the batter stands while at bat.

Batter-runner describes a batter who has just become a runner, until he is put out or that play ends.

Batting order, also called the lineup, refers to the sequence in which players will come to bat.

Bunt occurs when a batter doesn't swing at a pitch but holds the bat to tap the ball, intending it to roll slowly into play.

Called game (terminated game) is a game prematurely ended by the umpire.

Catch occurs when a fielder secures a batted or thrown ball in his hand or glove.

It is *not* a catch if:

- that player immediately collides with another player or a wall, or falls, and loses possession of the ball.
- a fly ball touches a fielder, then contacts an umpire or a member of the offense, and is then caught by another fielder.

To qualify as a catch the fielder needs to have control of the ball. If he subsequently drops the ball while in the act of throwing it, it is still considered a catch.

Note: On a fly ball a runner may take off from his base as soon as a fielder touches the ball, even if the ball is juggled or not yet in the fielder's control.

Catcher interference also known as defensive interference, occurs when a catcher interferes with the batter.

Championship season (regular season) is the period during which the teams play their 162 scheduled games, prior to the playoffs.

Coach is a team member assigned specific responsibilities to help improve the team's performance.

Dead ball is a ball no longer in play because the action on the field is temporarily suspended.

Defense is the team that is pitching and fielding.

Defensive interference occurs when any fielder (typically the catcher) interferes with the batter.

Designated hitter (DH) is a player named to bat for the pitcher throughout the game.

Double play is a play in which two outs are made, with no error made between the putouts.

Doubleheader refers to two games between the same two teams played on the same day.

Earned run average (ERA) is the average number of runs a pitcher gives up in 9 innings.

Earned runs are runs made by the opposing team for which the pitcher is responsible.

Ejection occurs when, as penalty for a serious violation, the umpire sends a team member to the clubhouse, banning him from further play.

Errors are charged when a fielder mishandles the ball, benefiting the offense.

Fair ball is a ball hit by the batter that:

- stops between first and third base — a ball is also fair if it lands in foul territory then bounces or rolls back into fair territory before passing first or third base
- lands in fair territory between first and third base (even if it goes into foul territory beyond those bases)
- touches first or third base
- lands in fair territory in the outfield
- touches a player or umpire in fair territory (even if it goes into foul territory after that)
- hits a foul pole

Note: The fouls lines are considered fair territory. A ball hitting a foul pole is also considered fair regardless of where it lands afterwards. Also see page 78.

Fair territory is the area within the foul lines. The foul lines and the foul poles themselves are within fair territory.

Field umpires are the umpires positioned at the bases.

Fielder is any one of nine players on defense.

Fielder's choice describes a situation in which a fielder decides to make a play on a runner other than to put out a batter running to first base.

Fly ball is a ball hit by the batter that travels up into the air and has not yet touched the ground. Also see *ground ball* and *line drive*.

Force play is a play in which a batter or runner is at risk of being put out because he is forced to advance when the batter becomes a runner.

Forfeit is a situation in which the umpire-in-chief declares one team the winner, with an automatic score of 9-0, as penalty for a serious rule violation. See page 150 for examples.

Foul ball is a hit by the batter that:

- lands outside the foul lines.
- lands in fair territory but crosses the foul line before passing first or third base.
- bounces off the pitcher's rubber, then crosses the foul line before passing first or third base.
- touches an umpire, player, or any object in foul territory.

Note 1: A ball that lands in the outfield in fair territory is fair, even if it then bounces or rolls into foul territory.

Note 2: If a hit ball touches the ground outside the foul lines, but then bounces or rolls into fair territory before passing first or third base, it is fair.

Foul territory is the area outside of the foul lines, and outside the foul poles.

Foul tip is a ball that is barely hit by a batter's swing and travels directly into the catcher's mitt.

Grand slam home run is a home run made with a runner on every base.

Ground ball is a hit ball that bounces or rolls along the ground. Also see *fly ball* and *line drive*.

Ground rule double is an award of two bases for a hit that bounces or is deflected out of play — i.e., over the back wall.

Ground rules are special rules that cover situations unique to a ballpark. In Wrigley Field, for example, two bases are awarded if a ball gets stuck in the vines that cover the back wall.

Hit see *base hit*

Illegal pitch is a pitch that violates some aspect of the rules — for example, a quick pitch.

Infielder is a fielder playing one of four fielding positions — first, second, third base, or shortstop.

Infield fly is a ball hit high into the infield that can be easily caught by a fielder.

Infield Fly Rule is a call by the umpire, made while an infield fly is still in the air, that automatically puts out the batter.

Inning is a segment of the game in which each team has a chance to bat. Typically games are eight and one-half or nine innings long.

Interference is an act that illegally hinders a play. They include:

- Offensive interference
- Defensive interference
- Umpire interference
- Spectator interference

Others on the field, like police or photographers, can also be the cause.

Judgment call is a call that is based on an umpire's decision — e.g., if a pitch is called as a ball or a strike.

League is a group of baseball teams. Major League Baseball consists of the American League and the National League.

League President is designated by the Commissioner to ensure the rules are enforced. Among other duties he may impose fines, solve disputes, and rule on protested games.

Line drive is a ball hit sharply by a batter that travels horizontal to the ground. Also see *ground ball* and *fly ball.*

Manager is the person designated by a club to direct the team and to communicate with the umpires.

MLB Major League Baseball — the organization that controls professional baseball in the United States and Canada.

Obstruction occurs when a fielder unfairly blocks or otherwise impedes a runner's advance.

Offense is the team at bat.

Offensive interference occurs when a member of the offense interferes, intentionally or not, with a live ball or a fielder making a play.

Official scorer is an official appointed by Major League Baseball to record the events of a game.

Official statistician is a person appointed by the League President to calculate the statistical records of a game.

Out occurs when a batter or runner is disqualified from advancing the bases. Three outs ends a team's turn at bat for that inning.

Outfielder is a fielder playing one of three positions in the outfield — left, center, or right.

Passed ball is a pitch (not thrown wild) that is missed by the catcher.

Pickoff is a play by the pitcher in which he throws to a base to put out a base runner who is not touching his base or is attempting to steal.

Pinch hitter is a substitute batter, and may be any player who has not yet played in the game. (Not to be confused with the designated hitter, page 100.)

Pinch runner is a substitute runner, usually put in place because he is faster or better at stealing bases.

Pitcher's mound is an eighteen-foot-diameter area in the infield, on which the pitcher stands.

Pitcher's rubber (plate) is a 6" x 24" hard rubber rectangle embedded into the pitcher's mound. The pitcher must touch it with his foot when pitching.

Pivot foot is the pitcher's foot that is in contact with the pitcher's rubber. It is the right foot for right-handed pitchers, the left foot for left-handed pitchers.

Plate umpire is another name for the umpire-in-chief, since he is positioned at home plate. Among other things, the plate umpire calls pitches as balls or strikes.

Protest describes a team's appeal to a League President to overrule an umpire's call that was not in keeping with the rules, and that affected the game. If upheld the game will be replayed from the point of the play in question.

Putout is an act by a fielder that causes a runner or a batter-runner to be out.

Quick pitch a pitch quickly delivered before the batter is ready.

Rain check is a ticket issued to a spectator for entry to a rescheduled game.

RBI see *runs batted in.*

Regular season see *championship season.*

Regulation game is a game that has progressed far enough to become official and be entered into the record books. This will happen sometime between the midpoint and the end of the fifth inning — see page 200.

Relief pitcher is a pitcher brought into the game to replace the current pitcher.

Removal refers to the ejection of a player from the game.

Retouch refers to a runner retreating to a base to touch it again.

Reverse force double play refers to play in which the batter hits the ball, forcing one or more runners to advance. The fielders throw out the batter at first base (removing the force) before tagging out a runner ahead of him.

Rubber see *pitcher's rubber*.

Run down occurs when a runner is caught between bases by fielders who throw the ball among themselves to try to put out the runner.

Runs batted in (RBI) is a measure of batting performance, referring to the number of runs that scored due to a batter's performance.

Sacrifice bunt occurs when, with 0 or 1 out, a batter bunts, putting himself out but allowing one or more runners to advance. The bunt will not be scored as a sacrifice bunt if any runners are put out on the play.

Sacrifice fly occurs when, with 0 or 1 out, a batter hits a fly ball or a line drive that is caught for an out, but which allows one or more runners to score — even if other runners are put out on the play.

Set position is one of two pitching positions. (*Windup* is the other.)

Shutout is a game in which one team does not score any runs.

Spectator interference occurs when a spectator enters or reaches into the field, or otherwise impedes a fielder, affecting a play.

Squeeze play describes a play in which a batter bunts in an attempt to allow a runner on third base to score.

Stolen base (a steal) is an advance on a base, including home, not due to a hit or an awarded base.

Strike occurs when a batter swings at a pitch and misses, or fails to swing at a pitch that passes through the strike zone.

Strike zone is an area above home plate, defined by the width of home plate and the size of the batter. The strike zone defines whether a pitch will be called a ball or a strike.

Suspended game is a game in which play is stopped (due to poor weather, for instance) but will be resumed either later that day or on another day. See page 148.

Tag occurs when a fielder, securely holding the ball, touches a base with any part of his body, or touches a runner with either the ball or with his glove or hand holding the ball.

Note: The fielder must be in control of the ball. If he immediately drops the ball after the tag, the tag will not count.

Tag up is the act of a runner touching his original base, or returning to touch his original base. When a fielder catches a fly ball, a runner must tag up before advancing.

Terminated game (called game) is a game that must be prematurely ended by the umpire — due to weather, for example.

Triple play is a play in which three outs are made, with no error made between the putouts.

Umpire is an official appointed by Major League Baseball to officiate at a game.

Umpire interference takes place when a hit ball touches an umpire before it passes a fielder, or the plate umpire gets in the way of a catcher or his throw.

Umpire-in-chief is the head umpire. He is typically positioned at home plate, and is also referred to as the plate umpire.

Walk see *base on balls*.

Wild pitch is a pitch thrown too high, low, or wide to be caught by the catcher.

Wild throw is a throw that is too high, low, or wide to be caught by a fielder.

Windup position is one of two pitching positions. (*Set* is the other.)

Index

Note: Where multiple page references are listed, see the pages in **bold** first.

Note: Where multiple page references are listed, see the pages in **bold** first.

The Authors

Dan Formosa, Ph.D.

Dan Formosa spent his grammar school years in Hoboken, NJ, the site of baseball's first recorded game.

A consultant to a wide range of companies and organizations, he has received numerous design awards. He also helped create the Masters in Branding Program at the School of Visual Arts in New York City.

Dan travels the world frequently in his work. He spends the rest of his time in Piermont, NY, and in New York City — virtually within throwing distance of Hoboken's old Elysian Fields.

Like Paul, Dan grew up playing stoopball. Unlike Paul, he is a diehard Yankees fan.

Paul Hamburger

Originally from New York City, Paul Hamburger is a recent transplant to sunny Los Angeles, where he works as a creative director.

Growing up in the streets of Brooklyn, Paul was an accomplished player of stoopball. As a Mets fan, he is bitter and resentful toward the relative success of other local baseball organizations. He lives in the past, nostalgic for the glory days of the mid-eighties.

Photo credits:

Cover photo Pete Coscarart Striking Out at Ebbets Field © Bettmann/Corbis
Page 41 Willie Mays © Bettmann/Corbis
Page 41 1903 uniform © Bettmann/Corbis
Page 42 Catcher's mask and helmet © MIZUNO Corporation
Page 48 Juan Marichal © Bettmann/Corbis
Page 73 Pat Venditte © Charles Krupa/AP/Corbis
Page 81 Eddie Gaedel © Bettmann/Corbis
Page 81 Sammy Sosa © Andy Altenburger/Icon SMI/Corbis
Page 82 Emmet Ashford © Bettmann/Corbis
Page 131 Alvin Dark and Yogi Berra © Bettmann/Corbis
Page 134 Spectator interference © Warren Wimmer/Icon Sportswire/Corbis
Page 139 Buster Posey © John G. Mabanglo/epa/Corbis
Page 160 Earl Weaver, Emmett Ashford and Boog Powell © Bettmann/Corbis
Page 173 George Brett © Bettmann/Corbis
Page 194 Steve Bartman and Moises Alou © Amy Sancetta/AP/Corbis
All other photos and illustrations © Dan Formosa and Paul Hamburger

Visit us at www.baseballfieldguide.com